WORLD WAR TWO

D1169540

WORLD WAR TWO

THE UNTOLD STORY

PHILIP WARNER

CASSELL

Cassell Military Paperbacks

Cassell
Wellington House, 125 Strand
London WC2R 0BB

First published by The Bodley Head 1988
This Cassell Military Paperbacks edition 2002
Reprinted 2003

British Library Cataloguing-in-Publication Data
A catalogue record for this book is available from the British Library

ISBN 0-304-35849-5

Printed and bound in Great Britain by
Cox & Wyman Ltd., Reading, Berks.

CONTENTS

LIST OF ILLUSTRATIONS

The Allied Leaders[1]
September 1940[1]
The blitz[1]
Sherman tanks[1]
Churchill[2]
The evacuation of Dunkirk[2]
British troops return to Normandy [1]
General Douglas MacArthur[2]
General Dwight D. Eisenhower[2]
U.S.S. *California*[2]
American marines at Guadalcanal Island[1]
U.S.S. *Bunker Hill*[1]
The Allied leaders at Yalta[1]
Suspected Russian partisans[1]
Nagasaki[1]
Concentration camps[1]

[1]Copyright Robert Hunt Library
[2]Copyright BBC Hulton Picture Library

LIST OF MAPS

DATES OF EVENTS OF THE WAR
1939–45

1939
1 Sept   Germany invades Poland.
3 Sept   Britain and France declare war on Germany.
17 Sept   Russia invades Poland.
29 Sept   Russo-German agreement to divide Poland.

1940
9 April   Germany invades Denmark and Norway.
15 April   British force lands in Norway.
10 May   Germans invade Holland, Belgium and
           Luxembourg.
10 May   Chamberlain resigns, Churchill becomes Prime
           Minister.
14 May   Germans invade France. British Home Guard
           formed.
4 June   Dunkirk evacuation of British and French forces.
8 June   British troops leave Norway.
10 June   Mussolini declares war on Allies.
25 June   France surrenders to Hitler.
3 July   British destroy French naval squadron at Oran.
4 July   German air blitz on Britain begins.
13 Sept   Italians invade Egypt.
15 Sept   Largest daylight attack on Britain. Germans lose
           60 aircraft. End of German attempt to obtain
           air superiority.
12 Oct   Hitler cancels invasion plan for Britain.
12 Nov   Taranto battle.
14 Nov   Coventry bombed.

1941

5 Jan	Britain begins attack against Italians in North Africa.
22 Jan	Tobruk captured by Australians.
12 Feb	Rommel arrives with German troops in Libya.
9 March	Italians invade Greece.
6 April	Germans attack Yugoslavia and Greece.
17 April	Yugoslavia falls.
24 April	British begin to evacuate Greece.
2 May	Hess lands in Scotland.
24 May	*Hood* sunk.
25 May	Battle of Crete.
27 May	*Bismarck* sunk.
22 June	Germans invade Russia.
6 Oct	Germans reach and attack Moscow. Leningrad besieged.
6 Dec	Zhukov's counter-offensive. Germans retreat.
7 Dec	Japanese attack Pearl Harbor.
8 Dec	Japanese land in Malaya.
10 Dec	*Prince of Wales* and *Repulse* sunk.
26 Dec	Hongkong surrenders.

1942

15 Jan	Japan invades Burma.
23 Jan	Japanese land in New Guinea and threaten Australia.
15 Feb	Singapore surrenders.
9 Mar	Java surrenders.
6 May	Corregidor (Philippines) surrenders.
8 May	Battle of the Coral Sea.
10 May	Japanese in control of Burma.
26 May	Rommel attacks 8th Army.
4 June	Battle of the Midway.
1 July	Rommel, having captured Tobruk, is stopped by Auchinleck at Alamein (1st Alamein).
13 Aug	Mongomery given command of 8th Army.
15 Aug	Alexander takes over from Auchinleck.
19 Aug	Dieppe Raid.
7 Sept	Battle of Alam Halfa (2nd Alamein).

23 Oct	Montgomery defeats Rommel at Alamein (3rd Alamein).
5 Nov	Eisenhower at Gibraltar.
8 Nov	Anglo-American 'Torch' landings in North Africa

1943
2 Feb	Germans surrender at Stalingrad.
6 Feb	Japanese evacuate Guadalcanal. 1st Chindit expedition in Burma.
13 May	Germans surrender in North Africa.
10 July	Allies invade Sicily.
25 July	Mussolini overthrown.
3 Sept	Allies invade Italy.
8 Sept	Italy tries to surrender.

1944
5 Mar	2nd Chindit expedition begins.
7 April	Siege of Kohima.
4 June	Fall of Rome.
6 June	D Day invasion.
13 June	First VI bombs fall on England.
3 July	Russians retake Minsk.
9 July	British take Caen.
19 July	Battle of the Philippine Sea.
20 July	Bomb plot against Hitler.
1 Aug	Rising in Warsaw.
15 Aug	South of France invaded.
13 Sept	Battle of Gothic Line in Italy.
17 Sept	Arnhem 'Market Garden' operation begins.
5 Oct	British land in Greece.
23 Oct	Battle of Leyte Gulf.
24 Nov	Capture of Pelelieu.
16 Dec	German offensive in the Ardennes.

1945
3 Jan	Akyab (Burma) retaken.
17 Jan	Russians take Warsaw.
28 Jan	Ardennes battle completed.
7 March	Capture of Remagen bridge.

16 March	Iwo Jima captured.
20 March	Mandalay recaptured.
23 March	Montgomery crosses the Rhine.
6 Apr	Okinawa landings.
12 Apr	Death of Roosevelt.
1 May	Suicide of Hitler.
2 May	Germans in Italy surrender.
3 May	Rangoon recaptured.
8 May	Unconditional surrender of Germany.
6 Aug	Atomic bomb dropped on Hiroshima.
9 Aug	Atomic bomb dropped on Nagasaki.
14 Aug	Japanese surrender.

INTRODUCTION

Incredible though it may seem, it has only recently become possible to understand what really happened in World War II. As over forty years have passed since the war ended, that statement requires some explanation. The reasons for this are both numerous and complex.

In the first place World War II was not a single war but a series of wars in different parts of the world, occurring at different times, and on different types of territory. The war in the North African desert was a different war from that in the jungle, the war in Europe totally unlike that in the Pacific. There were wars in the air: over Britain, over Europe, over Russia, and in the Middle East and Far East. There was always a war at sea whether in the bitterly cold North Atlantic, or the hot but unpredictable Pacific. The war of a man in a tank was so totally different from that of a Coastal Command pilot that it could scarcely seem to be the same conflict. And apart from these open battles, there were the secret wars, the wars of electronics, of code-breakers, of spies and deception teams, of saboteurs working in enemy territories, of political manipulation and of physicists racing against each other to discover and develop new weapons and counter-measures.

It was a war in which many of those involved were sworn to lifelong secrecy. Some of them did not understand what they were doing, so complicated was the pattern in which they worked; others knew very well what their jobs were achieving but, being bound to secrecy, became somewhat bitter and frustrated when, soon after 1945, versions of events appeared in books and films purporting to be the truth, for they knew very well they were not, but could not say so. Additionally, thousands of secret documents which would have been of inestimable value to historians were destroyed, usually deliberately by civil servants 'weeding' (as it is called) files before releasing them to the public domain. Some of this unnecessarily ruthless 'weeding' was due to ignorance, some to a desire to protect reputations, some because it was not realised that the secret material had already been published in other countries. From this sweeping destruction of material which would have been of the greatest value to historians and analysts, something has now been retrieved by the fact that there were often duplicates which escaped the incinerators. Operation orders which should have been destroyed were sometimes retained by those concerned, perhaps for sentimental reasons but more probably because it was hoped that one day official secrecy would relax and memoirs would be permitted. Over the years much information has come to light and can be used to piece together what really happened.

The subject matter is of course enormous but, so that the reader will not feel overwhelmed, this book has been kept to a length which permits an overall viewpoint and understanding. For those who wish to delve more deeply there is a vast collection of papers, memoirs, recorded interviews and film. However, it is as well for those extending their researches in any subject to bear the following facts in mind. Many of the writings were produced when the restrictions still limited the material which could be included; some of those taking part may well have had too narrow a perspective to be able to make informed judgements; and very few of the writers were trained historians. This last point may seem somewhat condescending, but one hopes it will not be taken as such. Any historian worth his salt has learnt to check and analyse every fact. In wartime enormous variations of reporting occur all too easily. Facts about weapons, numbers and casualties are often inadvertently distorted. During wartime, victories and figures are frequently exaggerated for propaganda purposes: regiments are described as 'wiped out' when many members of them have survived as prisoners of war, aircraft are 'shot down' when they have been only slightly damaged, ships are 'sunk' when they have merely disappeared from the battle zone. Very often, figures which have been inflated or diminished for propaganda purposes become accepted as accurate because of constant repetition.

But eventually, as we shall see, truth is stranger than fiction. Some incidents of the war are so bizarre or so brave that no reputable fiction-writer would have dared to invent them. War brings out the worst and the best in human beings.

It should not be overlooked that the 'Ultra' secret was not disclosed until 1974. When it was revealed, it made every previous history out of date. Although earlier histories contain much interesting and valuable information, they are therefore incomplete and may be misleading.

Philip Warner, April 1988

I

CAUSES AND EFFECTS

When World War II began in 1939 millions of people were shocked and apprehensive. However, the majority soon comforted themselves with the thought that this was a local conflict between Poland and Germany and that, although Britain and France had also declared war on Germany, they had done so in order to put pressure on the German people to restrain Hitler and his Nazi supporters, rather than to involve themselves in full-scale conflict. Most people felt that the war would never affect them, and in Russia, America, Italy, Japan, China, Egypt, Greece, Yugoslavia and Scandinavia they continued with their daily routine, quite unaware that during the next six years millions would lose their homes, and often too their lives, in the war which had just begun, and that the world would never be the same again.

The reason why the war spread and became a global conflict can only be understood if one has a clear idea of causes and motives. The war began when Germany invaded Poland but that fact alone was hardly likely to involve countries as far apart as America and Russia, nor to produce a desperate, agonized fight to the finish in which Germany would be devastated and partitioned and Japan virtually burnt into submission. The origins of the war are therefore inseparable from the subsequent course of events.

It is said, with some truth, that the peace treaties of one war are the cause of the next. This was undoubtedly true in the past, but it is not a complete explanation of the outbreak of war in 1939. For that we have a combination of causes.

The first was the condition of Germany in the 1920s; the second the political and military ambitions of certain nations, notably Germany, Italy, Japan and Russia; the third was the apathetic tolerance which made Western democracies, such as Britain, France and America, blind to dangers until it was too late to avert them peaceably; and the fourth the widespread belief that a well-trained military machine could win a clear-cut victory and then dictate a durable peace.

Although the condition of Germany in the 1920s did not mean that the elevation to power of the demagogue Hitler was inevitable, it made it extremely likely. At the end of World War I Germany was in desperate straits. Even while the war was continuing the German people had faced near starvation, but they had endured it stoically with the thought that it was a necessary step to final victory. However, when, after the war, deprivation continued but hope for a better future had been removed, the German people were prepared to accept leadership from anyone, however bizarre, who looked likely to produce a solution to their problems. Even before the end of the war in November 1918 the German navy and part of the army had mutinied. Then had followed the imposed peace treaty, the Treaty of Versailles of 1919, by which Germany was shorn of her overseas possessions, which included colonies in Africa and the Pacific, and also lost territory (which she had originally taken by force) to neighbouring countries. Her army was reduced to 100,000 men, a force considered necessary for the preservation of internal order. There was to be no German Air Force. The navy was to be severely reduced and the manufacture of arms and ammunition was to be strictly limited. Part of the Rhineland was to be occupied to make sure Germany complied with the provisions of the treaty. Finally, as she had inflicted massive damage on France and other countries, she was to pay a huge sum in reparations. Britain waived her claim to reparations but even with that easement Germany was still left with a financial burden which seemed to be well beyond her means to discharge. The French, who were to receive the major portion of the reparations, pointed out that the claims she was making on Germany were no more than the totally unjustified burden Germany had inflicted on France at the end of the Franco-Prussian War in 1871. On that occasion the French had paid off the debt surprisingly quickly and therefore

The European and North African Theatres 1939–1945

they did not see why Germany should not now do likewise; all that was needed was firmness of purpose on both sides.

Unfortunately for this theory, Germany was already nearly bankrupt. When she had invaded Belgium and France in 1914 she had expected a short, successful war and the mark stood at 20 to the pound sterling. By 1921 the rate had fallen to 1,000 marks to the pound, and this was only the beginning of inflation in the 1920s.

In 1921 there was also a world slump. Even in Britain, victorious in the war and owner of a vast empire, there were three million unemployed. In the event Germany never paid more than a small proportion of the reparations bill. When in 1922 she defaulted on the payment for the second year in succession, France, who had been the chief sufferer in the war, occupied the Ruhr Valley, the centre of German industry. The Germans thereupon embarked on a policy of non-cooperation and the French retaliated by imprisoning mayors of towns and cities, and directors of industrial works. Up to this point the Germans had nurtured no special animosity towards France, although they had invaded and devastated that country twice in the last 50 years. The French, of course, had every reason to hate and fear the Germans and the result was consequently an atmosphere of bitter hostility and fear between close neighbours who were also potentially two of the most powerful countries in Europe.

The effect of the occupation and stoppage of Ruhr industry was soon shown in the behaviour of the mark. By mid-1923 it stood at 500,000 to the pound. In the following months it fell even faster and workers who were paid their wages in suitcases full of marks rushed off to spend them before their value should have decreased even more.

In a period when there is concern if inflation runs above five per cent, it is not easy to visualize the atmosphere in Germany at this time. Retired people and those who had been living off the interest on life savings were suddenly penniless and destitute. The middle class which, under normal conditions, would have formed a stable, house-owning, prudent sector of society, saw the results of a life's work swept away in a year. In such an atmosphere people with their lives, their finances, their careers and their hopes in ruins, clutch desperately at any solution to their troubles. When therefore an ex-soldier with a considerable gift for fiery oratory proclaimed in the 1920s that if Germans followed him and his policy Germany would be great and prosperous once more, people from every level of society listened. The name he used was Adolf Hitler, although he had been christened Adolf Schicklgruber, which was his mother's name.

As Hitler eventually became the principal cause of World War II, dictated Germany's military policy, and finally dragged Germany to ruin, we need to take a close look at him. His rise to power and his capacity for evil are both astonishing. Shakespeare's words, 'The evil that men do lives after them', are undoubtedly true of Hitler. Everything about him was unextraordinary. He had a poor physique and an unimpressive appearance; even his saluting was sloppy. He was not a German citizen, but an Austrian, and as such was regarded by the Germans as a person of inferior status. He had a poor record at school, and left at the age of 16 without the normal educational certificate. He had ambitions to become an artist, but failed to gain entry to the Vienna Academy of Fine Arts and drifted around Vienna painting postcards and advertisements to eke out the small allowance given him by his mother. In this unsuccessful existence lay the seeds of his intolerance, and his hatred of Jews and the prosperous middle classes; he was a failure and consoled himself by withdrawing into the paranoic world of fantasy.

Although he had originally been rejected by the Austrian army as being physically unfit, he was accepted by the German army for World War I. He was wounded and gassed. He won the Iron Cross in the first and last years of the war but never rose above the rank of corporal. He was said to have been extremely brave but it has been suggested that his service record was enhanced after he rose to be dictator of Germany. He certainly served in the front line and enjoyed the comradeship and discipline which was very different from his former rootless existence. After the war he became an army political agent and in 1919 joined the German Workers' Party in Munich. In 1920 this still small party was re-named the National-Sozialistische Deutsche Arbeitspartei, a title soon abbreviated to Nazi; in its 25-year existence this organisation would be responsible for almost unbelievable evil and destruction.

Hitler's talent as an organiser and propagandist was soon recognised and in 1921 he was elected President. His audiences were numbered in thousands and he collected around him several helpers whose names would be feared and hated later; they included Rudolf Hess, Hermann Goering, and Julius Streicher. He was supported by ex-generals who could see a future in a Nazi Germany: among them was the highly respected Ludendorff. He also began to attract finance from armaments manufacturers, not only in Germany but elsewhere. Armaments manufacturers do not compete. As the huge firm of Krupp had already demonstrated, if you can supply arms to one country, you, or somebody else, will soon be supplying another. Even if someone else supplies a rival country, you may be assured of further orders from your own. When Hitler announced that one day he would rearm resurgent Germany, it was good news for the munitions makers, even though Germany was still forbidden to have more than a limited quantity of arms.

The danger which this development foreshadowed lay in the fact that it was all happening in defiance of a properly elected, democratic government. The support of Germany's most prestigious general, Ludendorff (who was prepared to assist a corporal whose name he would never have known) gave the Nazi party respectability. Yet the Weimar Republic, as the government of Germany was called, was a moderate organization.

This liaison between ex-Corporal Hitler and General Ludendorff was to have consequences long after the latter had died a disillusioned man. Hitler was able to study the man who had been commander-in-chief of vast armies and to observe his weaknesses. In later years the dominance Hitler had been able to exert over the famous general gave him confidence that he himself was cleverer than the German generals of World War II. He overrode their natural caution and urged them to take risks which appalled them; nevertheless when, in the early part of the war, bold, dashing policies brought German victories they too began to share his belief that he had exceptional insight and strategic sense. Only later, when his decisions were clearly disastrous, such as for example allowing a vast army to be trapped at Stalingrad, did that confidence ebb. By then however, it was too late to stop Hitler. The ultimate humiliation of the generals came when, after the plot against him in 1944, he had 29 of them hanged from meat-hooks in the ceiling and watched them die slowly.

The Weimar government's embarrassment over its inability to cope with war debts and inflation, and the general hopelessness of the situation in Germany, made Hitler's claim that an alternative government was needed seem all the more sensible. Weimar appeared to abet its own destruction by showing an absurd degree of tolerance to dissident minorities, corrupting influences, and decadent practices. Hitler grasped the power of the press as an opinion-former, and used the party newspaper, the *Völkischer Beobachter* (the *People's Observer*), to disseminate exaggerated claims that would foment discontent with existing institutions.

Nevertheless, he made a serious mistake when he and Ludendorff tried to overturn the government in the 1923 Munich Beer Hall Putsch. It failed; Hitler was sentenced to five years in prison, although he only served nine months. This period in prison gave him leisure to work out future policies, most of which he wrote down in his book *Mein Kampf* (*My Struggle*). He decided that the only way to achieve stable power was to exploit the existing constitution and make it seem that his ultimate elevation was the will of the people. When he was released he found that his party had almost disintegrated during his absence and that Germany's economic situation was beginning to improve as a result of rescue attempts by other countries.

However, the party continued to grow in numbers, and saw a fresh chance in the 1929 slump. This slump has never been equalled in history. Following a dramatic and totally unjustified boom on the world's stock markets, there was suddenly a catastrophic fall which eventually led to 17 million unemployed in America, four million in Britain, and seven million in Germany. The cause of the slump, which began with doubts about land speculation in Florida, was mainly that money was being lent at rates of interest which could not possibly be justified by future earnings. The industrial world was living on borrowed money and once confidence ebbed, rapid collapse was inevitable. America had 1,000 million dollars on loan to Germany, and promptly began calling it in. Unfortunately for the American investors, much of the money was in unproductive areas and there was no hope of recovering any of it in the near future. The slump had repercussions in other countries, which subsequently affected events in World War II, and was, of course, an appalling disaster; however, for Hitler and his Nazi party it was the best news they could have heard. In his speeches Hitler laid the blame for the worldwide financial crisis on the machinations of unpatriotic Jews and the conspiracies of international communism. His diatribes had a considerable effect and by 1930 the Nazis polled six million votes in the national election. Two years later Hitler stood for the Presidency against Hindenburg, the veteran general who had won the legendary battle of Tannenberg. Hitler lost, but he polled 36 per cent of the votes. Subsequently he improved his party's position by ingratiating himself with Hindenburg: in 1933, the aged president invited Hitler to become Chancellor of Germany.

So far the worst evils of Nazism had not come to the surface, but their time was not far distant.

As Chancellor, Hitler was able to establish a dictatorship. In 1933 a mysterious fire burnt down the Reichstag – the parliamentary building. The blaze was said to have been started by a Dutch communist, but his trial was clearly bizarre and stage-managed. Hitler used this as an excuse to introduce numerous restrictions on individual freedom and, at the same time, began a campaign of violence against all those likely to oppose Nazism. It was now clear to most thinking people outside and inside Germany that Hitler's increasing power made another major war inevitable. This view was based partly on observation of the man, partly on the political philosophy which he represented, and partly on the fact that Germany's growing militarism was not matched by its neighbours; they, with their 'peace at any price' policy, offered an irresistible temptation to the German dictator.

Hitler's intentions became clear when in 1934 he arranged the assassination of several of his former associates. Some of these had been concerned with the Nazis' private army. This pleased the German regular army, who saw him as a leader who would bring many benefits in the future. The Allied army of occupation had left the Rhineland several years before and now there was no one who could prevent Germany openly defying the provisions of the Treaty of Versailles. The Nazi party creed could now be summarised as: anti-Jew, anti-profiteer, anti-foreigner, anti-Versailles. The emotional appeal of all these was skilfully exploited by Josef Goebbels, a Heidelberg Doctor of Philosophy who had a genius for propaganda. His theory was that if you are going to tell a lie it is no good telling a small one: it must be a big one and then everyone will believe you. Goebbels had absolute control over everything which was printed or broadcast or shown in cinemas. He could therefore blandly announce the sinking of Allied ships which were still afloat, blame the Jews for 'stabbing Germany in the back', and allege that most of the Allied leaders were of Jewish descent. He also tried to create disunity in occupied countries by lies designed to incite different groups such as Walloons and Flemish in Belgium to resent each other's presence. His was a policy of divide and rule.

Everything was now brought under the state. Trade unions were abolished, communists beaten up and put in prison. Jews subjected to intolerable persecution. One English visitor was told in the 1930s by a German family that four Jewish doctors had just been thrown out by the local hospital. 'But how bad for the hospital,' commented the visitor. 'But how good for the Jews,' was the complacent reply. Hitler took various steps to make the country look prosperous, even if the economic situation was still bleak. He created jobs by expelling Jews, by insisting that women should stay at home and be mothers rather than industrial workers, and by sending young men to labour camps where they lived a healthy life in the countryside. Terrorism towards his opponents combined with benevolence to patriotic, 'racially pure' Germans was his policy.

When Hindenburg died in August 1934, Hitler became

President as well as Chancellor, which gave him official command of the armed forces. Once again this was a move which was to have great repercussions in World War II. Every serving officer and man now took an oath of allegiance to Hitler personally. Whether they adored and worshipped him, or thought he was an upstart mountebank, would in the future make no difference. They were now bound to fight and not die for Germany but for Hitler personally. When, later, his actions showed him to be scarcely sane, the fact that they had once sworn loyalty to Hitler made them hesitate to take any action to remove him, however disastrous his continuation in power was going to be. For others, there was no such problem. They had sworn an oath of allegiance and nothing would ever make them break it. This was ultimately a major factor in enabling the army to fight to the death, long after the war was lost, and Germany had been invaded and overrun. Officers and men had sworn an oath to Hitler; as long as he lived they would continue fighting for him and obeying his orders.

The reaction of other countries to resurgent Germany varied. France regarded it with apprehensive gloom and built the Maginot Line with a view to keeping back a future invasion attempt. At the same time there were numerous peace movements, mostly left-wing inspired. The French constitution of that time was so ultra-democratic that governments could come and go within the space of days. In the background of French politics were sinister figures, such as Colonel de la Roque, whose Croix de Feu movement aimed at establishing a system akin to Nazism. Later in the 1930s a number of French newspapers passed under German financial and thus editorial control. France's will to resist a future German attack was steadily undermined at this time.

Britain had retired to a position of near isolation. It is said that a British newspaper had once carried a headline which ran: 'Fog in the Channel; Continent isolated.' Anglo-French relations were not notably harmonious. The British tended to regard the French as grasping, ungrateful and politically chaotic: the French saw the British as untrustworthy rivals and were said to have coined a phrase, 'England will always fight to the last Frenchman'. Russia, at this time, appeared to be far removed in thought, as well as in distance, from the European scene but, as we now know, was running a very effective espionage and subversion campaign in the Western democracies. Italy had a similar type of government to Germany, with Mussolini, an even more bombastic figure than Hitler, at its head.

The word 'fascist', which described Germany, Italy and several other states at this time, has now come to be applied by dissident groups to anyone who does not agree to their aspirations. Even more frequently it is employed as a simple term of abuse. In fact, fascism, whose roots go back to Sparta, is a doctrine which emphasises that the state is the centre and regulator of life, that it has complete authority, and that its leader has indisputable authority. One might wonder how anyone could ever have accepted such a thesis but, when a country is defeated and in chaos, everything is possible. Nicolo Macchiavelli, living in the chaotic conditions of Renaissance Italy, had expressed the fascist philosophy in his book *The Prince*, and this had subsequently been taken by many as a justification for the establishment of a dictatorship, even a tyranny, when a state was in turmoil. Macchiavelli's adherents believed that citizens needed a strong, authoritarian government, headed by a man who would exercise power with prudence. This, of course, ran directly contrary to the liberal attitudes which flourished in the eighteenth and nineteenth centuries and which were based on the assumption that every individual was entitled to dignity, independence and freedom to express any viewpoint, however anarchical. In the climate of the 1920s, when the freedom of the individual appeared to mean only the freedom to starve, and the absence of a strong central government seemed merely to lead to unproductive, petty, quarrelsome splinter groups, a growing number of people began to think wistfully of a firm, stable, authoritarian state. Those with more vision looked a little further and realised that the militarist link would almost inevitably take the fascist state to war, resulting in the end being worse than the beginning. Both fascists and communists believed that the end justified the means (if necessary: murder, betrayal, treachery, deceit, lying) but whereas the fascists were happy to see the state continue in perpetuity the communists affirmed that once power had been assumed, and the master plan implemented, the state would gradually 'wither away'. Most of the countries on which fascism or communism was imposed cared little for theories of government: all they wished for was security and adequate food.

There is however always an intellectual minority in all countries which believes firmly in theories (however bizarre) of government. They are recognised as important in preparing people for a new form of government but, once it is established, are quickly swept out of the mainstream of events; often they are treated with deep suspicion and 'liquidated'. After World War II had begun certain events were influenced by communist intellectuals, often working in Special Operations Executive or resistance groups. There is of course something enormously attractive to the frustrated or idealistic intellectual in the thought that he can exert unseen but immense power over unsuspecting people. In the 1920s there were plenty of intellectual theories to justify fascism in Europe and elsewhere. Hitler derived his ideas from Georg von Schönerer and Karl Lueger; Mussolini from Giovanni Gentile. Both fascism and communism had their roots in the teachings of the German Professor Hegel who lived from 1770 to 1831.

Fascism had adherents in many countries, but in most of them it lacked a sufficiently dynamic leader to put it into practice. In Britain there was Sir Oswald Mosley and his Blackshirts, in Spain Primo de Rivera and his Falange (and later General Franco), in Portugal there was Salazar, in Austria Dollfuss, in Hungary Horthy, in Norway Quisling, in Belgium Degrelle, in the Argentine Perón. The importance of these fascist groups in countries other than Germany was that, when war came, some of them were able to support Hitler and even act as saboteurs. (Some, of course, refused to betray their country when the time came.) To everyone's surprise, and to the disgust of many, the Nazis were able to recruit regiments of sympathisers who were then incorporated into the notorious Waffen S.S. Quisling, whose name became a synonym for treacherous collaboration, was a former Minister of War, and had a marked hope for the restoration of the former Viking empire.

However, no one travelled as fast and as far as Hitler. Having established a firm grip on Germany he turned his attention outside. Mussolini was a natural ally but France was an enemy which would have to be conquered before he could embark on adventures in the east. Rather naively he imagined that Britain would be persuaded to confine her attention to the problems of running an empire and leave Germany a free hand in Europe. His European ambitions were much facilitated by the peace treaties which followed World War I and which had left most of Europe seething with discontent. At that time, with the best will in the world, Woodrow Wilson, the American President, had proposed that the best way to eliminate the causes of war was to make 'every territorial settlement in the interests of the populations concerned, and not as a part of any mere adjustment or compromise of claims among rival states'. The outcome of this had been that when the Turkish and Austro-Hungarian empires had disintegrated the map was redrawn to create various small, independent states. (A state can include several nations; a nation can include several states.) However, in the years before the war when these new states had been parts of an empire they had acquired a very mixed population, including, generally, some Germans. Thus Czechoslovakia was composed of Czechs, Slovaks, and an element known as the Sudeten Germans. Czechoslovakia with its important strategic position, powerful armaments industry, and excellent army, was a covetable prize for anyone and Hitler had his eyes on it from the first. Many of the tanks which ravaged through France in 1940 and the Western Desert in 1942 had been manufactured in the Skoda works in Czechoslovakia. The tactics in which they were employed had been formulated in the German army more than 10 years earlier.

This brings us to a very important point. Although history states that World War II began in 1939, this was not the way it was seen by Hitler and his supporters. For them the war had begun in 1938, when Germany had forcibly absorbed Austria. A further step was taken when Czechoslovakia was brought into the German camp in the spring of 1939.

Surrounding countries viewed the rise of Nazi Germany

with dismay and apprehension. To the communists in each country the issue was clear enough: the Nazis were fascists and must be opposed by every possible means. Communists in Germany had to keep out of sight, but in other countries they did their utmost to pursue two contrasting policies. One was to encourage the governments of other countries, whatever their character, to oppose Hitler and the Nazis; the other – contradictory – policy was to undermine the governments of those countries with a view to making a communist takeover possible. The instructions from Russia said that Hitler and the Nazis were to be opposed by every means possible. This meant giving practical help to the Spanish Republican forces who were endeavouring to win the civil war which had been started by General Franco (the eventual victor). The Spanish Republican forces were left wing and were therefore assisted by the International Brigade whose members varied from lifelong communists to university undergraduates and other young idealists. Franco, backed by the Catholics and the right, was assisted by German and Italian forces who welcomed the opportunity to try out their new aircraft and tanks.

Even at the time, the policies of other countries seemed extraordinarily supine and muddled in the face of the German threat. In both Britain and France there was a belief amongst some elements of society that Germany was right to feel a sense of injustice over the Treaty of Versailles and should therefore be 'appeased'. This view was held by some members of the government in Britain, though strongly opposed by others, and was espoused by *The Times*, which in those days was far more influential than today; if *The Times* endorsed a policy, it must be right, was then a widely held view. Since the 1931 slump Britain had had a coalition, known as the National Government. It had an undistinguished sequence of Prime Ministers: Ramsay Macdonald, who seemed incapable of a coherent statement, Stanley Baldwin, a lethargic 'hope for the best' type, and Neville Chamberlain, a competent, responsible, but extremely naive man who constantly accepted the wrong advice. All through the 1930s there were alarming stories of what was happening in Germany and it was obvious that this ferocious and cruel regime was not going to settle down peacefully by being given a few strips of colonial territory in Africa as 'appeasement'. What astonished many people, even at the time and even more in retrospect, was how the Foreign Office, which was supposed to be supplying the Cabinet with an accurate, well-informed account of the situation in Germany and elsewhere, could have been so hopelessly misguided and incompetent. Certainly it harboured communists, such as Burgess, Maclean and Philby, but these might have been explained away as freaks. The administrative grade of the Foreign Office were chosen from the most intellectually brilliant university graduates. Unfortunately, when the recruitment system was altered after 1945 to broaden the intake and to ensure it was not too narrowly drawn from the older public schools and universities, the Foreign office gave no sign of greater enlightenment; if anything it seemed worse.

By 1935 Hitler was acting in open defiance of any restrictions which treaties had placed on Germany. Defying the Treaty of Versailles, he reintroduced conscription. In 1936 he reoccupied the Rhineland, which was allegedly a neutral buffer zone between France and Germany. It has been suggested that this was the critical time when Hitler should, and could, have been stopped, but that view is not held by French Intelligence (the Deuxième Bureau). In their view Hitler was already too strong to be held by any existing forces. Any confrontation would have resulted in a German victory, a fact too awful to contemplate. Instead the French advised a rapid policy of rearmament among the Western democracies, but failed to take proper steps to reinvigorate their own forces.

Undoubtedly there was much tacit approval of Hitler and his regime outside Germany. Many saw it as a bulwark against communism; others secretly sympathized with the virile image which the Nazis were projecting. They preferred to ignore the police state and the vileness of the persecution of the Jews in Germany, who numbered less than a million, even allowing for the Nazi insistence that anyone with one Jewish grandparent was a Jew. Hitler propounded the view of a pure Nordic race, to which Britain, suitably purged, should also belong. Together Britain and Germany could rule a better world. Hitler did not believe in compromise. When, during the 1936 Olympic Games in Berlin, an American black man, Jesse Owens, won the 100 yards race, Hitler left hastily before Owens could be presented to him as a winner. There was undoubtedly support for Hitler from industrialists, outside as well as inside Germany. In the early stages of the rise of the Nazi party German industrialists, believing he would stimulate industry, not least that of armaments, had paid for much of the cost of the police, the arms, the rallies and the officials. No armaments manufacturer ever wants a war. What he wants is a period of tension and anxiety in which potential enemies keep constantly updating their arms. War closes down one market entirely and disrupts the industry which is often taken over by the government. But undoubtedly it was more than the profit motive which made industrialists support Hitler. In several other countries, as well as Russia, communists had flourished, even if only for short periods. If communism ever took control in Germany, it would spell ruin for the German private arms manufacturer, who would simply become a servant of the state if he survived at all. There was, as most senior industrialists were well aware, considerable sympathy for a communist experiment in many countries. The Scandinavian group of Sweden, Norway and Denmark had already taken notable, though constitutional steps in that direction. Germany, if the Nazi party collapsed, would be very likely to follow the same path.

Hitler and his cronies were adept at playing on the fears of potential opponents and making them allies, even if unwilling ones. The Catholic Church had originally given a cautious welcome to the Nazis on the basis that they would be a bulwark against the atheism and anti-clericalism of communists. But once potential opposition had been blunted, Hitler's attitude soon changed. The Hitler Youth enrolled all boys and girls and made Catholic youth work impossible. They followed this up by closing Catholic schools and attacking priests, nuns and monks. In Germany there could be only faith in one God – Nazism and Hitler. Men and women seemed to need something to worship and Hitler did not intend to allow any conflict of loyalties to inhibit support for the party.

The Protestants were more numerous than the Catholics but less united. However, led by Pastor Niemoller (who was eventually to be sent to a concentration camp) they refused to become the Reich church and thus a government department. They were persecuted but neither they nor the Catholics gave up their resistance to Nazism. During the war the fact that Hitler was opposed by the religious elements in his own country made it impossible for the Nazis to pose as the upholders of religious freedom in the face of communism. This robbed Goebbels of a potential propaganda weapon but perhaps more significant was the fact that resistance groups in countries which the Germans overran were able to enlist sympathy and practical help from people with deep religious convictions. That Hitler was evil was clear to anyone with intelligence, but when he also proclaimed it by his policy towards religion it was obvious even to the most obtuse and unobservant. This eventually led to resistance groups opposing Hitler for two diametrically opposite reasons: one element hated him because he was anti-communist; another element detested him because he was the enemy of Protestantism and Catholicism. Unfortunately, some of the resistance groups which opposed him hated each other more than they hated the common enemy and wasted time, ammunition, energy and opportunity by feuding with each other.

Hitler was an early and skilled practitioner of what is now known as psychological warfare. Whenever he made a threatening or merely disturbing move against other Europeans, perhaps in the form of a belligerent speech, he always chose the weekend. This invariably caught the British government, in particular, by surprise, as members of the Cabinet, including the Prime Minister, liked to regard Friday evening till Monday as a time to be devoted to rest and recreation. A blood-curdling speech by Hitler on Saturday night would be very unsettling and unnerving for ministers or senior government officials if it implied that some form of precautionary action should be taken immediately. Mussolini was also an expert at timing his most bellicose speeches to make the maximum impact on other countries' Sunday papers. Although by no means as powerful as Hitler, Mussolini and his Italian fascist party posed a considerable threat.

Italy had no special reason for falling under the spell of a charlatan such as Mussolini. By deserting her former German ally in 1915 and joining the Allies, she had eventually emerged as a victor, though a somewhat battered one, of World War I. In the 1920s her economic position was no worse and considerably better than that of many other countries, yet her internal government was chaotic. Mussolini, the son of a blacksmith, and a former socialist, journalist and soldier, decided that the future of Italy lay with a strong man (himself) and a dictatorial regime. He formed a fascist party, known as the Blackshirts, and stood for parliament. In 1921 his party gained 35 seats. A succession of Italian prime ministers now showed themselves incapable of commanding national confidence and imposing order on the anarchy to which Mussolini's Blackshirts were actively contributing. The latter made socialists their special targets, while Mussolini at the same time declared his loyalty to the King and the Catholic Church, whose safety and property were guaranteed. In 1922 the Blackshirts marched on Rome (while Mussolini prudently awaited the outcome in Milan) and when they had occupied the city Mussolini was proclaimed Prime Minister.

He tightened his grip on the country quickly but, unlike Hitler, he remained on good terms with the Church. Meanwhile his followers behaved with the utmost brutality to any critics or opponents of the regime: a favourite form of persecution was to pour a pint of castor oil down the victim's throat, sometimes followed by jumping on his stomach. He proclaimed himself '*Il Duce*' – the leader – and by vigorous policies drained and cultivated marshes, built factories and roads, balanced the budget, and in what seemed to many the greatest miracle of all, made the trains run on time. All this while he was building up the army, navy and air force and glorifying war. Military indoctrination began in infancy and Mussolini, in theatrical speeches and poses, proclaimed that Italy would soon have as great an empire as in Roman times. He referred to the Mediterranean as '*Mare Nostrum*' (our sea) as the Romans once had done.

Those bellicose statements were usually timed to match and support Hitler's similar outbursts. However, Mussolini was conscious that Italy was far from adequately supplied with modern aircraft, tanks and naval craft, so when he picked his opponents they tended to be people incapable of much resistance. A typical example was Abyssinia (Ethiopia) in 1935. Italy already had territory in Somaliland, from which it was comparatively easy to invade Abyssinia. The action was regarded with disgust by other European nations, as he used both poison gas and military aircraft against tribesmen whose only weapon was a spear. The League of Nations, which had been created in 1920 as part of the Treaty of Versailles, with the aim of assisting the preservation of peace, condemned Mussolini's aggression but could not rally any of its 54 members to take effective action. The League had had some earlier successes, and some failures, and had done much to alleviate the social and economic conditions which are said to be a principal cause of war, but it failed over Abyssinia and thereby lost the credibility which might have enabled it to prevent World War II. At that moment its efforts were also sabotaged by the infamous Hoare-Laval Pact. Sir Samuel Hoare, the British Foreign Secretary, secretly agreed with Pierre Laval, Prime Minister of France, that any action against Italy would drive Mussolini into alliance with Hitler, and that therefore it would be best to buy off the Italian dictator with the permanent cession of a large piece of Abyssinian territory. This seemed a cheap and convenient way to prevent an alliance which would make both countries more powerful, but the public outcry was so great when it was published that Hoare had to resign in ignominy. Laval, who was said to be so cunning that his name spelt the same backwards as forwards, hung on for a short while longer before being forced out; he regained power in World War II in the Vichy government which collaborated with the Nazis. In 1945, when Germany had been defeated, Laval was tried for treason in the French courts and subsequently executed. Hoare's career was not damaged by the pact fiasco and he held other ministerial appointments later.

By the mid-1930s it seemed unlikely that Germany would ever be defeated again in view of the reluctance of other countries to face the challenge which Hitler's regime clearly presented. The League was to all intents and purposes defunct and equally there was no sign that a reinvigorated organisation would be created 10 years later and become the United Nations.

During those years all the initiative seemed to be with Hitler and Mussolini. Both practised what became known as sabre-rattling. Britain and France, both slowly recovering from the slump, were horrified at the thought of having to fight another war and hoped that the regimes in Germany and Italy would collapse of their own accord in some miraculous way. Unfortunately they showed no signs of doing so. In 1936 Hitler and Mussolini made a formal alliance which they described as the Rome-Berlin Axis. Even Hitler was deceived by Mussolini's bombastic oratory and believed that he would be a strong and reliable ally. Thus encouraged, Hitler pressed on even more confidently with his policy to establish a German hegemony in central Europe, and in due course extend his conquests into Russia. The first stage of this was to weaken potential opposition by presenting a case in which there appeared to be an injustice in need of rectifying. As we saw earlier, the Treaty of Versailles and other treaties which had dealt with Austria-Hungary and the Turkish empire had all aimed at creating states of similar ethnic origins. In the event this was found to be easier said than done, for almost all those new states had pockets of people who lived in the area in which their ancestors, through wish or coercion, had settled many years earlier. Czechoslovakia was an obvious case for 'rectification'; Poland would come later. Austria was less of a problem: it was forcibly absorbed in February 1938 by the simple process of bullying the Austrian Chancellor into submission. Before Hitler presented his ultimatum, all the Austrian hotels found themselves booked up by healthy-looking young men all carrying almost identical suitcases. When the moment of 'Anschluss' arrived, the holidaymakers unpacked their suitcases and donned uniforms all adorned with the swastika badge of the Nazis. From then onwards Austria was virtually part of Germany.

There was considerable sympathy for Czechoslovakia in

other European countries. The country had been formed by the efforts of two greatly respected Europeans, Thomas Masaryk and Eduard Benes, and consisted of Czechs inhabiting what had been Bohemia, and Slovakia in what had formerly been a part of Hungary. The northern area of Czechoslovakia was mountainous and contained three million Sudeten (southern) Germans. As the total population of the country was only 14 million and the district in which the Sudeten Germans lived was the vital defensive area, as well as being on the German frontier, any inroads here would seriously weaken the fledgling state. The Sudeten Germans were very content with their lot until Hitler began stirring up trouble, complaining about totally imaginary wrongs and oppression: 'I weep for the wrongs of my unhappy compatriots, these tortured souls.' For some years there had been a Nazi party organisation in the Sudeten lands and this now instigated rioting just as Hitler's threats to 'liberate' the oppressed Sudetens implied that he was about to invade. As the other European powers could see that this might well be the beginning of another major war, it was decided that Neville Chamberlain, the British Prime Minister, should fly to Germany to see what personal discussions with Hitler could achieve. Chamberlain, who had never in his life flown, now did so three times in a fortnight. Unfortunately, the courage of this gesture was somewhat marred by the fact that he cut an unimpressive figure with his winged collar, stooping figure and umbrella. When he returned from the final visit and stepped out of his aircraft waving a piece of paper on which he and Hitler had both agreed their two countries would never go to war again, there was an element of the ludicrous. As the conversation at the meeting was kept secret, ribald versions were soon circulating in Britain. Thus: Hitler, 'I warn you that if we go to war we shall have the Italians on our side this time.' Chamberlain, 'Well, that's only fair. We had to have them on our side last time.'

But there was nothing humorous about the settlement. Chamberlain had originally agreed that there should be a plebiscite to decide whether or not the Sudetenland should be transferred to Germany, but Hitler had then increased his demands, abandoned the plebiscite, and threatened simply to march in. Mussolini then intervened to ask Hitler to postpone this move and, as a result, Chamberlain, Daladier (of France), Hitler and Mussolini all met at Munich. By this time Britain and France had mobilized for war and London was digging trenches in the parks as a precaution against air raids. Hitler flatly refused to allow Stalin to attend the Munich conference, which, in view of the pact he made with him a year later, was to say the least ironic. Britain had not guaranteed Czechoslovakia's territorial integrity but France had and this seems, in retrospect, to have been a pointer to the way France would behave when, later, she herself came under pressure.

For all practical purposes, World War II had now begun. After Munich those who had been called up from their various reserves were released again, but Britain was gradually moving on to a war footing and thinking people did not consider that actual fighting would be long delayed. Conscription, called National Service, was introduced in Britain in April 1939; this had never before been done in peacetime. Plans were made for the expansion of factories and orders were placed for essential equipment but in relation to what was really needed these were hardly more than gestures. The naiveté of those in positions of authority who still thought they could come to terms with Hitler and Mussolini was, and is, astonishing. Sir Nevile Henderson, the British Ambassador to Germany, was completely deceived by the flattery and assurances he received. For several years newspaper correspondents had been reporting on what was really happening in Europe. Writers such as Douglas Reed with his *Insanity Fair* and *Disgrace Abounding*, John Gunther in his *Inside Europe*, and G. E. R. Gedye in *Fallen Bastions*, wrote trenchant, warning best-sellers, but these were dismissed by many as expressions of the exaggerated views of journalists. A few years later their books were considered to be understatements.

When, in March 1939, the German army overran the rest of Czechoslovakia which included the huge Skoda armament works, the hollowness of Hitler's protestations about merely liberating oppressed Germans was clearly exposed. In Czechoslovakia he had acquired territory to which he could have no possible claim. This, however, presented no problems to Hitler. He was now talking about '*Lebensraum*' – living space for the German nation. This means that every country was at risk, particularly those which possessed colonial empires.

Mussolini, who had originally whetted Hitler's appetite for foreign conquest by his own annexation of Abyssinia, now felt jealous of his former pupil. On 7 April 1939, without any excuse for doing so, he invaded the barren and mountainous country of Albania. The conquest only took 24 hours: King Zog and his family hastily removed themselves to Greece and thereafter lived in exile.

So far all attention had been focussed on the dictators in Europe but there was another country, far distant, which would eventually play a considerable part in World War II. That country was Japan. Her presence on the scene requires some explanation.

At the end of the nineteenth century Japan, with a rapidly growing population, looked for an opportunity for expansion, and found it in China. In 1895, following a short war, she wrested Formosa (Taiwan) and the Liaotung Peninsula, which was a part of Manchuria, from the Chinese. However, France, Russia, and Germany reacted strongly and forced Japan to grant Korea its independence, and hand back the Liaotung Peninsula to the former owners. Russia thereupon leased the peninsula from China and made its port (Port Arthur, now renamed Lushun) the terminus of the Trans-Siberian railway. The stage had been set for a future conflict between these four powers. Meanwhile Britain, mistrusting every aspect of Russian policy which she felt was aimed eventually at the acquisition of China and India, signed a treaty with Japan in 1902 saying she would remain neutral if Japan went to war with one other power, and would aid her if she confronted two. In 1904 Japan suddenly attacked Port Arthur and followed this up with a series of victories over Russian forces. In the subsequent peace treaty, Russia gave up its rights in Manchuria to Japan, and Korea was recognised as being independent, though a Japanese protectorate.

The indirect results of this war were to have a significant influence on the future. Japan had now emerged from isolation and was recognised as a major power. Russia was humiliated and resentful, as well as being impotent – for the time being. And the victory of an oriental power (Japan) over a European one (Russia) stirred the imagination of Far Eastern peoples who had previously been made to feel they were so inferior to Europeans that a military victory was not possible. This thought profoundly influenced potential insurgents in India, and was reinforced in 1941, when Japan's surprise attack on Pearl Harbor and other colonial territories around the Pacific finally demolished the white man's legend of invincibility. In 1910 Japan quietly annexed Korea and put it under military control. In World War II they used Koreans as guards on Allied prisoners-of-war; the Koreans, already brutalized by Japanese treatment of themselves, were delighted to have someone on whom they could vent their own feelings with impunity.

Next, Japan virtually destroyed the League of Nations by defying it in the early 1930s. Following an incident on a Japanese-owned railway in Manchuria, Japanese troops overran the whole of that country which she then declared to be an independent state with the name of Manchukuo. When China appealed to the League of Nations, Japan simply ignored all its protests and resigned from membership. She was well aware that the United States, which might have taken effective action, was not a member of the League and could not be called upon to help it; also that the European powers were much too concerned with keeping an eye on Germany and Italy (as well as coping with economic problems) to have much time for an obscure piece of territory on the other side of the world.

Nevertheless the 'Manchukuo incident', as it came to be known, was one of the most important factors leading to World War II, and certainly encouraged Japan's active intervention in it. What began in Manchuria in 1931 ended in the ashes of Hiroshima in 1945. But much more happened between those two dates. In 1936 Japan signed what was known as the Anti-Comintern Pact with Germany and Italy. 'Comintern' was an abbreviation for 'Communist International' and was a Russian-financed organisation with the mission of spreading communism throughout the world.

Japan was now part of the Rome-Berlin-Tokyo Axis; the alliance was strengthened by a tripartite pact in September 1940 (when Europe was already under the control of Germany); this was mainly directed against the United States which was not yet in the war, though soon to be so. Furthermore, in 1937 Japan had attacked China in a full-scale war in which they captured Hankow, Nanking and Canton, and overran much of Mongolia. In 1938 and 1939 Japanese and Russian armies also clashed along the borders of Manchukuo. These campaigns took place far away in distance as well as in thought from the War Office and the Pentagon, and tended to be dismissed as half-hearted warfare in which men went to battle carrying umbrellas and stopped fighting if it rained too hard. This bland complacency met its merited reward when the Japanese launched their attacks on British, Dutch, French and American territories in 1941. At that point it was discovered that these endless battles in China had produced armies of highly experienced and toughened soldiers who, in a sharply revised assessment, were considered the equal of any in the world. So far from being an inchoate force of amateurs who could be bluffed by a few token forces, they were now seen as a conquering army, assisted by a modern air force and navy.

Meanwhile Hitler, having bamboozled the other European powers about the nature of his regime and his ambitions, was poised to produce his most dramatic stroke of all. This was little short of incredible. On 23 August 1939, Stalin and Hitler signed a non-aggression pact. If it had not actually happened, it would have seemed impossible.

Throughout the entire history of the Nazi party the principal enemy had been communism, and communism meant Russia. Russia, 'the sleeping giant', had established a communist government in 1917, following the collapse of the Russian armies fighting Germany. Communist Russia began with a reign of terror, in which the secret police, at that time named the OGPU, later the NKVD and finally the KGB, penetrated all levels of Russian society. In spite of enormous economic difficulties leading to famine, the Bolsheviks, led by Lenin, consolidated their control. Communism was based upon the writings of Karl Marx, a German Jew who had been exiled from Germany in the mid-nineteenth century and written most of his books in the Reading Room at the British Museum. Lenin died in 1924 and was replaced, after considerable internal strife, by Josef Stalin (his real name was Djugashvili, but he preferred Stalin which means steel). Stalin removed all real or imaginary rivals by a series of purges and established a regime of immense brutality and oppression. However, the fact that this was being done in the name of, though not through the practice of, democracy, attracted many sympathizers outside Russia. The slogans of communism, 'Workers of the world unite' and 'From everyone according to his ability; to everyone according to his needs', gave an impression that communist Russia was at heart a benevolent regime which would eventually be a shining example to the world. It was especially attractive to intellectuals, who had a somewhat romantic view of the simple, earnest nature of the working man – a being with whom they had had little, if any, first-hand contact. They had even less idea of the mind of the Russian.

Stalin imposed communism on Russia with a degree of brutality which has seldom been exceeded and which is regarded with disquiet even by hard-line Russian communists today. Under his harsh regime Russia progressed by what were known as 'Five Year Plans'. The first dealt with the expansion of heavy industry; subsequent ones with the increase of goods. However, consumer goods have never been available in Russia to the extent they may be purchased in Western countries. The priorities in the Soviet Union have always been heavy industry and military production; the two were, of course, closely linked. The enormous importance given to building up military strength in the Soviet Union derives partly from the experience of 1919 when Western powers intervened in Russia to prevent the Bolsheviks appropriating goods which had been sent from the West for use against the German army and at the same time to assist the moderates in regaining power. The Bolsheviks won the resultant civil war, mainly through the 'Red Army' created by Trotsky.

In the 1920s and 1930s the Soviets incurred the distrust of the rest of the world for several reasons. They had nationalized property, including foreign-owned holdings, without compensation; they had established a closed society with secret police; and they had made it clear that their ultimate aim was the overthrow of the Western democracies. Lenin had warned the Soviets they must be prepared for attack by capitalist powers and when Hitler's Germany established its anti-communist regime the Soviets became extremely apprehensive. However, apprehension did not prevent Stalin launching a purge of the armed forces, which weakened them considerably.

Russia and Germany were separated by Poland, which was to be the first victim of World War II. For several years Hitler had realised that Poland was a plum ripe for picking. It had always been a vulnerable, unstable country with no natural defensive frontiers. In the eighteenth century it had even ceased to exist, having been partitioned between its three greedy neighbours: Prussia, Austria-Hungry and Russia. Having been recreated after the Napoleonic Wars, Poland was made a dependency of Russia. In the 1914–18 war some Poles had fought for Russia, some for France and Britain, and some had become conscripted into the armies of Austria and Germany: this meant that on some fronts Poles had been compelled to fight against other Poles.

In 1919, following the Treaty of Versailles, Poland became an independent state once more. Almost immediately it came into conflict with its neighbours and acquired small portions of territory from them on the grounds that these were predominantly Polish. Poland acquired Teschen from the new state of Czechoslovakia, and Vilna and Grodno from the Russians, who at that time had other, more pressing, matters to consider. These territorial gains were of little value but brought disadvantages in that on the Russian front they took in large numbers of Ukrainians and Lithuanians.

The surprise which greeted the announcement of the Russo-German pact in August 1939 would not have been so great if the events of the previous decade had been properly interpreted. Although Russia had watched Hitler's rise to power with apprehensive interest, it had never seemed to her that the West would be likely to bring it to a halt. Instead, the Soviets suspected that France and Britain hoped that

Germany would expand eastwards and Hitler would endeav-
our to prove that he was a more successful general than
Napoleon. The Soviet Union believed that the West's policy
of appeasement probably involved leaving Germany a clear
field to make conquests in Russia. Better still for the West,
the Soviets considered, would be Germany and Russia
fighting each other to a standstill and thus weakened being
unable to resist Western pressure in Europe. Over the
centuries Russia had developed a deep suspicion of the
motives of all foreigners and this attitude of latent hostility
had been inherited and developed by the Soviets. Long
before the 1939 pact they themselves had been trying to earn
good will in Germany. From the early 1920s they had
provided training facilities and military aircraft for German
airmen who were forbidden by the Treaty of Versailles to
have an air force of their own. They were to pay a heavy price
for the help they had given to the embryonic German Air
Force when the Luftwaffe pounded Russian cities in the
1940s. But the co-operation had gone further than air force
training; it included liaison visits by Soviet staff officers to the
German army. In retrospect, the Soviet-German pact of
1939, which came as such a shock to the outside world, and
particularly to communist supporters of the Soviet Union,
had long been foreshadowed. Paradoxical though it may
seem, it was Hitler's successes elsewhere which encouraged
the Soviets to conclude the pact. Austria had been swamped
by the Nazis, Czechoslovakia had been dismembered: the
pressing need was to ensure that Hitler did not overrun
Poland and bring his troops right up to the frontier of the
Soviet Union.

Hitler was indeed closing in. After swallowing Czechoslovakia, Poland and the Polish Corridor became the subject
of his white-hot speeches. When Poland had been recreated
in 1919 it had been given access to the sea by this 'Polish
Corridor', a strip of territory, most of which had formerly
been German and which reached the Baltic at Danzig.
Danzig had been declared a 'free city' under the administration of the League of Nations. Unfortunately for Danzig, in
1934 the Nazis in that city obtained control of the administration and simply ignored the protests of the League. From

then on Hitler began to make demands – addressed to no one in particular – that Danzig should be formally transferred to Germany and a strip of land across the corridor should accompany it; direct road and rail links would be made to East Prussia, which was now separated from Germany by the corridor. East Prussia had an almost sacred quality in the eyes of the Germans, for this was the district in which modern Germany had originated. It had formerly been a border state owned by the Order of the Teutonic Knights, which had developed into the Prussia of Frederick the Great and the Junker military caste. Emotionally the isolated status of East Prussia was an excellent topic for Hitler when he screamed invective against the treaty-makers of Versailles. Hitler's speeches, delivered at Nazi rallies of thousands of people, were stage-managed with storm-troopers, torches, swastikas and superb timing. The word '*Deutschland*', thundered out from the microphones, seemed to signify all that was noble and all-powerful; 'Danzig' in a hissing sneer was clearly both venomous and unclean.

Few people in the West knew or cared what or where the Polish Corridor was: those who had heard of it mostly thought it must be an underground tunnel. But in March 1939 when Hitler was busy dismantling Czechoslovakia, Britain took the fatal step which committed her to 'a war in the wrong place at the wrong time'; furthermore it was a commitment which she could not possibly honour effectively. However, Chamberlain was now tired of Hitler's bluster and broken promises and decided that a resolute step should be taken. He was, of course, quite unsuspecting of the extraordinary development of six months later, when the two arch-enemies Russia and Germany would sign a non-aggression pact. He seems to have been equally unaware that any pledge to help another country preserve its independence is worse than useless when both guarantor and possible aggressor know that it cannot be implemented. In Britain at that time there were absurd armchair strategists who believed that the RAF could take off from Britain, bomb Berlin, land in Poland, be refuelled and rearmed, and bomb Germany again on the way home.

The pact was signed on 23 August. It was supposed to

remain valid for ten years. In the event it lasted for less than two, for Hitler broke it unilaterally when he invaded Russia on 22 June 1941, but by then both the signatories would have agreed it had served its purpose.

2

THE PHONEY WAR

Without any formal declaration of war, German troops and aircraft crossed the frontier into Poland during the night of 1/2 September 1939. France and Britain promptly demanded their withdrawal and on 2 September Chamberlain sent an ultimatum declaring that unless Hitler withdrew at once Britain would declare war. Hitler was given 24 hours to reply, but simply ignored the ultimatum. In consequence, Chamberlain made a broadcast on 3 September, explaining what he had done and announcing that Britain was now at war with Germany. It was an extremely uninspiring broadcast and it was only just over when the air raid sirens began wailing. It seemed to many at that moment that all the doomsday prophets had been right and that Britain would immediately be flattened and gassed by bombers. In the event it was a false alarm caused by someone mistakenly supposing that a flight of our own aircraft was an enemy bomber squadron. The wartime sirens had a particularly chilling, wailing note which wavered up and down; a more likely morale-destroyer would have been difficult to find. The 'all-clear' was a long continuous note, unmusical but comforting. At first, everyone stopped work (or was supposed to) and took shelter when the sirens went. However, as this was soon found to be stopping vital war production quite unnecessarily, work was authorized to continue until whistles were blown; these meant that bombers were virtually overhead. Later in the war bombs were treated philosophically, 'If it's got your number on it, it will get you,' and men and women carried on with their tasks, industrial or domestic, while bombs thumped and crashed all around them.

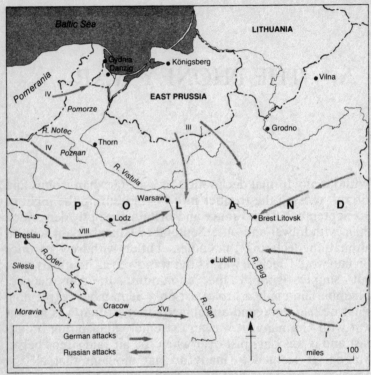

Poland 1939

However after the first scare life in Britain settled back to
near normality. In the expectation that the main towns would
be bombed, children and their mothers were evacuated to
what was believed to be safe areas (this had begun two days
before the declaration of war). They were billeted on people
who were considered to have accommodation to spare. This,
though true, did not mean that they relished being the hosts
to families of children who had been brought up in a different
environment, with a different standard of behaviour, and
sometimes with lice in their hair. However, the resentment of
the billeters was probably matched by the boredom of the
evacuees (as they came to be called) who much preferred the
excitement of a deprived life in the city to the dreariness and
restrictions of the countryside. In a short time many of them

drifted back; when the real bombing started better preparations had been made.

Meanwhile air raid wardens reported for duty and busied themselves in enforcing the blackout; this gave great scope to petty bureaucrats and frustrated tyrants. The blackout regulations decreed that it was an offence to show any light which might be visible from the air. This meant thick curtains over all windows and doors, with special arrangements for the entrances to public houses, no street-lighting, car lights reduced to one small cross in blacked-out headlights: the glow of a cigarette was said to be visible to an enemy aircraft a mile above, and to strike a match in the street was a very serious offence indeed. A Swansea man whose excuse for striking a match was that his false teeth had fallen out of his mouth while he had a coughing fit in a dark street had his reasons dismissed; he was heavily fined.

Hospital beds were cleared for the expected bombing casualties, vehicles requisitioned for ambulance and rescue work, public shelters, above and below ground, were opened. Food stocks were dispersed; essential points such as telephone exchanges were guarded against sabotage; cinemas and theatres were closed and public gatherings, as at football matches, were forbidden. The country had mobilized; food rationing was introduced, thousands of restrictive regulations were introduced (about 15,000 a year) and enforced. When the expected bombers failed to arrive, these restrictions became particularly irksome and some of them, such as for football matches and dances, were relaxed. Stories of what was happening in Poland continued to be broadcast, and sounded very unpleasant, but soon it began to be felt that Poland was a long way away and Hitler would not be so foolish as to try those sort of tricks on the British. From another 3,000 miles away, in America, it all seemed positively bizarre and journalists nicknamed it 'The Great Bore War' or 'The Phoney War'. However, there were American journalists in London and Paris who had given warnings about Hitler in the 1930s and they now waited and watched for some of their prophecies to come true. The RAF was sent on missions to release thousands of leaflets over German territory warning them that they should stop fighting; all ended with the ominous words, 'This might have been a bomb'. The recipients had, of course, no power to stop Hitler, even if they had wanted to do so. All the British armed forces had more recruits than they needed and it was said that you needed influence even to join the army as a private. Trains, also blacked out, were always overcrowded. Soldiers in uniform had to carry a rifle and kit bag if they were travelling, which added to the congestion. People were admonished to stay at home if their journey was not really necessary. As the weeks passed, the initial enthusiasm waned and was replaced by apathy and irritation. Rationing and regulations caused some inconvenience; timber became (to use a phrase which had widespread use) 'in short supply'. Later in the war this first year was looked back on as a period of unbroken happiness, but by then people knew what war involved.

In Poland the people knew well enough what war involved. The Germans had launched their vaunted '*Blitzkrieg*' (lightning war) on them. *Blitzkrieg* was a new concept in warfare: the combination of surprise, speed and terror tactics. The initial surprise was achieved by attacking without declaring war, the speed was the result of using fast vehicles and crashing through potential gaps without troubling to protect flanks, and the terror tactics were implemented by machine-gunning and dive-bombing civilians and refugees. The German effort was greatly helped by the fact that there were two million Germans living in Poland and from these the Nazis had built up a 'Fifth Column'. The term derived from the Spanish Civil War when Franco's forces were said to have been advancing towards a citadel in four columns but had already a fifth column of supporters inside it. During World War II the term was applied to previously infiltrated troops and also to potential sympathizers ready to betray their own side. Fifth Columnists spread false rumours, stimulated panic, guided bombers with ground signs, and generally hampered the resistance.

The Polish Air Force, such as it was, was destroyed on the ground within the first two days. The Polish army was hopelessly out-gunned and out-generalled, but fought valiantly nevertheless. At one point Poles even charged German

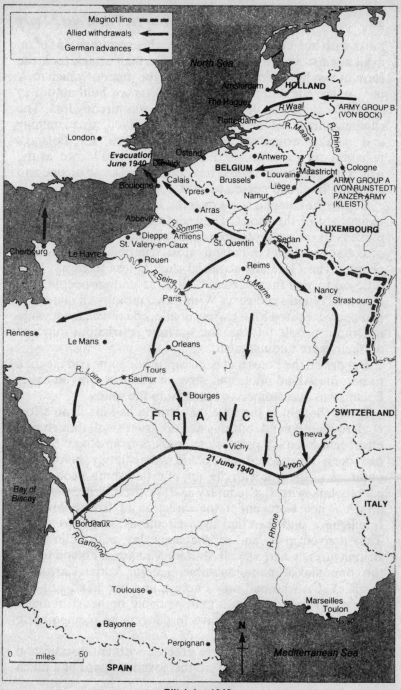

Blitzkrieg 1940

tanks with horsed cavalry. However, sheer courage was of no avail against weight of metal. The German attack took the form of two huge pincer movements, the inner of which took in Warsaw, the outer Brest Litovsk. Warsaw held out till 27 September, but for the Poles the war was already lost. The campaign had cost the Germans 10,572 killed, 5,029 missing and 30,322 wounded, which speaks well for Poland's response to an undeclared war, but Poland's own army, which fully mobilized could have numbered close on one and a half million, had ceased to exist.

Before the campaign was over the Russians had leapt in for their share of the spoils. They sent their armies in a pincer movement on 17 September. This enabled them to acquire 77,000 square miles of Poland, most of her oil, and 13 million people. The Germans acquired slightly less territory, very little oil (which they needed badly), 22 million people, and most of Poland's industry. Within two months 18,000 Poles had been executed for a variety of alleged crimes; meanwhile in Britain people felt that the wartime restrictions imposed on them were unduly harsh.

But not all the Poles had been captured. Some had escaped to become Allied pilots and serve in a Polish army-in-exile. Poland was accustomed to rising from the ashes.

It was thought at the time that Britain had made no effort at all to help Poland, but this was not true, small though that effort had been. A party of 12 soldiers from Royal Signals had been despatched to Poland immediately before the outbreak of the war with the aim of establishing a communications link with that country in case the Germans should attack. They were under the direction of British Military Intelligence and travelled by a circuitous, overland route. They arrived in Poland on the same day as the Germans. Britain already had a small Military Mission in Poland under the command of the redoubtable General Adrian Carton de Wiart, V.C., who had only one eye and one hand and had been wounded more times than he could bother to remember. He was not merely brave in danger, he seemed quite unaware of it.

On arrival the Signals were greeted with enthusiasm and the expectation that they were the advance guard of a much larger force. Sadly, this was not true. They became the first British troops to see action in World War II, for they were soon caught up in machine-gun fire from low-flying aircraft. They were also the first – and last – British troops to be caught in a gas attack, for at one point the German aircraft, flying low, sprayed an unidentified liquid which created a white mist. This choking gas was fortunately kept out by army respirators and there were no lasting effects from the first sniffs.

Although the position of the Signallers would have been difficult enough if the invasion had been limited to German troops, with the intervention of the Russians it became impossible. The Red Army overran all the areas where the Signals could have found 'safe' hiding places, and thus become a rallying point and link for the Polish resistance. But as the German and Russian armies moved closer to each other there was clearly nowhere for the Signals to go but out of Poland – a journey which they made with considerable difficulty.

As this brief, brutal and successful campaign drew to its close the British and French High Commands pondered its lessons. Unfortunately they did not treat them sufficiently seriously. The assumption was made that the German success had been entirely due to Polish unpreparedness and lack of equipment. There was an element of truth in this, but it was rash of the Allies to decide that such tactics could not be repeated as successfully against stronger opposition. It was not realised at the time that the German forces were infinitely better equipped, better-trained and more highly motivated than they had ever been. Furthermore, they were using a new tactical concept.

The irony of the situation was that the German tactics had been learnt entirely from British experiments and British writers; while the Germans were absorbing the lessons from these two sources, the British War Office dismissed them as being impracticable.

The story had begun in November 1917, as World War I was entering its last year. In that month, the British High Command, shaken by the enormous losses caused by the blood and mud bath of Passchendaele, decided to allow the tank pioneers to try out tactics in the nearby sector. At that time tanks were very slow, averaging about 3½ miles an hour, but at Cambrai, 381 of them, unannounced by the usual preliminary bombardment, rolled forward on 20 November and made a gap five miles deep in the German line. Nothing like it had ever been seen before in this war: it was the end of stalemate and a foretaste of victory. Unfortunately for the British, the attack then petered out. There were insufficient British infantry to hold the newly won ground. The Higher Command's plan for the battle had been unimaginative and soon drifted into chaos. The Germans, who had been shocked and beaten in the first 48 hours, took advantage of the pause in the British surge to counter-attack. They infiltrated the newly won British positions with columns of infantry and they harassed the British infantry, which had been left too far behind, with low flying aircraft. With a few adjustments, the tactics which would later destroy the Poles, French, Belgians, Dutch and British, had been born. The enormous potential of a tank thrust preceded by low-flying aircraft and closely followed by mobile infantry columns was now firmly impressed on the German military mind. All that remained was to develop it.

When World War I ended, almost exactly a year after the Battle of Cambrai, the British and French had too much on their minds to dwell on the past battles except sentimentally. They had won the war, they had beaten the Germans; they now had other problems, mainly with their imperial responsibilities, to occupy their thoughts.

For the Germans it was a very different story. The German army had been reduced to a fraction of its former size, the German fleet had been scuttled, and the air force had been abolished. But the generals and the staff officers still remained. They had lost this war; the vaunted Schlieffen Plan had miscarried; their armies had been out-fought; they had sustained enormous casualties. But soon a new generation would be growing up and while it did the Allied victors would begin quarrelling among themselves as Allies usually do when the fighting is over, sometimes even before. History would repeat itself. But in one particular it must not repeat itself. Next time Germany would use newer and better methods and this time she would win.

The German officers discussed and debated every battle of the war, analysing what had gone wrong, where, and why. There was little to learn from most of them, but Cambrai was different. Germany, which had paid little attention to tanks in the last war, must have them for the next.

There were, however, problems to be overcome. Germany was forbidden by the Treaty of Versailles to have tanks. She was also forbidden to have military aircraft. These problems were not difficult to overcome. As we mentioned the Soviet government secretly agreed to allow German pilots to train on military aircraft on an airfield near Moscow; the Swedes, neutral in theory but in fact biased towards Germany, supplied them with two real tanks for training purposes in 1926. The Swiss, also neutral, agreed to allow factories to manufacture arms for the embryonic German army.

Even so, the tank pioneers of Germany did not have matters all their own way. Even in the small German army of the 1920s there was an element of conservatism, particularly among those who had been trained in the old cavalry regiments. There is a natural tendency in every generation to believe that the methods by which you yourself were trained in your youth are inherently better than those which succeed them. However, Hans von Seeckt, who was the German army commander between 1920 and 1926, was progressive and encouraged a young captain called Heinz Guderian, of whom the West would hear more later. Guderian wrote articles in military journals, expounding the virtues of armoured vehicles. His disciples could not use the genuine article at first because of the treaty restrictions, so instead they simulated them with canvas and plywood structures mounted on wheels. The other European nations laughed derisively when they heard of these experiments, and found the German preoccupation with these absurd structures proof that German militarism had now become farcical. The jokes about the German 'cardboard tanks' lasted well into the 1930s, when there was always someone who knew someone who had been travelling in Austria or Germany in an Austin 7 (then the smallest British car) who had had a head-on collision with a formidable-looking German tank. To the traveller's astonishment the 'tank' had distintegrated on impact and was found to be made of canvas and wood. However, these stories ceased suddenly in 1940 when British soldiers found that none of their existing anti-tank weapons could stop a German tank unless the gun could be fired through one of the observation slits: the Panzer armour, then and later, made a mockery of most British anti-tank weapons.

Guderian admitted that many of his ideas were drawn from two British writers, B. H. Liddell-Hart and J. F. C. Fuller. Both these visualized the tank not as a subordinate vehicle to be called on when needed, but as the leader on the battlefield with other arms, such as infantry and artillery, subordinate to it. This did not commend itself to elite regiments which had always seen themselves as superior to other units, particularly those with wheeled transport. This attitude was slow to change and even affected some of the events during World War II itself. Similar military conservatism had prevailed during World War I and had eventually led to huge numbers of infantry soldiers being slaughtered by machine-guns which the High Command had for long refused to believe were a serious threat.

However, it would be unfair to say that the War Office completely neglected the opportunity to examine potential tank warfare between the wars. In 1927 and 1928 two Experimental Mechanized Forces exercises were held in Britain. A report was produced but it was apparently not a secret one and no doubt copies found their way to Germany. One which undoubtedly did was supplied by Captain Baillie-Stewart who gave it to a German girl friend, an act of treachery which led to his being arrested and becoming the mysterious 'Officer in the Tower'. Baillie-Stewart was given a five-year jail sentence and after release went to Germany and became naturalized in 1940. He then broadcast Nazi propaganda, aiming it particularly at British troops.

Of greater long term importance was the fact that in 1927 the Germans and Russians inaugurated a joint tank school at Kazan in the USSR. Here officers from the two armies examined all the latest prototype tanks. As both countries were still deficient in military expertise they drew on British and American designs. Before long this meant that the best features of the British Vickers and the American Christie tanks were being incorporated into German and Russian designs. When, in 1941, the Russians produced the T-34 (based on the Christie design) and the KV1, the West was astonished. No one should have been surprised: the Russians had made the necessary deductions in the 1930s and when Hitler closed down the Kazan co-operation in 1934 the Russians were well capable of operating on their own. In the event Hitler was probably the loser by breaking off co-operation just when the Russians were beginning to forge ahead. Had they continued with it a little longer, they might not have been quite so surprised when they met the T-34s and KVs in 1941.

One other event of the 1930s had a significant effect on the Russo-German tank battles of the 1940s. At the end of the 1930s Stalin launched a ferocious and apparently senseless purge on the upper ranks of the Red Army. To many this appeared to have weakened it to a point beyond which it would not be able to recover. Subsequently it seemed that what had happened in Russia was what would, in a more kindly manner, occur in the Allied armies. All were full of senior officers who refused to give serious consideration to a totally new form of warfare. It was not surprising. Tank warfare, which led to breakthroughs with long exposed flanks, relied on the avoidance of mechanical breakdowns and required imagination and initiative by subordinate commanders, was anathema to officers who believed that ground should be consolidated as it was won, flanks should be protected and armies should advance in line at a speed at which the supply train could keep up. The essence of tank warfare was that you had either an enormous success or an appalling disaster. To avoid the latter, if matters went wrong, much local initiative was required. We shall see the results of this later when we look at some of the great battles of the war.

The Poles were the first to find out about the revolution in armoured warfare but, as we saw, the unfortunate Polish experience was not quite enough to convince the Allied Higher Command.

The French in particular did not want new ideas. Their

commander-in-chief, General Gamelin, said to be suffering from the effects of venereal disease, was not interested in learning from or co-operating with allies. He spoke French very rapidly and almost inaudibly, indifferent to whether either colleagues or allies could understand him. This time the French wanted nothing to do with battles in the open field, whether with tanks or not. Since the 1920s they had been building the Maginot Line, a fortification designed to keep out future German invaders. André Maginot, after whom it was named, was Minister of War in 1929–31. He died in 1932 but the line continued to be built and was completed in 1938. Maginot was not a soldier but a politician. He had joined the French army in 1914 as a private but had been seriously wounded and had returned to politics in 1915. However, many French politicians agreed with him that the best way to protect France was to build an impassable barrier. The line itself was a masterpiece of underground fortifications, with tunnels, lifts, railways and guns of all sizes. However, when the Germans invaded in 1940 they initially ignored the line completely and came around the northern flank, much as they had done in 1914. Experience should have taught the French that if the Germans did not respect Belgian neutrality in 1914 they were still less likely to do so at a later date with Hitler in charge.

But the worst aspect of the line was not that it was too short but that it created what became known as the 'Maginot mentality'. Opposing aggression by sheltering in allegedly impregnable strongholds creates a feeling of timidity rather than security. The best antidote to fear of being hurt is to make some attempt to strike back at the aggressor. Submission to a more powerful opponent may work in the animal kingdom but it is a fatal policy for humans. The spirit of 'They shall not pass' which had inspired the French at Verdun in 1916 was not capable of surviving defensive entombment in concrete bunkers and tunnels. The Maginot Line gave the French army the totally false idea that it would never be called upon to fight battles in the open again. Worse than that was the malaise which gripped the entire French nation. This was a feeling of 'We are now protected by the Maginot Line. It is not necessary to concern ourselves with the state of our armed forces. At all events we must avoid being dragged into a different sort of conflict by our allies, notably Britain.'

The French tend to be sceptically realistic about governments, public figures, generals, diplomats, allies and big business. Schneider-Creusot was a massive French arms manufacturer. However, those 'in the know' were aware that it controlled Skoda in Czechoslovakia before Hitler invaded that country and also had links with Krupps. During World War I certain Franco-German border areas were neither shelled nor bombed; this was apparently by mutual agreement when the armies were otherwise locked in a fight to the death. Both sides benefited by their arms manufacture being uninterrupted, but the greatest beneficiaries were the financial controllers. Even if the average Frenchman did not know these facts, he would suspect them.

There was, of course, good reason for French apathy and disillusionment. France had been compensated for the damage that Germany had inflicted on her between 1914 and 1918, and Germany had subsequently been demilitarized. Now, however, Germany was stronger than ever, all the alliances which France had made with border states like Czechoslovakia and Poland were in tatters, the League of Nations, on which so many hopes had been founded, was now no more than a laughing stock. Admittedly the French themselves had done little to help the League, but that was overlooked. French people read newspapers avidly, but they do not always believe what they are told in them. It would have been surprising if they had done in the 1930s when papers were edited according to the amount of subsidy which was being paid to their proprietors – by Germans, Italians, Japanese, or even the French government itself.

Added to everything else was the instability of the franc. Even in French industry there is much of the practical attitude of the French peasant farmer, who likes to work hard, drive a close bargain, and accumulate savings. However, when the factory for which you are working cannot sell its products abroad because of some mysterious manipulation of the value of the franc you become impatient with your own politicians and exceedingly wary of all foreigners. The combined effect of all these matters was scarcely likely to produce a nation briskly ready to tackle yet another German aggression a mere 20 years after the last one had been defeated at fearful cost. The collapse of France in 1940 was predictable. Subsequently the wide variety in the quality of resistance movements was as inevitable as the hostility between various sectors.

In 1939 France did not realise that she was to be the next victim. She read about the German onslaught on Poland with awed horror. *C'était horrible, épouvantable.* Fortunately it could never happen to France. There was the excellent air force, the traditional navy, and a large conscript army. And above all there was the Maginot. No matter how many tanks and dive-bombers the Germans had they would not get past that.

The British thought the same about the English Channel, though a year later they were beginning to have doubts.

America took a detached view of these events. In the 1930s the British opinion of the United States was that at heart it was really still a part of the British empire. The fact that it had been an independent country for over 150 years and that Americans included millions of people whose ancestors had migrated from European countries such as Italy, Germany, Yugoslavia and even Russia, and thus had no feelings of affinity towards Britain, did not break into the consciousness of the average Briton. America's place in any conflict was right beside Britain in the front line, was the prevailing view. It did not occur to most people in Britain that Americans did not share this sentiment, and in fact most Americans hardly gave a thought to Britain. There, the assumption was that World War I had been won by America's intervention, 'they had pulled the chestnuts out of the fire' but received few thanks for it. Fortunately Woodrow Wilson's madcap scheme of involving them in the League of Nations and the tangled, quarrelsome politics of Europe which their ancestors had thankfully left behind them had soon been forgotten. The rise of figures like Hitler and Mussolini seemed inevitable after the slump of 1929, which had involved America, but for which Europe must take some responsibility. Europe was no business of America's; it offered no threat and if America needed a powerful defence force it would be against the 'Yellow peril' – the threat of the Japanese from the other side of the Pacific. The fact that the Japanese were 5,000 miles away and Europe only three did not affect the argument. When therefore Congress passed two Neutrality Acts in the late 1930s, clearly stating that America was not going to get herself involved in any conflicts outside her territorites, the American electorate approved strongly. America had enough to bother about without being concerned with other people's troubles: she was busy recovering from the long-term effects of the slump. The stories of events in Europe, reported vividly in the newspapers, made interesting reading but seemed increasingly remote to Americans as they travelled from the Atlantic seaboard, through the Middle West (which was never much interested in Europe anyway), and to California where they were only interesting as potential material for film plots. There was nothing surprising or blameworthy in this, whatever Britain may have thought; few Britons had any concept of events in Nebraska, Wyoming or Texas. To most Europeans an American was a rich tourist with a large hat and camera who came from a country which consisted of skyscraper cities and cowboys chasing Indians over the countryside. Only a handful of British people understood American politics or the constitution: most people assumed Americans operated the same system as the British, but less efficiently.

The agonies of Poland in September 1939 made little impact on the rest of the world and were soon forgotten. Many people thought that Hitler had now got war out of his system and, when he had counted his casualties, would begin to behave like a normal head of state should. The motto was 'Business as usual'.

Events were not, however, entirely as they seemed on the surface. For the Royal Navy the battle had begun immediately: there was nothing 'phoney' about the war at sea. It had, however, begun well. On 3 September 1939, Neville Chamberlain appointed Winston Churchill First Lord of the Admiralty and a member of the War Cabinet. The Board of the Admiralty signalled to the Fleet, 'Winston is back', and the news was well received. The last time Churchill had held that post was before the outbreak of World War I, when he had mobilized the navy and pursued an energetic policy up until 1915. In that year, however, the Gallipoli landings had gone badly wrong and Churchill, quite unnecessarily, shouldered the blame and resigned. During the 1930s he had written numerous articles, many of which were published in *The Daily Telegraph*, giving clear warning of the threat posed by the rise of Hitler and the rearmament of Germany. Nevertheless his warnings were ignored by the Cabinet, which preferred to believe that appeasement would solve the problem more easily than rearmament. The other great national newspaper, *The Times*, edited by Geoffrey Dawson, threw its weight behind the government policy and by that fact slipped from its position of authority which it has never regained. People used to say with conviction, 'You can believe what you read in *The Times*', but after the fiasco of appeasement they ceased to believe and say it. Beaverbrook's *Daily Express*, which was his mouthpiece, supported Churchill, but with inane stubbornness stated firmly that there would be no European war and was continuing to do so until the day it broke out.

Churchill was back, but not yet where he should be. His contemporaries regarded him as a dangerous maverick, a useful though turbulent member of the War Cabinet but a man to be removed as soon as his useful work was done. In 1939 the idea of his ever being Prime Minister was inconceivable.

The naval war began with the sinking of the *Athenia*, an unarmed passenger ship, on the day war was declared. The U-boat responsible gave no warning. 112 lives were lost, including those of 28 Americans. The sinking was said to have shocked the Germans as much as the British. The U-boat commander afterwards said that he had thought that the *Athenia* was an armed merchantman, and was too far off the normal shipping routes to be a mere passenger ship. The Germans subsequently issued orders that only freighters were to be sunk and even then only after their crews had been taken off. Passenger ships, unless troopships, must never be attacked, even if sailing in convoys. The *Athenia* atrocity caused a wave of shock through the Western world, but the feelings of outrage soon died down, much as they had done over Poland.

Both the British and the French navies were efficient, but the Royal Navy had been starved of money for so long that many of the larger ships were older than they should have been: 13 out of the 15 warships had been built before 1918. Four new battleships were under construction in 1939 but would not be ready for another 18 months. There were 69 submarines, mostly modern, and an adequate number of cruisers and destroyers. However, naval warfare had changed considerably since 1918, faster in fact than the Admiralty was prepared to acknowledge. Ships were now vulnerable to aircraft, both shore-based and those on aircraft-carriers. There was resentment in the Royal Navy over this, and it was not limited to the most senior ranks. When manoeuvres were held the multiple pom-pom guns on battleships and cruisers were usually judged to have shot down all of the attacking aircraft. The umpires were, almost invariably, on the ships. There would be a bitter harvest for this self-deception in 1941.

For a Royal Navy of Britain's size (numbering over 100,000 men) there was a grave deficiency in carriers. Of the six available, only one, the *Ark Royal*, was new and had been built for the purpose: the others were conversions from battleships. During the war the German radio constantly announced the sinking of the *Ark Royal*, hoping that this might provoke the Admiralty into disclosing her whereabouts. Nobody was allowed to say where a ship was or, if a sailor, which ship he belonged to. A sailor's cap simply bore the letters HMS: the name of his ship had been deleted.

An additional counter to the submarine threat was provided by RAF Coastal Command, which had only become independent as late as 1936. However, it had rather less than 300 slow, almost obsolete Ansons, and the crews had had no proper training in anti-submarine warfare.

Both the main bases for the navy were vulnerable: Scapa Flow had been demilitarized after 1918 and was poorly defended in 1939; Malta, the base for the Mediterranean Fleet, was all too close to the Italian airfields. In view of the vulnerability of Malta, the base at Alexandria was hastily expanded. Britain was entitled to the use of this Egyptian port by virtue of the Anglo-Egyptian Treaty of 1936. Had she not been, the position of the Mediterranean Fleet would have been far from easy. However, the foresight shown by the Anglo-Egyptian Treaty had been counteracted two years later when the Chamberlain government, anxious to gain Irish good will, unconditionally surrendered all rights to bases in Southern Ireland. The bases at Berehaven and Lough Swilly had been invaluable during World War I and there was no possibility that they could be adequately replaced by expanding the facilities at Belfast and Londonderry.

The French navy, although useful on paper, was destined to play an ineffectual part in the war and to be the cause of much Franco-British ill-feeling.

The German fleet had the advantage of consisting almost entirely of modern ships. According to some 'official' versions of German naval history, Hitler had no intention of going to war with Britain in 1939 and was shocked when he realised what had happened. His plan, it seems, was to continue building until 1944 and then, with every prospect of success, to challenge the combined British and French navies. However, the view that he did not expect war with Britain seems to conflict somewhat with the fact that by 19 August 1939, *a week before* the Russo-German Pact, and 12 days before Hitler ignored Chamberlain's ultimatum, 21 German U-boats had taken up station around the British Isles. These were all long-range submarines; a further contingent of shorter range craft had been sent to patrol the North Sea. A few days later the *Graf Spee* was in mid-Atlantic and the *Deutschland* off Greenland. Even so, the SKL (German Naval High Command) felt extremely unprepared. The fast battleships, *Scharnhorst* and *Gneisenau* were not complete, and the *Bismarck* and *Tirpitz* were still under construction. In the SKL opinions were sharply divided about the merit of battleships in a future war. Some believed they had a valuable part to play even in the era of aircraft and submarines; others, notably Admiral Dönitz, believed that the only way to win a naval war against Britain was by packs of U-boats. In the event, the latter nearly proved their case.

The most vulnerable aspect of Britain's war potential was that it all depended on imports. Of the population of Britain, at that time verging on 50 million, less than half could be fed from internal resources. Feeding the remainder, some 30 million, required that large quantities of food must be imported, mainly from Canada, New Zealand, Australia, and North and South America, but in order to pay for food imports Britain needed to earn money by exports. Exports were created by harnessing British energy and inventiveness to manufacturing goods which other countries wished to buy, but manufactured goods required raw materials and the only raw materials in which Britain was self-sufficient were coal and fish. Iron ore, manganese, chrome, nickel, timber, copper, etc., all had to be shipped in. It was clear therefore to any potential adversary that the quickest way to defeat Britain was to cut her sea routes. The resultant starvation would not merely be of foodstuffs but of all the other raw materials required to keep exports and armaments manufacture in a flourishing state.

Needless to say Britain, with grim experience of the submarine blockade of the previous war, was more conscious of the vulnerability of her position than anyone. Her lifeline, the sea lanes, must be kept open and for this purpose she had a substantial, but by no means complete, navy. Surprisingly enough, at the outbreak of war Britain had more submarines than Germany (69 to 56). In the coming conflict both sides would make extensive use of mines, the Germans to sink British shipping; the British to protect it. The aim of both sides was to lay as many mines as possible, by aircraft or submarine, in the enemy's coastal waters. Britain protected Dover with some 3,000 carefully positioned mines and therefore enabled the entire British Expeditionary Force to be transported to France without loss. Nevertheless, the Germans had the better of the mine war in the opening stages, for they sank nearly 200,000 tons of Allied shipping in the first three months. The secret of their success was the magnetic mine. This lethal device had been invented by Britain during World War I but had then been neglected. Subsequently it was further developed by German scientists and proved particularly effective when dropped by aircraft. Unlike other mines it did not require to be moored in a designated area, but could be dropped on to the sea-bed from which it would rise and collide with any ship which passed over it. Fortunately for Britain, one was dropped on land by mistake. It was taken apart by an extremely courageous naval officer and in consequence the Admiralty was able to install a counter-measure known as de-gaussing. Ships were provided with an energized electric cable which neutralized magnetic fields and in consequence the German mines did not detonate their charges.

The brisk naval warfare around Britain and France alarmed the US government, which was incensed by the British insistence on seaching neutral (including American) ships which were bound for Germany and suspected of carrying contraband (i.e. war materials). Congress therefore prohibited American shipping from entering the waters around France and Britain. However, the American President, Franklin D. Roosevelt, who was strongly pro-British and anti-Hitler, managed to put through a measure which enabled the Allies to buy war materials in America provided they could pay for them and would use their own ships to transport them. This was known as the 'Cash and Carry' Act and was the first of many steps which Roosevelt took to assist the Allied cause.

The ferocity of the war at sea should have been an adequate indication that the 'phoney' war on land was likely to be merely temporary. However, neither the British nor the French government seems to have made the necessary deduction.

By March 1940 the Germans had sunk 222 Allied ships, for the loss of one-third of their own U-boats. An early victim was the small British aircraft carrier *Courageous* (17 September) which was, unwisely, hunting U-boats in the Atlantic at the time. On 14 October Britain sustained another loss, which was, in fact, less crippling than it was thought to be at the time. The *Royal Oak*, a World War I battleship which was too slow for modern sea forays, was at anchor in Scapa Flow when it was torpedoed by a German submarine. The ship was of little value, but the 833 sailors who went down with it were a tragic loss. A daring U-boat commander had shown up the inadequacy of the Scapa Flow defences which were hastily strengthened; he became a German hero but was himself sunk by a British destroyer less than two years later. Although the U-boat's feat seems well enough authenticated, there is still some mystery attached to it and there are those who assert that the battleship was sunk by sabotage.

On 23 November the Royal Navy showed that it had lost none of its old fighting spirit when a converted liner, the *Rawalpindi* put up a gallant fight before being sunk by the German battle cruisers *Scharnhorst* and *Gneisenau*. As the Germans were reading the British naval codes, their two ships were able to return safely to port before a vengeful British force could catch up with them and hand out appropriate retribution.

It later became known, when the official history of British Intelligence in World War II was published in 1979, that Naval Intelligence was limited and ineffective at this stage. When successes occurred at sea they were usually the result of local initiative, rather than of plans by higher authority acting on good intelligence reports. A case in point was the *Graf Spee* battle. The *Graf Spee* was a German 'pocket battleship', which had been cruising around the South Atlantic during the first three months of the war, in the course of which time she had sunk nine British ships. 'Pocket battleship' was the term the Royal Navy applied to ships which the Germans were allowed to build under the Anglo-German Naval Agreement of 1930. They were larger than cruisers but smaller than conventional battleships. They were formidable and very fast.

A force of three British cruisers, under the command of Commodore H. Harwood, guessed that the *Graf Spee* would soon turn its attention to the shipping off the River Plate, and took station nearby. When the German ship appeared, Harwood's force, though out-gunned, gave battle. The German ship inflicted considerable damage on its opponents but not without taking heavy punishment itself. The *Graf Spee*'s captain was uneasy about the situation, thinking there must be other, heavier British ships in the vicinity, and therefore took temporary refuge in Montevideo, Uruguay. The Uruguayans, strongly pro-Ally, were not prepared to let him stay there more than 72 hours. Accordingly, the *Graf Spee* put out to sea and scuttled herself. This gave the British a useful nickname for German ships – 'Scuttleships'. The German commander committed suicide.

There was a sequel to this welcome victory of David's over Goliath. The *Graf Spee* had always been accompanied by a supply tanker, the *Altmark*. Whenever the *Graf Spee* had sunk a ship, its commander had scrupulously transferred all the crew to the *Altmark*. The latter now headed rapidly for home and by February was in Norwegian territorial waters. There she was being escorted by two Norwegian destroyers, who were alleged by the Norwegian naval headquarters to have searched her and found nothing amiss. The prisoners were said to have been concealed in the holds. Churchill was not convinced and therefore authorised the British destroyer *Cossack* to investigate. The *Altmark* resisted but was captured; 299 British prisoners were found to be on board living in squalid conditions. Boarding a ship in neutral territorial waters was an illegal action, as the Germans were quick to point out. The incident indicated that the Norwegians, or at least some of them, were considerably less neutral in their relationship to Germany than had been supposed. However, the significance of this discovery was lost on the British government which supposed that Norway would resent being taken into the German orbit, and would bitterly resist any attempt at invasion. This proved to be another miscalculation for which Britain would pay dearly.

Miscalculations were all too frequent at this time, many, no doubt, being due to wishful thinking. One was the assumption that Hitler now realised he had gone too far in attacking Poland and would be ready to come to a conference table. There was a firm conviction in the Ministry of Economic Warfare that Hitler had neither the manufacturing capacity nor the raw materials to continue in the war for more than another 10 months. In fact, in 10 months time Hitler would have captured all the assets he needed to wage war for 10 years, let alone 10 months, and would be hammering on the door of the United Kingdom.

Far from being intimidated by Britain and France, Hitler was contemplating launching an attack on those countries as early as November 1939. Military intelligence in both France and Britain, knowing that Germany had approximately 80 divisions on the western front, most of which were concentrated near Belgium and Holland, and having a Czech spy in German Intelligence, concluded that an offensive might begin on some date between 31 October and 15 November. In fact the Germans had chosen 12 November, but postponed it without giving reasons. Meanwhile the population of Britain was living in a state of blissful complacency. In December, military Intelligence suggested that Norway and Sweden might be the next targets for German attacks, but then decided that the blow, when it came, would probably fall on France. Confirmation of the latter view came when a German aircraft was forced by bad weather to land in Belgium. In the cockpit was a document referring to the instructions for the German Air Force during an attack on France in the near future. This document, which had been captured so easily, seemed highly suspect to British military Intelligence, but was in fact genuine. It should not, of course, have been taken into the aircraft at all, but, as students of military history know well, many a plan has miscarried owing to flagrant disobedience of such rules.

The capture of this document changed the whole pattern of the war. British and French Intelligence assumed correctly that whether or not the document was a 'plant', there was every reason to suggest that the Germans would launch an attack on Belgium and France in May or June 1940. The Germans, realising that the capture of the plan must inevitably cause the Allies to tighten up their defences in the areas mentioned, now changed their entire tactics. Instead of coming through northern Belgium, along the invasion route used in World War I, they would now break through the 'impassable' Ardennes. Everyone on the Allied side knew that the Ardennes countryside with its hills and forests was quite unsuitable for tanks. However, Guderian, von Manstein and von Runstedt firmly believed that the Panzers could break through in that area and after their plan had been tried out in War Games in February 1940 Hitler, and Halder (the Chief of the Army General Staff), agreed with them. The stage was thus set for an Allied surprise and a German victory.

Meanwhile another campaign had been taking place in an

area in which the Allies were almost helpless to intervene. Russia, now linked to Germany whom she did not trust, was apprehensive about any action which the Allies might take in conjunction with the countries on the eastern Baltic coast. Finland, which had a land frontier with the Soviet Union (with Helsinki a short distance from the vital port of Leningrad), represented in Russian eyes a very considerable threat. In its chequered history Finland had been under Russian dominance until 1919, after which it had become independent. Similarly Estonia, Latvia and Lithuania were former Baltic provinces of Russia which had only been independent republics since 1920. Lithuania did not have a common frontier with Russia, but she did have one with Poland. Stalin was able to absorb Estonia, Latvia and Lithuania into the Soviet Union by making treaties with them in 1939 and later turning these into annexation, but Finland refused to agree to a similar process. In consequence Russia sent Finland an ultimatum on 29 November 1939 and followed it up with an invasion on the 30th.

In view of the fact that Russia had a population of 180 million and Finland a mere three million, it seemed that Finland's fate would soon be settled. Much to everyone's surprise, the Finns held out for three and a half months. This was incredible, since the Russians outnumbered them in every department, with 3,000 tanks to a mere handful, and 2,300 aircraft to 96. The Finns had constructed a formidable barrier known as the Mannerheim Line, named after the able commander-in-chief, but it was the guerrilla work of the Finnish ski patrols which caused the most delays: they harassed the Russians mercilessly as the latter tried to press forward through forest and snow. The Russians eventually won the war by a desperate attack on the Mannerheim Line by 27 divisions. Although Russia had eventually won, her losses had been enormous, many of them caused by the climate and the terrain on which the war was fought. Both the Germans and the Allies were interested in the Russian performance in its attempt to defeat a small, heavily outnumbered neighbour, and found it unimpressive. However, these conclusions about the military ability of Russia were premature, as the Germans were soon to find out. The Russian army had been fighting an extremely courageous opponent over terrain on which it was difficult for them to bring their full strength to bear. The Russian generals learnt much from the campaign and carried out reforms in the army accordingly.

The nearest that Britain came to being involved in the Finnish campaign was the raising of a volunteer force of experienced skiers. In order for this to be able to give effective help it needed to travel through Sweden, and the Swedes, cherishing their neutrality which allowed them to supply goods to all the belligerents, refused permission for it to do so. Unfortunately, at the end of the Finnish campaign, this volunteer force was disbanded. Had it been kept in being a further month it could have been of inestimable value in assisting in the Norwegian campaign.

However, there was more going on during the 'Phoney War' than was realised. Britain was trying desperately to expand her war potential in every field. The conscripts, the volunteers, and most of the territorial army, all required training facilities, whether for sea, land or air. In order to accommodate large numbers of young men, holiday camps, race courses, cricket and football grounds, and public buildings were commandeered. The majority of these places were totally inadequate for their new purpose, lacking heating and most other facilities. Holiday camps, which had been suitable for temporary summer occupation, were mainly constructed of plywood, and most had been built to accommodate a few hundred, not a few thousand. The winter of 1939 to 1940 proved to be exceptionally severe. Rationing was in force and extended not merely to food, clothes and petrol but also to all forms of fuel. Some camps had no heating at all, and when snow was on the ground the lack of facilities for drying clothes soon caused a mounting toll of sickness. The main problem with the rapidly expanded armed forces was that no one had experience of handling large numbers of recruits.

Although those who experienced the hardship of military service in the early days of the war would be surprised to hear it, conditions were vastly better than they had been for those who joined up in 1914. The greatest handicap from the training point of view was lack of the latest equipment. Every recruit, whatever his arm, learnt to handle and fire a rifle, but there were insufficient automatic weapons, as well as instructors skilled in their use. Cold, confused and disorientated though they may have been, thousands of young men and women were learning how to march, shoot, conceal themselves, cook, repair machines, maintain and fly aircraft, handle boats, read morse, parachute, and work in teams. In retrospect it seems something of a miracle that an entirely new structure could be built within society, as potential leaders were identified and trained, and enormous numbers were received, clothed, fed, transformed into sailors, soldiers or airmen and then sent to various destinations throughout the world. As the trainees gradually, then in a flood, emerged from the camps, they had to be linked to the tanks, artillery, aircraft, ships, and other machines of war with which they would have to fight. Fortunately there were no German air attacks to impede progress at this stage in the war: however, the 'blackout' imposed to guard against aerial attacks created problems enough. Travelling on roads in complete darkness was hazardous for both pedestrians and motorists, and the accident toll rose so sharply that there were suggestions that the blackout should be lifted until the German bombers actually appeared. The government shrank from taking this backward step. Later, when the bombers did come, there was usually plenty of light from burning buildings to enable motorists or pedestrians to avoid each other, if either wished to travel at the height of an air raid.

Needless to say, the public found something to joke about. Detested though air raid wardens were, there were plenty of ribald stories about them. A humorous style was found to be effective in making people take note of matters which it was important for them to understand. One was against 'careless talk'. Germany was credited with having an extremely efficient network of spies in Britain who, when not spying on their own account, would be listening to conversations in pubs, trains, and cafés. As it was inadvisable that Maisie should tell her friend Gladys that she had an important job in the converted factory up the road, making secret bomb guidance systems, the walls were plastered with notices saying that 'Walls have ears'. Fougasse's drawings of Hitler and Goering eagerly listening from the luggage racks of trains, or behind the chairs of people in pubs, were undoubtedly effective. Fifty years later many of these restrictions may seem bizarre to people who have never experienced the feeling that their country is at war and that the intention of some 80 million foreigners is to kill you as quickly as possible. In the first six months of the war the danger of actually being killed or wounded did not seem very great to the average unimaginative citizen, but when the bombs and the rockets began to fall the situation needed no further explanation. It has been aptly said that nothing clears the mind of man faster than the prospect of immediate and violent death. The unfortunate British public was doomed to live with pettifogging restrictions until six years after the war had ended, making nearly 12 years for most of them, but the one which most people were happiest to see go was the blackout in 1944. One of the more poignant wartime songs was:

> When they sound the last All-Clear
> Oh, how happy my darling I'll be.
> When they turn on the lights
> And the long, lonely nights
> Are only a memory.

Many who sang that song never lived to see it happen.

One of the most irritating restrictions of the time also related to air raids. From the beginning to the end of the war there were no weather forecasts. Most people had listened attentively, and hopefully, to the BBC weather forecasts and a larger number also read them in the newspapers. But now neither German pilots nor British farmers, submariners or English fishermen were to be told whether fog was expected in the Channel, clear skies over the Midlands, or storms in the north-east. War had become not merely a matter of killing or being killed, or losing relatives and friends, it had become an infuriating dislocation of everyday life, of everything sane and normal. People knew that things would get worse before they got better and suspected that, whatever the government complacently said, the war was going to be a long and gruelling business from which the country would take years to recover, if recover it ever did.

The complacency of the government was, in fact, more assumed than real and there was much going on behind the scenes which would have beneficial effects on the future. One was the urgent building programme for radar stations, of which there were far too few. The principle of radar had been discovered early in the 1930s. The technical details need not concern us more than to say that it was a process by which an electro-magnetic beam swept the atmosphere around it in an arc. As soon as the beam met a reflective substance it recorded the fact on a screen. Obviously this would have enormous value in locating approaching aircraft, ships or even vehicles. Radar would occasionally give false signals through encountering some natural object, perhaps a high wave, but in general it was extremely effective. Britain believed that the secret of radar was unknown to the Germans but this was subsequently found to be incorrect.

In addition to the expansion of radar installations there were ventures into unorthodox weapons and means of acquiring information about the enemy. However, in the first year of the war when it seemed that time, as well as everything else, was on the side of the Allies, very little encouragement was given to inventors or others who offered unorthodox plans or machines to the War Office. But one secret device of 1939 had its importance recognised immediately. This was the Enigma machine.

For an instrument which was a revolution in secret communication, Enigma was unimpressive in appearance. It resembled a typewriter with two keyboards. The keyboard on the German machine was the same as an ordinary typewriter except that there were no numbers or punctuation marks. Behind this was another keyboard of a slightly different type, with the alphabet set out identically, but appearing within small glass holes. On this second set of letters, one would light up when a key on the front board was pressed. If an operator pressed the A key, a different letter of the alphabet would appear in the opposite hole. If he pressed the key a second time, another, different letter would appear. This ingenious system was produced by a system of plugs and drums, any of which could be changed for the given setting of the day. Enigma would thus encode a message into a random system of letters which could not be interpreted by any other existing machine, for it involved thousands of possible combinations. But the message was easily translated back into clear German if the receiving operator had a machine with the correct setting for the day.

Although the machine had been invented by a Dutchman named H. A. Koch in 1919, he had been unable to make a working model himself. However, in 1923 a German firm manufactured a machine to his design and called it Enigma. Unfortunately for the manufacturers, the machine did not appeal to the business world, which thought it was too complicated for the simple purposes of protecting business correspondence, and the firm went bankrupt. However, the machine had roused interest in the German armed forces, which were very much alert to the reception of new ideas and a few machines were made in 1926 for the German navy. In 1928 the German army also took delivery of some machines. Germany was not the only country to possess Enigma, for it was a commercial venture, and the Chief Signals Officer in Washington also bought one in 1929. Commercial machines did not, of course, incorporate the German improvements.

Long before German rearmament had got into its stride, Poland regarded its large neighbours, Russia and Germany, with apprehension and suspicion. The Poles knew very well that there were many Germans who resented the separation of East Germany from the rest of their country by the Polish Corridor and would seek an early opportunity to change the map of Europe at Poland's expense. The Poles had formed many of their views from reading German codes, but in 1926 found themselves no longer able to do so. This did not surprise them, for they had one of the original commercial Enigmas themselves, but to their dismay they were unable to respond to the German settings. By espionage and considerable persistence the Poles came near to doing so once again, but then the Germans made further adjustments and the Poles were lost once more. However, when the Germans invaded Poland the Polish cryptographers escaped with their two machines and began working with an Allied team, 70 strong, at Vignolles, near Paris. This team included expert cryptographers, some of whom had that touch of creative genius which can ultimately lead to detecting something comprehensible in an otherwise unbreakable code. The Vignolles cryptography school maintained close links with another immensely important organisation, the Government Code and Cypher (as it was then spelt) School at Bletchley Park. The GC and CS had been founded in 1922 when the Services and the Foreign Office had felt a need to establish a centre where cryptography could be studied and practised, and the coded messages of potential enemies could be deciphered.

The name given to the process of deciphering Enigma messages was Ultra; it would eventually involve as many as 6,000 people at Bletchley Park, as well as hundreds of interception radio operators from the army, navy and air force, whose collective work formed the Y Service. Intelligence summaries would then be forwarded to the appropriate addresses by Special Liaison Units. These were teams of radio operators who received the summaries of the decrypted messages (once more encrypted for safe transmission) and passed them in clear English prose, in absolute secrecy, to officers of the very highest ranks only.

The degree of secrecy involved in these operations was unprecedented, for it was obvious that if the Germans once had the least suspicion that their messages were being read they would adjust the system to make decrypting impossible once more. Everyone concerned was bound to secrecy and the existence of Ultra was not made public until 1974, 29 years after the war had ended. Some aspects of Ultra, mainly its methods of interception, have never been divulged and probably never will be.

The preceding paragraphs provide an example of the difference between a cipher and a code. Ciphering is the process of substituting a figure or figures for a letter. One method of doing so is to send blocks of meaningless figures with one occasionally being relevant. This is a time-wasting process and one mistake can ruin the entire operation. An efficient operation, such as the Enigma machine or a modern computer could provide, would mean that the enciphered

message need be no longer than the original, but totally
baffling. All that was needed was a version which could not
be deciphered by a logical process.

Coding has an even longer history than ciphering and in
previous times has often been a device for concealing a
totally different message within an apparently innocuous
letter. The morse code, which substitutes dots and dashes for
letters of the alphabet, is not a code in the normally accepted
sense. It is, however, invaluable for sending messages (often
enciphered) in atmospheric conditions which would make
transmission by voice impossible. Code words continued to
be used by all sides during World War II and are still in use
today. All operators in the war were given code names – the
Germans used 'Sealion' for their projected invasion of
England in 1940 and the Allies used 'Overlord' for theirs of
France in 1944. Neither of these seems particularly subtle.
'Torch' was used for the North African landings and 'Market
Garden' for the Arnhem operation. However, even though
every attempt is made to use the most absurd and irrelevant
words, the supply eventually seems to become exhausted and
great efforts have to be made – not always successfully – to
prevent the use of the same code word for different
operations. The problem with many code words is that they
have to be sufficiently obscure to deceive the enemy, but to
have some clue in them which will make them recognisable
by one's own side.

It was clear in 1939 that the general public was going to
make a contribution to code words, often as a means of
disguising something which might be very unpleasant. The
bombing of Britain, when it began, became known as the
'blitz', although this was not what the Germans envisaged
when they used the word in '*Blitzkrieg*'. The deeds of
bureaucrats were an obvious target. Those conducting a
wartime social survey became 'Cooper's Snoopers'.

Secrecy tended to become an obsession which could defeat
its own purpose. An American war correspondent (John
Gunther), who asked to see a copy of one of the leaflets
which the RAF dropped in millions over Germany, met with
refusal. Enquiring why, he was told it was not policy to
disclose information which might be of value to the enemy.

His startled response was that if they were meant for the enemy to read they could not be very helpful to them. His request was still refused.

But in 1939 and the early days of 1940 the British public did begin to feel there was some truth in the mocking description of this as 'The Great Bore War': there appeared to be no danger but a vast number of petty restrictions, few but increasing shortages, much inconvenience and discomfort which seemed premature, if indeed necessary at all, and a bore because most people were forced to take part in activities which did not interest them. They listened to BBC programmes and exhortations which often seemed puerile and futile, and they were unable to travel and take themselves 'away from it all' for a restful few days. Most of the best hotels seemed to have been requisitioned and were now occupied by schools or businesses. Anything, people began to think, would be better than this. But they were wrong.

3
THE WAR WIDENS:
NORWAY AND DENMARK,
THEN BELGIUM, HOLLAND,
LUXEMBOURG AND FRANCE

April 1940, with a foretaste of spring, was welcomed in Britain; the winter had been worse than any which even the oldest inhabitants could remember. Longer days would make the blackout less tedious and problems of heating would be alleviated with the warmer weather. The more optimistic thought that the summer might bring Hitler to his senses. He would realise he could never win and the war would drift to an end.

Awakening came on 9 April 1940 and at first was not believed. On that day German troops invaded neutral Denmark and Norway. Once more there had been no declaration of war but the Allies were not so completely surprised this time, for they knew that Hitler had made up his mind to invade Norway sooner or later. In fact Hitler had decided to do so as early as 18 February, but for various reasons had postponed the move. By April the Allies had decided that the time had come to stop ships using Norwegian territorial waters to carry contraband materials, mainly iron ore, from Narvik to Germany. The only effective way of doing so was to mine the area known as the Leads, and permission was sought from the Norwegian government to take this step. The Norwegians, anxious to avoid provoking Germany, refused, although they knew that German submarines were already operating there and had sunk a British ship. Meanwhile, Hitler had been assured by a Norwegian Nazi sympathizer named Quisling that Norway would welcome a German occupation. Quisling had in fact done more than sympathize; he had organised a sizeable Fifth Column, and also advised the Germans of the best ways to infiltrate troops. Hitler had 12 divisions available and a large fleet of surface ships, many of which he was to lose. Denmark, with an army smaller in numbers than a single German division, had no chance from the start, and after a token resistance surrendered (under their King's orders) within a day. The German move had begun on 8 April, which was also the date the British had originally chosen to begin mining, irrespective of Norwegian displeasure; the traffic of nine million tons of iron ore from Sweden via Narvik must be stopped by fair means or foul.

Nevertheless the German move caught the Allies by surprise, and most British ships were elsewhere when the invasion began. This may seem strange in view of the fact that Britain was already reading Enigma signals. In fact, at this stage, the Enigma decrypts were not being particularly helpful and more information was coming from agents on the ground. Although the Y Service and Ultra were working well, full and proper use was not being made of the information gained. This was due to lack of knowledge and expertise among the staff handling the messages and without military or naval knowledge some of the important clues were missed. Clearly more time would elapse before Ultra would perform to its fullest ability.

However even when, later, Ultra could produce a reasonably full version of radio traffic, there would still be enormous problems. One was that it would be impossible to intercept, decrypt and understand the implications of the vast mass of traffic between the German sets, which eventually numbered 100,000. 100,000 is not a large number of encrypting sets for an entire army, but it is enough to produce a huge volume of traffic. Furthermore there was an enormous range of German communication which was outside the range of Ultra, for it was conveyed by line or messenger and not by interceptable wireless.

There is nowadays an absurd but firm belief that, because the British were able to intercept and read many of the German army wireless signals, winning the war should have been simplicity itself. This was, of course, far from the truth. If a man who is pointing a gun at you announces that he is going to shoot you, the fact of knowing this will make no difference if you have no effective counter-measure. All too often, during World War II, the Allies learnt what their enemies were about to do, but had no effective means of stopping them. Sometimes, when they knew what the Germans intended, they dared not react to it because in those particular circumstances to take any counter-action might disclose to the Germans that their code was broken. On such occasions an elaborate ploy of sending up a reconnaissance aircraft, or inventing a message from an alleged spy, might have to be devised if any action was to be taken.

Earlier in the book it was stated that the Armed Forces often regarded Intelligence officers and their products with varying degrees of scepticism. Sometimes they were right to do so, but on many other occasions they were not. The material from Ultra certainly came into the latter category.

There is a well-known service expression – 'the fog of war'. As soon as the first shots are exchanged confusion begins to mount. Reports of successes and failures are both exaggerated, units lose their way, become tangled with each other, may perhaps even fire on each other by mistake, and often make gains or losses which have not been envisaged in the original plan. The fog of war, supplemented at times by normal fog, certainly operated in Norway. The situation was exacerbated by the amount of iron in the hills, as this made radio communication difficult.

Radio communication, whether decrypted or not, can be an effective instrument of war. Between 1939 and 1945 millions of bogus messages were sent with a view to deceiving the enemy. Non-existent divisions radioed thousands of messages to other non-existent divisions simply by using a few wireless operators. The absence of wireless traffic in an area might mean that radio silence was now in force in order to deceive the enemy about one's intentions, or might simply mean that the bogus traffic had now been moved to another point.

The Norwegian campaign quickly became a disaster for the Allies and a striking victory for the Germans. However, in the long run, Norway proved to be a very doubtful asset to the Germans. Hitler was obsessed with the idea that the Allies would open a second front in that country and therefore allowed 300,000 soldiers to be immobilized waiting for an attack which never came. In the later stages of the war those soldiers could have been enormously valuable to Germany in other theatres of war. An even more damaging effect was that the Germans began relying on the Norsk Hydro plant for 'heavy water', a substance essential for the production of atomic bombs (when these could be perfected). When the plant was put out of action by an American bombing-raid, the Germans decided to transport the stocks of heavy water to Germany. However, when these were being ferried over Lake Tinnsjoe, the boat was sunk by saboteurs. In consequence, German experiments were set back for so long that the Allies perfected the bomb first. Had Hitler been able to use an atomic bomb before the Allies, the war would have had a very different conclusion.

The Norwegians themselves could not hope to stave off a German invasion, for they had an even smaller army than Denmark, and a population of only three million. Their only hope of preserving their independence was through the Allies coming to their aid in time. Although once again Hitler had invaded without declaring war, on this occasion his opponents were not caught entirely by surprise. The British Home Fleet was at sea, although it was deployed to prevent a German breakout into the Atlantic, where her larger ships could do great damage, and was not expecting to be countering a German invasion of Norway. The fleet was too late on the scene to prevent the Germans landing, but not too late to sink most of the German fleet subsequently. Unfortunately for the Allies, by that time the Germans had captured Oslo, Bergen, Trondheim and Narvik, as well as many airfields and nodal points. The Norwegian shore batteries made the Germans pay a stiff price for their unheralded invasion. At Oscarsborg (a 100-year-old fortress) they pounded the German cruiser *Blücher*, the pride of the German navy, set her on fire, and sank her with a loss of 1,000 men. The pocket battleship *Lutzow* (formerly called the *Deutschland*) was badly damaged. However, Oslo was captured by six companies of German airborne troops, and Stavanger was taken by a single company of parachutists. Narvik and Kristiansand could put up very little resistance. When the British arrived

on the scene all the main ports were in German hands and
landing an expeditionary force was going to be very difficult.
However, the Royal Navy attacked with some vigour. While
this was happening, Chamberlain was breaking the news to
the British parliament, but softened it by saying that he did
not believe that Narvik had fallen; he thought it must have
been mistaken for Larvik, down in the south. Alas for hopes,
it turned out to be Narvik after all and the gaffe represented
one more blow to Chamberlain's diminishing prestige.
Narvik was however the scene of a naval battle equal to
anything in Britain's history. Captain Warburton-Lee, commanding a flotilla of five destroyers, had received an uncon-
firmed report that a German ship had been seen in the region
of Narvik. Warburton-Lee decided to investigate. He found
the report to be a classic understatement. There were 10
destroyers at Narvik, all more heavily armed than Warburton-Lee's five. In two spirited actions he managed to sink
two and damage seven of the German ships, for the loss of
two of his own. Warburton-Lee, who was killed in the battle,
was awarded a posthumous Victoria Cross.

Three days later, the Royal Navy came to Narvik again
with a larger force, which included the battleship *Warspite*,
and prepared the way for Allied landings. These were
eventually made at various points but the Allied expeditionary force was too small, too badly equipped, and too much
out-gunned to make a success of the fight back. Narvik was
captured on 28 May, but by that time the situation in France
and Belgium had changed the whole complexion of the war,
and the Norwegian expeditionary forces were withdrawn.
The campaign had been a brave but far from happy story.
The British government knew so little of Norway that it
appealed to the public for railway timetables, tourist maps,
or even postcards, in order to build up a general picture of the
country. (Subsequently certain British officers who knew
Norway well from fishing and climbing expeditions voiced
their disgust that their offers of help had been spurned by the
War Office.) There were many tales of deficiencies, of
aircraft being frozen on to the lakes they had used for
emergency airstrips, and of totally unsuitable equipment.
The Germans, who had been planning their campaign for

years, had every advantage. In summer and winter young German soldiers had spent special 'leaves' climbing and walking in Norway, and had got to know the country very well indeed. This was to be expected when one country was determined to wage aggressive war and its victim was simply concerned with peaceful co-existence. Previous reconnaissance such as this is of great value for surprise attacks, but is soon cancelled out if both sides settle down to a long struggle.

The British government's reaction to the rush of events in April 1940 was probably the best which could be expected in the circumstances, although in retrospect it seems bizarre. Auchinleck was undoubtedly the best available commander for the expeditionary force, but the main reason for appointing him was that he had had experience of mountain warfare on the North-West Frontier of India. Mountains near or in the Arctic Circle do not bear much resemblance to mountains in sub-tropical areas, as he pointed out. Carton de Wiart, mentioned earlier in Poland, explained his own appointment as being due to the fact that Norway was a country which he had never visited and knew nothing about. On the other hand, it is difficult to think of two better appointments than those of Auchinleck or Carton de Wiart.

Fortunately the Norwegian merchant navy, which was the fourth largest in the world, escaped to British ports. The Norwegians had fought better than expected and had sustained 1,335 casualties. The total Allied casualties were under 5,000, the German slightly over that figure. The Germans had lost 242 aircraft but had gained valuable airfields from which they could bomb Britain and attack Atlantic shipping. The German navy had suffered heavily in both cruisers and destroyers, but their most damaging loss had been in surface shipping and escort vessels. When, later, historians pondered why Hitler had never tried to invade Britain, the answer was to be found in the heavy shipping losses which had been sustained in the Norway campaign. Britain, on the other hand, had now realised the importance of landing craft and amphibious warfare training, both of which would be needed on many occasions later in the war. When Churchill stood up in the House of Commons on 11 April 1940 and declared that the invasion of Norway had been a strategic blunder by Hitler, few believed him and some scoffed openly. But in this, as in so many other matters, he was proved right. Hitler had taken an enormous risk in calculating that he could defend and occupy Norway before he launched the next stage of his campaign. In fact he succeeded, but by a very narrow margin. A further delay could have jeopardised his grand design to conquer France.

The most significant event of 1940, which was of great importance for the whole war, took place on 7 May when the House of Commons was debating the Norway campaign. Leo Amery, a Conservative, rose to his feet and, pointing at Chamberlain, dramatically quoted Cromwell. 'Depart I say and let us have done. In the name of God, go.' Chamberlain resigned, a coalition government was formed, and Churchill was appointed Prime Minister. Britain's darkest hour was approaching but fortunately for the Allies the one man who could lead like a torch through the gloom was now in the position to do so.

It was not a moment too soon. On 10 May 1940 the Germans invaded Belgium, Holland and France. This again took the victims by surprise, although subsequently there was said to have been so much aerial activity on the frontier areas that they should have realised that an invasion was imminent. Perhaps they preferred not to know, rather than face facts.

The facts were not encouraging. In Poland and Norway the German army had shown itself to be devastatingly successful. It had won two clear-cut victories and won them quickly. German morale was undoubtedly very high indeed.

Regrettably, morale in the Allied land forces was far from high. The French believed that the Maginot Line would protect them; they had therefore dedicated much of the defence budget to building it and too little money and time to equipping and training their soldiers. The French air force was hopelessly outclassed by the Luftwaffe. The French army possessed 3,000 tanks, which was 300 more than the Germans, but General Gamelin, the French commander-in-chief, had no idea of how to use them and therefore spread them along the whole line of his front. There was therefore no reserve of tanks for a counter-attack if the Germans broke through. In fact Gamelin had made no provision for defence

in depth, even without tanks. It was a situation to make any
would-be conqueror feel confident.

The British Expeditionary Force was unimpressive. It
numbered a mere 10 divisions (approximately 200,000 men).
For a war which would see attacks by 50 or more divisions,
this was a pathetic figure. Even worse was the fact that it
contained only one armoured brigade. The divisional commanders, who included Alan Brooke, Alexander, Dempsey
and Montgomery, were men of outstanding ability but
whereas the German troops were battle-experienced and
highly trained, the majority of the soldiers of BEF lacked any
form of military experience except digging trenches and
practice firing.

Holland took the first blow. At 4 a.m. on 10 May the
German armies crossed the Dutch frontier, two hours before
the Germans delivered their ultimatum. The small Dutch air
force was annihilated. German parachutists, some wearing
Allied uniforms, seized strategic airfields and bridges. The
Dutch fought back to the best of their ability and hoped to
check the Germans by flooding large areas, but in vain. After
four days the Nazis blitzed Rotterdam, an 'open city', killing
40,000 civilians. This was meant to knock the spirit out of
further Dutch resistance, and undoubtedly did so, for the
Dutch army, which had lost a quarter of its fighting strength,
surrendered the same day and the Dutch government
escaped to England.

Meanwhile further south the Germans were pouring into
Belgium. The Belgians had put great faith in a substantial
fortress at Eben Emael. It commanded the bridges on the
Meuse and the Albert Canal and was believed to be impregnable. The Germans, who had trained on a full-scale model,
dropped parachutists on to Eben Emael on 11 May. The
surprise of this audacious manoeuvre was so great that the
garrison of 11,000 was virtually shocked into surrender,
though it did sustain 100 casualties. A powerful German
force which included von Runstedt's Army Group A and von
Kleist's Panzer Army was now the main instrument of
German victory. The Belgians were still fighting, but had
fallen back to link up with the British, who had come up to
Louvain. Because the Belgians had wished to do nothing to

provoke the Germans, they had steadfastly refused to allow British troops to set foot on Belgian soil during the 'phoney' war, or even to co-operate with them. Now that they had no option it was too late, and they fell into the German trap. Bridges, such as that at Maastricht, were not blown before the Germans reached them, and worse still, von Kleist's Panzer Army was reported to be advancing without difficulty through the Ardennes.

THE ARDENNES. The whole basis of Allied strategy was now undermined. The Germans crossed the Meuse and opened up a gap 50 miles wide between Namur and Sedan. This was in the French sector where, of course, there was no reserve. Guderian, one of von Kleist's leading Panzer commanders, asked for permission to press on and with reluctance permission was granted. There was no alternative for the British now but to withdraw hastily, abandoning Brussels and Antwerp in the process. This was on the morning of 16 May; the same evening Guderian reached a point 55 miles beyond Sedan. His brilliant stroke was almost too much for the German Higher Command (the OKW) to swallow and they ordered Guderian to halt. They could not believe that success could be as easy as this and suspected an Allied trap and probably devastating counter-attack.

But there was no trap, still less a counter-attack. Guderian managed to comply with orders by 'halting' but at the same time conducting 'reconnaissance'. Other German forces soon followed. The Panzers were in St Quentin on 18 May and were still advancing. The Allied defence had been sliced to ribbons; the Germans were now miles behind the Maginot Line; the British Expeditionary Force was being surrounded and was well on the way to being caught in a closing trap. Rommel, whose name would become a household word to many British soldiers later, was pushing deep into France with his 7th Panzer Division. Everywhere the Panzers were advancing at the rate of some 40 miles a day. This was too fast for the artillery support which tanks often require to demolish obstacles, but this was no problem for they used Stuka dive-bombers instead.

Dive-bombers had never before been employed in the way the Germans were using them. In theory, a dive-bomber is not a particularly effective instrument of war, because it may be shot down at the lower altitude, or be unable to pull out of its dive. But the people who constructed such theories have not usually had the experience of being the target of an attack by a dive-bomber and may fail to realise that bombers hurtling noisily out of the sky are more disruptive to morale than aircraft which aim bombs more carefully. The dive-bomber was particularly effective against civilians. When the German armies advanced, many French families abandoned their homes and rushed onto the roads seeking safety. Doubtless they hoped to return later when the danger had passed, but if the worst came to the worst, and France was once more crossed by trench lines, they hoped to be on their own side of them. The presence of huge crowds of civilian refugees, occupying almost every inch of available road space, made the movement of Allied military traffic almost impossible. To the inevitable confusion and congestion, the German Air Force added its not inconsiderable contribution by bombing every bridge and crossroads it could find, as well as machine-gunning the helpless refugees. This was the total war which Hitler had promised. Fifth Columnists spread alarmist rumours that German parachutists disguised as nuns or priests had been dropped in rear areas and were blowing up bridges and water supplies. Some 95 per cent of the rumours were untrue, but this did not inhibit their effect.

On 19 May Gamelin was dismissed from his command and replaced by Weygand. The new C.-in-C. was 72 (Gamelin was 68) and was a veteran of the earlier war. It was said that he had a formidable memory which could recall the slightest detail. Unfortunately, more than a good memory was needed now. He needed soldiers, but most of his soldiers had already been cut off by the German advance. The only problem the Panzers were facing was attacks from their own dive-bombers, who could not believe their tanks had now reached the coast.

The fighting was, however, by no means over. The BEF made a counter-attack at Arras on 21 May but had only two infantry divisions and 74 slow, under-gunned tanks; some had a machine-gun only, others had a 2-pounder gun and a machine-gun. The two-pounder gun was highly esteemed by the British War Office on account of its performance in trials, but confidence in its abilities did not extend to the soldiers who had to rely on it. The British army at the time, and for a long time in the future, was without adequate anti-tank guns which could take on the German tanks with confidence. Many of the Panzers had been manufactured in the Skoda works in Czechoslovakia which Hitler had acquired in the previous year.

Dazzling though their success was, the Germans were taking enormous risks and were highly vulnerable. If Gamelin had not deployed his tanks and most of his troops so stupidly, there would have been a reserve which could have come in across the rear of the German columns and effectively cut off the heads. At the end of their tether in every sense, down to the last drops of petrol and badly in need of maintenance, the Panzers could have found that their success was their undoing, but it was not to be. The only chance of cutting a swathe through the German line of communication lay with an armoured division commander named Charles de Gaulle. He was not popular with the higher command owing to his critical and imperious manner, but he had often predicted that the modern way of warfare was the method which the Germans were now employing and it seemed advisable to give him a chance to counter it. Unhappily for de Gaulle, the hastily improvised force at his disposal lacked air support, infantry and artillery, but it did cause Guderian to divert some troops to deal with this small threat to his flanks. Perhaps the least satisfactory aspect of this was that de Gaulle carried away the impression that if he had been in charge of the French army instead of Gamelin, disaster would not have overtaken France. He may have been right, but when later he decided that in consequence he should be recognised as the leading Allied strategist, his relations with his allies became strained.

Boulogne held out until 25 May; its dour resistance to the Panzers was greatly assisted by the Royal Air Force. The latter was in a difficult position. It had taken heavy losses in heroic battles to assist the army and what remained was now vital to the defence of Britain itself. Nevertheless the RAF continued to apportion a substantial part of its diminishing strength to helping the beleaguered BEF.

But while Guderian was hammering away at the ancient walls of Boulogne, on 24 May von Runstedt took a decision, supported by Hitler, which became one of the most controversial of the war. He halted the panzers outside Dunkirk, to which most of the remnants of the British Expeditionary Force and a considerable number of French soldiers had now retreated. They were not completely finished as a fighting force, but they were in poor shape, having had to abandon much equipment while scurrying back to avoid being trapped by the Panzers. It was a tired, dispirited, defeated army, which was totally baffled by the predicament in which it found itself and how it had got there. Viscount Gort, V.C., the British C.-in-C., had decided there was no hope of recovering and winning this particular battle, but thought it might be possible to evacuate some 35,000 men before the Luftwaffe made further action impossible. He informed the Cabinet of his views and on 26 May 'Operation Dynamo' (another code word) was authorised. The following day Gort withdrew the BEF more tightly into Dunkirk and Admiral Ramsay, Vice-Admiral Dover, began the evacuation which, a few days earlier, he had foreseen might be necessary. In the event 338,226 soldiers were evacuated, of which one-third were French. The French were undoubtedly bitter that the BEF, which had come over to defend French soil, had failed to do so and then disappeared back home, but the British were not pleased either when the majority of those French soldiers who had taken up valuable shipping space opted to return to France, rather than serve in the Allied armies which were continuing the war.

The story of the 'Miracle of Dunkirk' has been told many times in books and films. Although large numbers of amateur sailors took part, the bulk of the evacuation was done by the navy, but not without cost. Six destroyers were lost, 19 were badly damaged. Nine passenger boats were sunk, eight severely damaged. Many small craft were lost. There was a knock-on effect, for the concentration and loss of destroyers in the Channel gave the German submarines welcome opportunities against sparsely defended convoys in the Atlantic. By the time the evacuation was complete, on 4 June, those on the beaches had had an experience they would never forget. There had been the inevitable scenes of great courage and of depressing cowardice. The morale of this defeated army, beaten by an unexpectedly better organised and equipped force, was at a very low point, but recovered somewhat when it found itself regarded as a band of heroes by the British public. Unfortunately improved morale did not compensate for its having left all its equipment behind. Re-equipping and re-training would be needed before the BEF could be a fighting force again. Had the evacuation not been successful, Britain, perhaps even Churchill, might have sought peace terms if any were available. Subsequently, when the British army was heavily defeated on other fronts – Crete, Hong-kong, and Singapore in particular – it was not realised that those were labelled as disasters because no further retreat was possible, yet Dunkirk, which involved greater numbers than all the others put together, was regarded not as a disaster but as a triumph. The successful evacuation had saved face.

Dunkirk was not, in fact, the end of the fighting in France, as the French were quick to point out. De Gaulle's armoured division continued fighting, and the French cadets at Saumur put up a fight in which courage compensated for lack of experience. The 51st Highland Division, under French command, fell back on St Valery, where it held out till 12 June. The 52nd Highland Division managed to get out from Cherbourg. The French government left Paris and went first to Tours and then to Bordeaux. Winston Churchill made a surprising offer of complete union between Britain and France, but by this time Reynaud, the French Prime Minister, was on the point of resigning and his successor, Marshal Pétain, a hero of World War I, promptly asked for an Armistice. On 22 June Hitler accepted the French surrender in the railway coach which had been used for the German surrender in 1918. It was also in the same place in the Forest of Compiègne.

All north and west France, on a line running from Geneva to Bayonne, was to be occupied, and the cost would be borne by the French. The French forces were to be demobilized.

The French government, firmly under German control, was to be allowed to have its own capital at Vichy, in the unoccupied zone.

France was stunned by the shock but the French thought the country had been let down lightly in defeat. Time would decide whether this view was correct. There were many questions still to be answered: how could it have happened? Why did Hitler allow the Panzers to be halted outside Dunkirk, and thus made possible the evacuation? What part had treachery played in the French disaster? Were the Panzers and the Luftwaffe as good as they seemed to be?

The long-term effects of this brief but decisive campaign could not be foreseen at the time, but would eventually affect most of the world. When France collapsed, Hitler felt that his hands were now free for the attack on Russia which he had long had in mind. It would be launched a year later. The German successes in France, and in the early stages of the Russian campaign, encouraged the Japanese to think that it was now their turn for a share of the spoils. They too would omit to declare war before they attacked Pearl Harbor, and the speed and enterprise of their assaults in the Pacific owed something to the German example. But, like Germany's challenge to Russia, Japan's challenge to America was ill-conceived. Nevertheless, having seen the successes her Axis partner was having in Europe, Japan could not wait to make an empire for herself in the Far East.

Hitler's action in halting the Panzers outside Dunkirk also had a long-term effect. Like the rest of the German Higher Command Hitler was excited but slightly bewildered by the German victory. The Panzers had achieved miracles: they had broken through 'impassable' country, they had crossed unexpectedly large distances, they had brushed aside all opposition. But now they had crowded an entire army into a corner, and Hitler was well aware that cornered animals – and armies – can be much more dangerous than those met in the open. He remembered how tough and resolute the British soldiers had been when he himself fought against them. To risk the Panzers, which must be desperately in need of maintenance and fuel, against such a potentially formidable enemy might well be a gamble which could lose the war. If the British came out of Dunkirk, fighting with the desperation of the doomed, they might easily overwhelm the weary Panzers and turn the tide of the campaign. The French, as Hitler knew, were now fighting in the south and fighting much better than they had earlier. Although he permitted the Luftwaffe to harass the BEF whenever the weather and the RAF allowed, he did not wish the evacuation to stop and the BEF to return to the fight.

If the Panzers had not been halted, there is no doubt that there would have been no miracle of Dunkirk but an even greater German victory. An invasion of Britain would probably have followed quickly and then, with no need to fight on two fronts, Hitler would probably have beaten Russia before winter set in in 1941. German power would have been supreme. That failure of nerve at Dunkirk undoubtedly saved the Allies.

The French forces in the south were in no condition to reverse the battle. Undoubtedly German Fifth Columnists and German propagandists had been at work in the French army, but the real cause of the débâcle was poor leadership. France in 1940 was expecting to be beaten if the Germans attacked. It was not treachery which caused the overwhelming defeat of the French army, but collapse of national morale. The army had no stomach for fighting and France was glad when it seemed to be over. A German soldier remembers that when his battalion marched into Paris they received a more enthusiastic welcome than when they returned to Germany and marched through Berlin. The French were not so much welcoming German conquerors as cheering the end of the war.

France was down but not out. Many years would pass before she became a great nation again, but eventually she recovered her former prestige and dignity. Unfortunately there was one more embittering phase before the battle of France was truly over. On 10 June Mussolini, the 'Italian Jackal', as he came to be known, declared war on the Allies, hoping by this gesture to gain Hitler's good will and a share of the spoils. It was an adventure which was to cost him dearly in the future.

A more worrying matter for Britain was the situation of the

French fleet. One of Pétain's first moves had been to appoint Admiral Darlan as Minister for the Navy. Both the British and the French trusted Darlan not to hand over the French navy to the Germans. On 18 June Roosevelt took the step of asking Darlan to ensure that the French navy did not fall into German hands. As America was not involved in the war at this point, the request was surprising. Darlan gave his word that the ships would not be handed over and everyone guardedly believed him; the question was, would he be able to keep his promise? Churchill felt that the Germans might seize the ships in a surprise move using subversives.

The stakes were high. Britain possessed a navy which was superior to the Germans', but which could still be challenged. If the French navy remained neutral, or an ally, that superiority could be maintained. But if, by some trick, the German navy was able to add the French fleet to its own, a very different picture would emerge.

Britain felt the risk of that happening was too great. Darlan was undoubtedly trustworthy and would, if left to his own devices, have scuttled the ships rather than hand them over. But, from experience of Hitler and his promises, there was little reason to suppose he would be left alone. Reluctantly the British government felt that it must act.

The first step was to seize the French ships which were in British ports and then prevent them from putting to sea, possibly under the orders of the Vichy government. It was a task which the Royal Navy found distasteful, and the French crews, who were temporarily interned before being repatriated, found unforgiveable. However, the ships in British ports represented only one-tenth of the French naval strength. Most of it was in the African port of Mers-el-Kebir. As the French refused either to hand over their ships or scuttle them, a strong British force was sent to disable them. The result was that, although some French warships were sunk, many escaped to Toulon, and the French navy now became more hostile to the British than it had been towards the Germans. The French submarines at Oran would have torpedoed the British ships if they could have got into range before being depth charged.

All this took place in July. Bitterness and rage against the

British swept through the French navy and at one point it was suggested that Gibraltar should be attacked as a reprisal. Hitler hoped that this feeling could be exploited to allow German troops to be landed in the French possessions in North Africa, but, although he had the French mainland at his mercy, he did not have the resources to take North Africa by force. Darlan, although unhappy with this turn of events, realised that there was no future for France in allying her own navy with the Germans. He realised that, if Hitler's next objective were Russia and if France could play for time until Germany was well and truly locked in desperate conflict with that country, then there could well be a chance of assisting the Allies to achieve France's liberation from German occupation. To this end he had to appear to be co-operating with Hitler, even though in practice he was delaying doing so as long as possible.

Meanwhile, the crews of the ships which had been seized in British ports for the most part resisted invitations to join the Free French and instead opted to return to France. Both nations had reason to feel aggrieved by the conduct of the other and tended to forget that they both faced a more dangerous opponent than each other. There were large numbers of British people who were prepared to sacrifice their lives to help to liberate France and very many French who risked – and sometimes met – a particularly unpleasant death for helping British airmen to escape after they had been shot down.

So, by August 1940, before the war was a year old, much of Europe had been brought under German domination. British convoys were now coming under German attack in the Channel. The Battle of Britain had already begun with the Germans making probing aerial attacks, many in the Thames estuary. The threat of a German invasion had now become very real: the German army was only 21 miles away at the nearest point, and already invasion barges were being assembled on the other side of the Channel. During July the Luftwaffe had refrained from bombing Britain, as Hitler believed that Churchill, when he considered how desperate his situation was, would be likely to agree more readily to peace terms if he had not been goaded into fury. However, as

Churchill showed little sign of falling in with Hitler's wishes, the order for full-scale bombing was given on 23 July and 'Sealion' (the invasion plan) was put into operation. The landing would take place between Ramsgate and the Isle of Wight, and extend north and west subsequently.

However, as Hitler and his chiefs of staff knew perfectly well, no invasion would be possible until the Luftwaffe gained complete air superiority, enabling it to sink all British ships opposing the landing and also to cover the German assault troops as they went ashore. By mid-August it was clear that the Luftwaffe was a long way from acquiring this position, although the Germans now had enough barges to move 60,000 men, dive-bombers were being stationed on airfields close to the coast, and long-range guns were being concentrated around Calais. Aerial reconnaissance brought in reports that the Germans were practising embarking and disembarking from the barges.

On the English coast hasty preparations were made to protect the beaches with blockhouses, barbed wire and tank traps. Long stretches of the coast were declared 'No go' areas and civilians were prevented from visiting them without reason. A call for volunteers, first called the LDV (Local Defence Volunteers) and later the Home Guard, produced a response of over a million men within two months. Many years later the Home Guard was the theme of a television series called 'Dad's Army'. The programme was very amusing and sound in detail, but may have given the impression that service in a volunteer unit of mixed ages in 1940 was less demanding and potentially dangerous than it was in reality. The Home Guard had many problems, not least being the lack of weapons likely to have any effect on a German invasion force. It was reported that some units were armed either with pitchforks or with lances borrowed from nearby museums, though most had obsolete rifles, a few hand-grenades and a collection of home-made bombs. No one who was not in Britain at the time can have any idea of what it really felt like to know that a ruthless and powerful army, which had already defeated the British, French, Polish and Norwegian armies, was waiting to cross the Channel, escorted or preceded by parachutists and dive-bombers.

Although it was known that the Royal Navy would exact a heavy toll on anyone who tried to cross the sea, and that the army which had been evacuated from Dunkirk was being rearmed as quickly as possible, neither of them were such obvious defenders as the Spitfires and Hurricanes which could occasionally be seen like autumn leaves whirling about the skies. The ordinary citizen felt that the protective screen was a thin one and that, even if the German soldiers did not burst through, the German bombers undoubtedly would. Britain would have to 'take it' for a long time before matters improved. Later a wartime slogan was 'Britain can take it'. However, 'taking it' does not win wars unless you can also give it. As the American general Patton remarked, 'Patriotism is not dying for your country but making some other poor bastard die for his!' However in 1940 Britain had little option but to take it.

The naval situation, which was not fully revealed to the general public, was not too happy. Many of the naval escorts were too slow to catch surfaced U-boats, naval tactics were not very highly developed at the time and were none the better for the fact that, unknown to the British, the Germans were reading their naval codes.

In mid-August Hitler declared a total blockade of Britain and announced that neutral shipping travelling in British coastal waters would be sunk on sight. This had the advantage of arousing American indignation, as her ships were still neutral, and while feelings were running high the United States agreed to send Britain 50 obsolete destroyers in exchange for the lease of bases off the eastern coast of America. Two of the destroyers were so ancient that they could only be used as jetties, but the remainder were made serviceable and were of great value in supplementing Britain's limited stocks of escort ships.

Although ration books had been issued at the beginning of the war, they had not been brought into use until February 1940. Butter, sugar, bacon and ham were the first things to be rationed; later, when shipping was short and U-boat attacks extremely effective, there was virtually nothing which was not rationed or 'in short supply'. The situation in the autumn of 1940 was very different from that in the previous spring.

For those in the towns it was possible to supplement one's meagre rations with a meal in a 'British Restaurant', a government-sponsored institution or, if working, in a factory canteen. The food rationing system was controlled by the Ministry of Food, an organisation consisting of some 50,000 Civil Servants, and ensured that throughout the war nobody starved, although many people had much less to eat than they would have wished. The 'Black Market' was small, mainly, perhaps, because it was kept so by government vigilance. As the war ground on, everything to eat or drink became officially or unofficially rationed. Retailers such as butchers, fishmongers and grocers often found themselves with a little more in hand than was required by the exact ration. The small surplus could then be sold to favoured customers, who were of course those who did not mind paying a little more and were suitably deferential to the lordly creatures which some shopkeepers became. But in August 1940 rationing had scarcely began to have much effect, and people were less concerned with what they might have to eat than with whether they would survive to eat it.

Subsequently it was learnt that one reason why Hitler did not order an invasion of Britain immediately after the fall of France was that he was still surprised by the speed at which his previous successes had been won and had not quite decided how fast and far he should try to press on. Preparation for an invasion was one thing: launching it was another. The German Air Force reported that bombing Britain was much more difficult than had been anticipated. Not only were the Spitfires and Hurricanes more formidable than had been imagined, but they seemed more plentiful: whenever a German aircraft made a probe it was likely sooner or later to encounter a British fighter.

The explanation was twofold. Britain was now operating an efficient Y Service and had a rapidly increasing number of radar screens.

The Y Service was the organisation, with separate branches for the navy, army and RAF, which monitored all enemy air traffic. This, of course, meant listening to all possible signals sent by the Enigma machines, but also to all the low-grade cipher, high-grade cipher, radio telephone or non-morse transmissions. Although German aircraft were supposed to keep radio silence whenever they were near or over the British coast, they often broke this rule and chatted to each other. Intercepting and understanding this fragmented talk required that the listener in the Y Service had a good knowledge of colloquial German. The German pilots were well aware that their conversations were being overheard and would occasionally address remarks to the British operator in English. Nonetheless these intercepts were invaluable and often gave help to decipher some of the more obscure Enigma messages.

Radar had been developed by several countries in the 1930s, but Britain had been well in the lead and had built a chain of radar stations around the coast of Britain, mainly in the south-east. The information gained from these stations was priceless in the autumn of 1940, for it enabled the diminishing number of pilots in the RAF to intercept large forces of German bombers. So effective was this interception that the Luftwaffe was diverted to knock out the airfields near the coast, rather than targets further inland. When this proved to be not as effective as had been hoped, daylight raids were abandoned temporarily and the towns and cities began their long experience of night bombing.

How long Britain could have endured German pressure without Churchill's dynamic leadership is impossible to assess. His defiant yet constructive speeches, his bulldog-like appearance, even the angle of his ever-present cigar, symbolized British grit and determination. Even when the country was reeling from the shock of the collapse of France and the evacuation of Dunkirk, he could make his listeners face the worst and at the same time have a glimpse of a better future. On 4 June 1940:

Even though large tracts of Europe and many old and famous states have fallen or may fall into the hands of the Gestapo and all the odious apparatus of Nazi rule, we shall not flag or fail. We shall go on to the end. We shall fight in France, we shall fight in the seas and oceans, we shall fight with growing confidence and strength in the air. We shall defend our island whatever the cost may be. We shall fight on the beaches, we shall fight on the landing grounds, we shall fight in the fields and the streets, we shall fight in the hills; we shall never surrender; and even if, which I do not for a moment believe, this island or a large part of it were subjugated and starving, then our Empire beyond the seas, armed and guarded by the British Fleet, would carry on the struggle, until, in God's good time, the new world, with all its power and might, steps forth to the rescue and the liberation of the old.

Three weeks earlier, when the battle of France was beginning and he had just become Prime Minister, he had told the House of Commons, 'I have nothing to offer but blood, toil, tears and sweat.' In his speech on 4 June, when the situation was much worse, he had offered 'a faint shred of hope'. On 18 June he said: 'Let us therefore brace ourselves to our duty and so bear ourselves that if the British Commonwealth and Empire last for a thousand years men will still say, "This was their finest hour".' On 20 August, referring to the courage and skill of the fighter pilots of the RAF, he said, 'Never in the field of human conflict is so much owed by so many to so few.'

Churchill's genius lay in his ability to present the most brutal facts or the most encouraging news in correct proportion. Over two years after the Battle of Britain, he was able to comment on the British victory at Alamein in North Africa: 'This is not the end. It is not even the beginning of the end. But perhaps it is the end of the beginning.'

In most of his speeches there was poetic vision. When matters looked like improving he warned his people not to be prematurely optimistic but mentioned that he could see a gleam of light at the end of a long tunnel.

Astonishing though it may seem, planning for the return to Europe began in the summer of 1940. As was clear later, the scale of the D Day operation was so vast, and the range of equipment so complicated, that four years does not seem overlong for its collection and preparation. But Churchill did not intend to let the Germans settle down comfortably with their gains. One of his first orders was to 'Set Europe ablaze'. This meant both commando raids ('butcher and bolt') on the coast and SOE (Special Operations Executive) agents further inland. The earlier commando raids were more of a symbol than a military threat, but they caused enough havoc to infuriate Hitler, who ordered that commandos should be shot if captured rather than be treated as normal prisoners of war. When the commandos, who were trained to hitherto unknown degrees of physical fitness, got into their stride, they achieved considerable success in Norway and at St Nazaire, but rather less at Dieppe. Commando training and raids provided invaluable experience for the amphibious operations which took place later in the war on D Day, in Burma, and in the Mediterranean. SOE played a less obvious part. The aim of SOE was to form a link with local resistance groups in countries which the Germans had overrun, to ensure that they received the right information and supplies and that their efforts were properly co-ordinated. Many of those who volunteered for SOE were abruptly surprised by the firm military note of their training. They were disconcerted to find that they would not merely sit in cafés establishing a few links with local leaders but would be required, if the occasion demanded, to use some of the skills they had been taught. Those skills included the ability to live in harsh conditions for long periods, to parachute, canoe, or swim, to kill with a gun, knife or noose, to use explosives, and to resist interrogation if captured.

Some 20,000 SOE agents were eventually recruited; among the best of them were women, whose daring, resilience and fortitude surprised even themselves. When Churchill had referred to 'the Gestapo and all the odious apparatus of Nazi rule' he was using a word which became the epitome of terror in occupied Europe, and even in the German armed forces themselves. Everyone, whatever his rank or position, feared and hated the Gestapo, who might arrive at a person's house in the middle of the night, order him into their car, and refuse to tell him the reason for their visit. Often the victim would know only too well and would realise he would be lucky if he ever saw his family or home again, and even if he did it would only be after a prolonged 'interrogation', which would include torture, beatings, lack of sleep, brutal discomfort, and near starvation. When the

Gestapo entered a restaurant all conversation stopped temporarily and all eyes watched apprehensively. It was not necessary to have committed any sort of crime to fall foul of the Gestapo.

From all this Britain was defended in August 1940 by a handful of resolutely brave, cheerful, very young men, who had learnt to fly their aircraft either in the Royal Air Force, or one of the Dominion air forces. Some had even learned to fly in their own spare time and at their own expense. The RAF contained a high percentage of short-service commission pilots and air crew who had joined for adventure and the joy of flying, not for the career prospects it might offer, which were very limited. These were the men Churchill praised in his speech on 20 August and who would thereafter always be known as 'The Few'. Living on forward airfields which often came under attack, outnumbered in the air, fighting not merely highly skilled German pilots but also their own increasing tiredness and frayed nerves, they never gave up. Not least of their achievements was that they set a standard of courage and flying skill which was equalled, though never surpassed, by other pilots in other theatres later in the war.

At the beginning of August the Luftwaffe tried to sink every ship in the Channel. It then moved on to attack coastal radar stations and airfields, and other targets in the south-east. By the end of August the Luftwaffe had lost 602 fighters and bombers, and Fighter Command had lost 239 fighters. At the beginning of September the Luftwaffe shot down 185 British aircraft, though losing 225 of its own. By this time the RAF strength was getting low and desperately needed a few days to recover. Fortunately, the RAF had made a raid on Berlin on 25 August 1940 and had so infuriated Hitler that he ordered Goering to stop destroying the RAF airfields in the south-east and instead to attack London and other towns. This was rash, for Goering was almost at the point of establishing sufficient air superiority to make just possible the invasion, which had already been several times postponed. It was unfortunate for London on 7 September to be subjected to a raid by 1,000 bombers, for many people were killed and many homes were destroyed by fire, but Fighter Command was now recovering fast. Another German raid on

London on 9 September was a virtual failure because it was broken up by Fighter Command. On 15 September, Goering launched his final blow in a daylight raid involving 1,000 bombers and fighters. Some got through and inflicted heavy damage on East London, but 60 were shot down for the loss of 26 RAF aircraft (of which half the pilots were saved). The German losses were originally given as 185, a figure probably due to several pilots claiming the same aircraft, but numbers meant less than effects. It was clear, even to those watching from the ground, that the RAF was winning the battle. It was also clear to the Germans and two days later Hitler postponed the invasion 'till further notice'. On 18 September he agreed that the invasion barges, most of which had been brought from the Rhine, should be returned to their normal duties for which they were urgently required (they were, in fact, unsuitable for crossing the Channel). On 12 October the 'Sealion' invasion was postponed until the following spring, and by January 1941 Hitler ordered that it should be postponed altogether. His eyes had now turned to what he thought was an easier conquest in the East – Russia.

Although Hitler was unaware of it, Poland had already begun to avenge what he had done to that country. One in every 10 pilots in Fighter Command was Polish; there were also Czechs and one or two American volunteers. He had now lost his first battle and ironically it was to a force which included a combination of nationalities.

But the cost of victory was not light and for the most part it was paid by non-combatants. In the first three months of the Blitz (as the air raids came to be called) a total of 12,696 Londoners were killed. There may have been more, for many were caught in buildings which were burnt to the ground. During the next four years thousands more would die by bombs or rockets, and not only in London. From now on most of the bombing would be done by night. The RAF had prevented the invasion of Britain but it could not hope to stop the German bombers which came night after night, their presence easily recognisable by the rhythmic rise and fall of the note from their purposely de-synchronised engines. Anti-aircraft guns blazed away into the dark, having a good effect on morale, but little on the Luftwaffe, and searchlights criss-crossed the sky, occasionally catching a German aircraft in the beam from which it tried to twist and escape. Balloons like enormous sausages surrounded the main towns; these, like the AA fire, achieved a purpose in making the Germans fly so high they found it difficult to bomb their appointed targets. Ordinary men and women hurried home from work to get a meal and then go to a shelter – sometimes the London Underground – before the sirens went. The sirens (often mispronounced 'sireens') with their chill, ghastly wailing, spoke of horrors to come, and during the long night people would hear the thump and crash of bombs and hope to God the next one would not have *their* number on it. In the morning they would get up somewhat bleary-eyed from disturbed sleep (if indeed they had had any) and make their way to work through streets lined with damaged buildings, broken glass on the roadway, an occasional fire, and little groups of anxious people watching the fire brigade and air raid wardens digging in the rubble of what had once been a house. Sometimes they would see a living body drawn gently out, perhaps a child, and would give a cheer; at others they would turn away and walk on silently.

September was a month when Britain seemed to have wrested some of the initiative from the Germans, but this achievement was partly offset by shipping losses which amounted to 160,000 tons. The general public was not aware of this, but one loss could not be concealed. The *City of Benares*, carrying children to Canada in a government-sponsored scheme, was sunk by a U-boat on 17 September; the government scheme was therefore abandoned. However, on 2 October the *Empress of Britain*, also carrying children bound for Canada, was sunk. There seemed to be something especially vile about the murder of innocent children, no matter what excuse the U-boat commanders might try to make. Inevitably the public felt that the best way to teach the Germans a lesson was to do the same to them.

Southampton, Bristol, Liverpool, Birmingham, Plymouth and Coventry now joined the list of target areas for the Luftwaffe. King George VI, Churchill, and various members of parliament toured the blitzed areas, often showing considerable courage in this morale-raising exercise. The most spectacular raid was on Coventry on the night of 14–15 November. The raid had begun with incendiaries which illuminated the targets for the bombers. The cathedral was destroyed, two hospitals were hit, 554 people were killed and 865 seriously injured; the centre of the city was pounded to rubble. Coventry was, of course, an industrial city, with factories manufacturing vehicles, tanks, and radio equipment, but the indiscriminate viciousness of the attack, combined with the fact that the Germans described it as 'Coventrieren', disposed of any impressions that the Luftwaffe might have chivalrous aspects. Eventually the Germans may have realized that the Coventry raid was counter-productive, for it removed any inhibitions that Bomber Command may have had about similarly 'coventriering' German cities, which ultimately suffered far worse, and it demonstrated a very effective technique for blitzing large industrial targets. The Luftwaffe had started so many fires at the same time in different areas that the fire services were unable to cope with them all.

The Coventry raid subsequently became a vehicle for post-war attacks on wartime government policies. When the Ultra secret was revealed in 1974, it was learnt that the War Cabinet had learnt from a decrypt that a massive raid was to be expected in November and that this would serve as a sample of the sort of raid the Luftwaffe would thenceforward use to knock out Britain's centres of war-material production. Goëring, the commander of the Luftwaffe, had already made his boast in one of his public speeches. Obviously, nothing which came from Ultra could possibly be acted on at this stage, still less revealed, but it was also known that a prisoner-of-war had mentioned that a huge raid, preceded by incendiaries, would take place on a Midlands town on 15 November. On the strength of the latter information, defensive precautions were taken by the RAF but presumably not enough of them. Such as they were, they were available for the 14th rather than the 15th which the prisoner-of-war had mentioned. However, there was another cloak of secrecy here. As soon as raids had begun over Britain, Air Intelligence had become aware that the bombers were using a beam guidance system. A brilliant scientist by name of R. V. Jones had become extremely interested in the beam theory, and soon found confirmation of some of his theories in papers recovered from a shot-down Heinkel. These referred to Knickebein, which means 'crooked leg'. Jones' theories were considered nonsense by some experts but he soon proved that the beam guided pilots by the simple process of sending a string of dots along one side of the beam and a string of dashes along the other. At a point above the target, the guiding beam would be crossed by another, and the pilot would take this as an instruction to unload his cargo of bombs. This, of course, prevented him from dropping them short of the target, or even in the sea, if he felt inclined to go home early and avoid trouble. However, when Jones began to cross their beam with his own system, or even send them off course with false beams, they began to believe that the diabolical British had perfected a means of bending their beams. At the worst they might find themselves directed into a waiting group of British fighters. By November the Luftwaffe was using X Gerät, a more sophisticated beam than Knickebein, and this in fact was used over Coventry. However, the success of the Coventry raid was not because the British government had let it happen for fear of disclosing its knowledge of Enigma, but because the Enigma decrypt had been imperfectly understood. The code name of the raid was 'Moonlight Sonata' and from this it was deduced that it would be in three stages and at the time of the full moon. The decrypt had also said that the beams would intersect over Wolverhampton, Birmingham, and Coventry. However, the significance of the word 'Korn' which had appeared in the German seems to have been missed. Air Intelligence was by no means sure that the raid would not be on London. By 9 p.m. on 14 November it was discovered that the beams were in fact intersecting over Coventry. Although the message was sent out promptly, the defences did not work as they should and 449 of the 509 bombers the Germans launched reached their target.

London had its turn on the night of 27 November, when the city was set alight. This was the raid during which huge stores of ancient books were burnt, the Guildhall destroyed, and eight of Wren's churches were set alight. It is recorded in a famous picture which shows St Paul's miraculously preserved among the surrounding flames. It was said that watching this orgy of destruction hardened the resolve of (the then) Air Vice-Marshal 'Bomber' Harris to repay the Germans a hundredfold.

During November, 4,558 people were killed in Britain, thousands more seriously injured, and the centres of whole cities, such as Coventry and Plymouth, reduced to rubble. Joseph Kennedy, founder of the Kennedy dynasty and ambassador to Britain in 1940, frequently reported to Washington that Britain was well and truly beaten. His view was upheld by other American politicians, notably Senator Wheeler. Even in Britain there were those who held similar views, among them Lord Beaverbrook who, while enjoying Churchill's friendship and the important office of Minister of Aircraft Production, was secretly putting out peace feelers towards Hitler.

Fortunately, Franklin D. Roosevelt, re-elected President for a third term on 5 November 1940, did not believe Kennedy. Nor did many American journalists who chose to stay in London, where they marvelled at the stoicism and resolve of the citizens. The brightest event of the month was the attack on the Italian fleet at Taranto on 11 November. The Fleet Air Arm lost two aircraft; the Italians lost half their fleet.

4
BRITAIN ALONE:
1940–1941

As the winter of 1940 approached, the grim reality of Britain's position was all too obvious. From the strong position with which she had begun the war, allied to an apparently powerful France, and surrounded by friendly neutrals, she had suddenly become the last piece of northern Europe to be holding out against Nazi domination. With airfields in Scandinavia and France, the Luftwaffe was able to pound British cities nightly. The Royal Navy appeared to be holding its own but had not yet got the measure of the U-boats and was well aware that some very large German ships must now be ready to put to sea. The RAF had acquitted itself well in the Battle of Britain, but needed rapid expansion if it were to cope with future commitments. The most worrying factor was the quality of the army. If Britain was to win this war it must ultimately be through soldiers invading Europe and forcing the Germans back. Its recent performance in France, when it appeared to have been bewildered by the German thrusts, gave little ground for confidence that it would be able to match German tactics and determination in the near future.

Britain was not entirely alone, of course. The Dominions, as the self-governing members of the Commonwealth and Empire were then called, were sending troops to the battle-fronts. Canadians, Australians, New Zealanders, and South Africans were standing by 'the old country' but were not going to be ordered around as they had been in the previous war. The South Africans, whose presence in the war was almost entirely due to General Smuts' persuasive powers, were not, for the moment, prepared to fight anywhere except on African soil. In spite of – or perhaps because of – their governments' attitudes, large numbers of Australians, Canadians, New Zealanders and South Africans had joined the British armed forces. In time there would be troops from what was then known as the dependent empire: India, West and East Africa, and other colonies. There were large numbers of Irish from Eire in the British army, and a number of British generals were of southern Irish descent. In London there was a remarkable variety of uniforms and badges: Poles, Free French, Norwegians and Danes were but a few. It was said that a humorist dressed up in a German officer's uniform he had hired from a theatrical company and walked around London all day in it: all the attention he received was a few salutes.

Instructions on what to do in every possible circumstance poured out from the ministries. Many of their original suggestions, such as putting a piece of wood between one's teeth to avoid the effects of blast, were ignored, although people remembered to use sand, rather than water, to extinguish incendiaries. People were tending to grow more vegetables and to organise themselves to avoid possible waste. Although Britain was said to be an island built on coal and surrounded by fish, both those commodities seemed very short. The merchant navy and fishermen were having a rough and dangerous war. They were liable to be attacked by German aircraft, drafted into mine-sweeping, or lose their lives transporting vital goods across the Atlantic. The courage of the merchant seamen was legendary, and needed to be. German submarines no longer had to traverse the North Sea to reach British shipping: they could berth in French ports and sally out to meet their intended victims at short range. The future outlook was grim and looked like becoming grimmer. If the Germans increased the volume and frequency of their bombing, war production in Britain could well become paralysed; if the submarines sank more shipping in the Atlantic, the country might be starved into surrender. Even so, a shaky optimism existed. 'We are not interested in the possibilities of defeat; they do not exist.' Shopkeepers who had had their windows blown in would board them up and paste a notice outside saying, 'Business as usual during altercations'.

It was inevitable that Mussolini would now try to make his impression on the war. For years he had been boasting about the strength and potential of his armed forces and in the summer of 1940 Britain had even taken his boasts seriously enough to consider buying him off by ceding territory – even Malta. The Italians had an army of 250,000 in Libya, and one of 350,000 in Abyssinia. On 5 August 1940, Mussolini's troops invaded British Somaliland, which contained a token British force of 1,500 men. British forces in the Middle East were commanded by General Archibald Wavell, and numbered altogether approximately 80,000 men. These were all he had to defend territory ranging from Palestine and Cyprus to Kenya, Egypt and the Sudan. He decided to evacuate British Somaliland and concentrate his forces elsewhere. On 13 September Marshal Graziani brought a force of some 100,000 men up to the Egyptian frontier and dug in. Mussolini viewed the prospects with growing confidence and decided that before he demolished Wavell's forces in the Middle East he would advance into Greece and thereby both impress and forestall Hitler at the same time.

On 28 October 1940, Mussolini launched an invasion force into Greece without declaring war. 150,000 strong, it therefore outnumbered the Greeks two to one, and it also had an excellent supply base at Koritza on Albanian soil. However, the Greeks, who had been supplied with some anti-tank guns flown in by the RAF, did not respond as expected. Instead they checked the Italians and went on the offensive themselves. In less than a month they had captured Koritza, and continued to overrun most of Albania. In the meantime, as mentioned above, Mussolini had lost half the Italian fleet at Taranto. To add to his problems, Britain now took the offensive in Libya on 9 December 1940. Two days later five Italian divisions were out of action. On 5 January 1941 Bardia was captured and on the 22nd Tobruk fell to the Australians, who took 2,500 prisoners. Benghazi was captured on 6 February. By the end of the month British forces were in Italian Somaliland, and a week later had captured the capital, Mogadishu. It was now all too clear to Hitler, that the Italian 'sawdust Caesar' was more of a liability than an asset, he decided that steps must be taken to stop Britain entering

Tripoli and clearing every Italian off African soil. He sent an experienced general with an armoured division. The general's name was Erwin Rommel.

The despatch of a leading general to North Africa was a sign that Hitler had now decided to come to the aid of his uncertain ally and that, if necessary, he might send enough reinforcements for Rommel to capture Alexandria and Cairo. If Rommel could do that, Germany would be within striking distance of the Iranian and Iraqi oilfields. But meanwhile he was having to keep a watchful eye on his own sources of supply in Roumania. Britain was helping Greece, who was her ally, and there seemed to be a good chance that the RAF might establish sizeable air bases there and be able to interfere with Germany's access to Roumanian oil.

In order to save Mussolini's face, he was allowed to try to re-take Albania with his own forces, but Hitler decided that Greece must be brought into the German orbit. Initially he decided to do this by coercing Bulgaria and Yugoslavia to agree to the passage of German troops by linking them with the Tripartite Pact which had been signed on 27 September 1940 by Germany, Italy and Japan (the Berlin-Rome-Tokyo Axis). However, in late March Prince Paul, the Regent in Yugoslavia, was ousted by a military *coup d'état* which made his young nephew, Peter, king. Hitler, sensing that the new government might ally itself with Britain, decided to act before the situation deteriorated further.

At this moment the British Cabinet put pressure on Wavell to send troops to Greece. Wavell was dismayed at having essential troops removed at the critical point of his 'rags to riches' victory, and apparently the Greeks were not happy at receiving them. In the event it turned out to be a disastrous decision, for many of them were taken prisoner either in Greece itself or later in Crete. On 28 March 1941 the Italian fleet suffered another blow. A force which included the battleship *Vittorio Veneto* and several large cruisers and destroyers was moving to intercept the British convoy of reinforcements for Greece, when it was spotted by Admiral Cunningham's battle fleet, which was in the area after an Ultra decrypt had indicated this would be advisable. In the subsequent brisk engagement off Cape Matapan, North

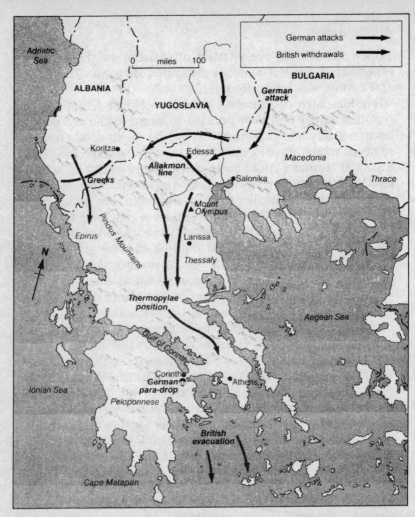

Balkans Campaign

Africa, three large Italian cruisers and two destroyers were sunk, and the *Vittorio Veneto* was badly damaged. Admiral Sir Andrew (later Viscount) Cunningham's fleet lost one aircraft.

On 6 April, Germany invaded Yugoslavia with 33 divisions, including the normal component of tanks, dive-bombers, and ancillary troops. The Yugoslavs had nothing to match them and the campaign was over in 10 days. Although the Germans did not realise it at the time, this campaign was a deceptive success for in the future up to 20 divisions would be needed to contain the guerrilla activity in Yugoslavia.

An attack on Greece was launched simultaneously via Bulgaria. The main body of the Greek army was already engaged with the Italians, and 14 divisions were in Albania. The remainder was deployed at various strategic points, but was nowhere able to hold out against the German onslaught. The rapid collapse of Yugoslavia made a difficult position impossible in Greece. The British Expeditionary Force had to retreat hastily to avoid being cut off. Of 60,000 men, all but 11,000 were evacuated to Crete. The Germans took Athens on 27 April, but the Greek destroyers and submarines had all left Greek ports and joined the British forces.

The loss of Yugoslavia and Greece was a blow, but not a totally unexpected one: the next setback reinforced the view that, although the British might be able to out-fight the Italians, they were as yet no match for German forces once the latter set out on a path of conquest. However, although there were private misgivings, there was no serious doubt that in the long run they would be.

The force which now held Crete, which was commanded by Major-General Freyberg, V.C., numbered some 60,000, but had only 35 aircraft and nine tanks. It was also initially short of ammunition but this was remedied. The German general entrusted with the task of capturing Crete was Kurt Student, an expert on airborne assault tactics. For this purpose he had at his disposal 500 transport aircraft, 70 gliders, and an adequate supply of bombers. The assault began with attacks by the bombers, mainly on the air defences. It was followed by parachutists and glider-borne troops. Casualties among these early arrivals were very high but they were soon replaced by other invaders. Maleme airfield was captured on 21 May 1941 and from that point Freyberg's force was swamped. Student planned to follow up the airborne troops with a seaborne force in Greek caiques, escorted by an Italian destroyer. A British force consisting of three cruisers and four destroyers sank every ship in the convoy. A second convoy was heavily protected by aircraft from the nearby Dodecanese islands and this sank two of the British cruisers and three destroyers. However, by this time the Germans had decided that seaborne reinforcements were too costly to pursue the idea further. By the end of May the attempt to hold Crete had clearly failed and the Royal Navy had the onerous task of evacuating as many survivors as possible. Eventually they took off 15,000, though had to leave 13,000 British and 5,000 Greek troops behind.

However though this was yet another failure for Britain, the long-term effects of the battle put it in a better light. Firstly the casualties among the German airborne forces had been so high that the Germans decided never to try this form of assault again. Secondly, while German forces were engaged in these somewhat gruelling battles in southern Europe, Hitler thought it unwise to launch his attack on Russia. The latter had originally been planned for 15 May. In the opinion of various German generals, the delay of five weeks cost the German army the Russian campaign. That month which had been lost in the summer would have enabled the German army to penetrate so deeply into Russia before the winter began that the Russians would never have been able to dislodge them. Moscow and Leningrad could have fallen and Russian recovery would have been made virtually impossible. There were, however, as we shall see shortly, other reasons why the Germans found the Russian campaign more difficult than they expected.

Ultra played an increasingly important part in the Mediterranean area but was not as informative about Italian moves as had been hoped. When information was acquired it had to be used with extreme discretion. However, when a decrypt disclosed that the Italian navy had every intention of intercepting the convoy of troops bound for Greece, Cunningham employed an unusual deceptive ploy. He was a keen golfer and played every day at the Alexandria club; the Japanese Consul-General was also a member, and when not playing golf would relay to his superiors any movement of the British fleet. On the day before Cunningham encountered the Italians at Matapan, he played golf in the afternoon and ostensibly left his overnight bag so that he could go round again in the morning. In consequence, Ultra was pleased to learn from an Italian decrypt that the Italians thought that the majority of Cunningham's force was still in Alexandria harbour late that evening. The truth, as we know, was somewhat different. Furthermore, the heavy losses which the Italian fleet suffered at Matapan made it impossible to interfere effectively with the evacuation from Crete two months later.

There was a very experienced Y unit in Greece, most of whose operators could read German and Italian. However, although this produced much helpful information, it could not of course compensate for the ground forces' inability to cope with the strength of the German onslaught. Subsequently there was plenty of information about what was in store for Crete. In consequence, Freyberg was able to deploy his forces where they would most easily be able to inflict the damaging casualties referred to above.

Although the loss of Greece and Crete seemed to suggest that the chronicle of humiliation would go on until the war came to an end, there were distinctly encouraging developments elsewhere. On 7 March 1941 British troops invaded Abyssinia. On 11 March the vital Lend-Lease agreement was signed in the United States. Lend-Lease granted the United States the power to supply munitions to 'any country whose defense the President deems vital to the defense of the United States'. This of course meant Britain and the Dominions and came at a point when Britain was at the end of her resources for buying goods on a cash and carry basis. Lend-Lease was later extended to Russia, where it was both a help and an embarrassment. It was a clear sign that the United States realised that the war was not just a remote European conflict but one which, with the assistance of Japan, could quickly reach its own territory. Although America had tended to distance itself from the affairs of

Europe, a mere 3,000 miles away, it was acutely conscious that Japan, 5,000 miles away, could pose a real threat. The reality of that threat would be all too clear before the end of 1941.

March 1941 saw a fresh surge of activity in the war. The Germans had begun raiding London intensively (of the 60,586 people killed and 86,175 seriously injured in air raids on Britain during the war, 30,000 were Londoners), Russia made an undertaking to support Turkey if she was threatened by an aggressor and this could hardly be anyone except Germany, U-boats intensified their attacks on merchant shipping, and Rommel began an offensive in Libya. Owing to the despatch of British forces to Greece, the British line in Libya was now thinly spread. Positive gains were that the British force in Abyssinia captured Kerean and Harrar, and early in April would take Addis Ababa and Massawa.

It was now becoming clear that in signing the 1939 pact with Germany Russia had simply been buying time. Now that she realised that time was running out Russia offered a treaty of friendship to Yugoslavia and signed a neutrality pact with Japan. Her friendly gesture to Yugoslavia did nothing to help that country when the Germans overran it but established a useful link with the communist partisans who would fight under the leadership of Marshal Tito.

From time to time Hitler spoke menacingly of a 'secret weapon' which he would soon unleash on Britain. Initially this had been thought to be the magnetic mine. In view of the fact that Hitler's more boastful utterances tended to be taken seriously, there was some speculation about what it might be. Opinion varied from a new form of gas to new tactics in submarine warfare. Hitler probably had rockets in mind, for research on these was proceeding rapidly, and no doubt he planned to equip them with atomic warheads. However, the first rockets did not land in England till June 1944, so his threats at this stage were probably no more than bluster designed to affect British morale.

As Commander-in-Chief Middle East Land Forces Wavell had a daunting task. Fortunately large numbers of Italians had been taken off the battlefield in his earlier victories; many of them were set to work on farms in Britain, to the mutual satisfaction of them and their hosts. However, Rommel's Afrika Korps now had two good Italian divisions as well as the original German one, and his equipment, particularly in tanks and anti-tank guns, was superior to the British. Meanwhile further trouble came from an unexpected quarter. On 3 April there was a revolution in Iraq (Mesopotamia) in which the pro-British government was ousted and a pro-German one, led by Rashid Ali, took its place. This was a particularly sinister development, for Iraq contained vital oilfields and pipelines; there was also an RAF base at Habbaniya. This crisis had apparently been foreseen by the Special Intelligence Service (MI6) which complained that its warnings had been ignored by Whitehall departments and the Cabinet. This was certainly true, if in fact they had received them. The official history of British Intelligence in World War II, on page 367 of Volume I records: 'The SIS claimed that the fault lay with the failure of the Eastern Department of the Foreign Office to forward its report to the Whitehall Service Department.' In retrospect this does not seem surprising. Philby, Burgess and Maclean were all members of the Foreign Office at that time, and Blunt was working in MI6. As Germany and Russia were then allies and all four spies were intent on furthering Russia's interest at the expense of Britain, it does not seem surprising that large numbers of reports advising Britain to take action to safeguard her interests should have been 'lost'. There were unlimited opportunities for papers to be 'lost' in the Blitz; wage packets in transit seemed to have an uncanny attraction for bombs, or so their custodians often seemed to think. It seems unlikely that this ex-Cambridge coterie of traitors were working entirely alone in the Foreign Office without some helpers and sympathizers. This does not, of course, mean that the whole of the Foreign Office had been corrupted by subversives. The majority of its members were highly intelligent, loyal and industrious, but neither they, nor anyone else at the time, suspected that this evil little group was busy at work undermining the British position.

Nevertheless, when the crisis occurred the British response was admirably resolute. Wavell sent as many men as he could spare, although that was few enough. Fortunately the Arab

Legion, commanded by Sir John Glubb (Glubb Pasha) was available and knew how to fight in the desert. Rashid Ali's attempt to impose a pro-German government on Iraq was quickly nipped in the bud and he himself had to flee to Turkey. The following year the new government of Iraq declared war on Germany, Italy and Japan, but the country did not become involved in any further hostilities. However the arrival of Rashid Ali on the scene in April 1941 when the Germans were just about to invade Greece had given the Middle Eastern scene an ominously dangerous look.

Syria posed an even greater threat than Iraq, for since the fall of France Syria had agreed to take its orders from the Vichy government. Syria was a former Turkish colony which had been put under French admistration after World War I and, like other mandates (as such territories were called), was being prepared for its self-governing independence. As we saw earlier, the French colonial empire did not automatically join the Allies and Free French and take up arms against Germany after the fall of France, but adopted a 'wait-and-see' policy. The Vichy government quickly appointed General Dentz as High Commissioner and, when the British were involved in the campaign against Rashid Ali in Iraq, Dentz allowed the Luftwaffe to establish air bases at Damascus, Palmyra and Rayak. When the Iraqi campaign was safely over, Britain decided that the Syrian situation was too potentially dangerous to remain in its existing state: the next Axis thrust in that area could well be to make it into a base for attacks on Palestine and Iran. In consequence, with the approval of General de Gaulle, a mixed force was sent to invade Syria and to put it under Free French control. The force, commanded by the British General Maitland Wilson, and the Free French General Catroux, was surprised to find that the Vichy French in Syria put up a strong and bitter resistance inflicting many casualties on the British and Free French forces. However, after five weeks the campaign was over and the country put under Free French control. (Syria received its full independence in 1946.) Ultra was now producing a large volume of valuable information, and during the Syrian campaign the decrypts revealed that the Vichy government had seriously considered sending French infantry to Syria by seaborne convoy protected by the German Air Force. The operation was only cancelled because the war in Syria was thought to have been lost already.

On the home front in spring 1941 there was a general feeling of relief that things were not worse. Paradoxically public confidence was raised when the government increased income tax to 10 shillings (50p) in the pound. In a curious way this gave the impression that if the British were paying their way they must be winning the war. The public certainly needed something to stimulate confidence; in April Coventry was blitzed once again, and the House of Commons was destroyed by a bomb on 10 May. Fortunately the Chamber was unoccupied at the time. Outside the Houses of Parliament there is a statue of Richard I (Coeur de Lion) on horseback, brandishing his sword in the air. In one of the raids the sword was bent, but not broken, by a piece of flying metal. This seemed highly symbolic. Britain was bent but not yet broken either. The second Blitz succeeded in being boring as well as terrifying. On the first occasion it had seemed almost unbearable; now everyone hated it for the general misery and discomfort it caused. Everyone seemed to have a bomb story to tell and patient listeners became hard to find. People eventually began to wear buttons printed with the words, 'I am not interested in your bomb'. The stories varied from the horrific to the merely bizarre. Blast could kill you without leaving a mark on your body; it could also strip off all your clothes as you moved along the street, yet leave you unharmed. However, it was seldom so benign. Soldiers found that the effects of the blitz were harder to bear than experiences they had had in battle. Dead children, homeless people, houses ripped apart and pathetically displaying what had once been a private home; all this seemed unfair. Soldiers killing other soldiers was one thing and could be unpleasant enough, but bombing helpless civilians seemed an obscene act. Then there was the smell. After a raid there was always a nauseating smell of dust, decay and death.

The month of May 1941 brought one of the most extraordinary events of the war. Rudolf Hess, Hitler's deputy, flew solo to Scotland where he tried to make contact with the

Duke of Hamilton, whom he claimed to have met previously.
Hess had been a pilot in the German Air Force in World War
I, so the flight itself was no problem for him. He had
subsequently been a founder member of the Nazi party and
strongly anti-Semitic. In 1941 he was head of the Nazi party
organisation, but his position and prestige was being undermined by Martin Bormann. When he arrived he disclosed
that he had proposals for ending the war; these required that
Britain should allow Germany a free hand in Europe in
return for Germany leaving Britain and her empire intact.
The British government promptly dismissed his proposals
and made him a prisoner-of-war. However his record during
the first part of the war brought him to trial at Nuremberg in
1945 as a war criminal. Although many felt that this record
deserved the death penalty (which was handed out to 12 of
the defendants), he was sentenced to life imprisonment.
Subsequently he was interned in Spandau Prison until he died
in 1987 at the age of 93; by then he had long been thought to
be insane. Spandau Prison has now been demolished in order
to dispel any lingering traces of Nazi mythology.

An equally dramatic event that May was the sea chase of
the new German battleship *Bismarck*. The Royal Navy
already had its hands full with the task of preventing German
submarines sinking British merchant shipping, which they
were doing faster than replacement ships could arrive. That
spring the Royal Navy was able to derive some satisfaction
from the fact that the U-boat commander who had ordered
the torpedoing of the *Athenia* on the first day of the war was
killed, but rather less when the commander of the submarine
which had sunk the *Royal Oak* suffered a similar fate: the
latter was admired as a brave and resourceful seaman. Since
the episode of the *Graf Spee*, the larger German warships
had only made sporadic excursions into the Atlantic. *Scheer,
Scharnhorst, Hipper* and *Gneisenau* had made occasional
forays from Brest, doing considerable damage, but *Bismarck*, with eight 15-inch and 12 5.9 guns, was a newcomer to
the scene. She sailed out of Gdynia on 18 May, accompanied
by a heavy cruiser, the *Prinz Eugen*, also new. She hoped to
be joined by *Scharnhorst* and *Gneisenau* from Brest, but the
latter two had been immobilized by the RAF. *Bismarck* was

spotted by the heavy cruiser *Suffolk*; a British battle squad-ron, which included a 20-year-old unmodernised battleship, HMS *Hood*, and a new battleship, the *Prince of Wales*, now endeavoured to intercept the German ship. This plan was upset by poor visibility which caused contact to be lost. On 24 May, the German squadron was sighted by the *Hood*, and everyone opened fire – at ten miles range.

The *Hood* was caught by a full salvo from the *Bismarck*, one shell of which penetrated a magazine. The *Hood* blew up and sank with 1,416 officers and men; there were only three survivors. The *Prince of Wales* was hit by seven shells, but had hit the *Bismarck* twice; the new British battleship was still on trials, had a number of civilians on board, and had not yet got her guns working properly. She therefore broke off the action and slipped away under smoke, hoping the Germans would not follow; fortunately, the *Bismarck* was more intent on reaching Brest than completing a possible major naval victory.

The Royal Navy then set itself on the path of revenge. *Bismarck* was spotted by aircraft from the carrier *Victorious*, but their torpedos could not penetrate the German ship's armour-plating. The battleships *Ramillies* and *Rodney*, with cruiser and destroyer escorts, began the pursuit; the aim was to stop the two German warships from reaching Brest or St Nazaire. While this desperate chase was going on, the German navy decided to concentrate every available sub-marine in the area to torpedo any unwary British ship. The weather strongly favoured the *Bismarck*, but aircraft from the carrier *Ark Royal* caught sight of her through the mist and hit her with two torpedoes. One damaged the propellors and jammed the rudder. It was now 26 May and that night destroyers attacked and hit the *Bismarck* with two more torpedoes, though without much effect. The following morning the battleships *King George V* and *Rodney* arrived on the scene and after a two-hour exchange of fire sank the Bismarck with 2,100 men: 115 were rescued. The *Prinz Eugen* had escaped.

The British government heard the news of the sinking with relief. Had the *Bismarck* escaped after sinking one capital ship and badly damaging another, it would have been an

appalling setback, not least because she would then have
been free to sally forth from Brest at a later date and sink
innumerable unarmed merchant ships. German warships
were not noted for being compassionate to weaker and
smaller craft and the prestige value of the *Bismarck*, claimed
by the German navy to be so well-armed as to be unsinkable,
would have been as big a boost to German morale as it would
have been damaging to British. Ultra decrypts had already
learnt that when the *Bismarck* was put to sea with *Prinz
Eugen* it was not for the purpose of engaging the British fleet,
but to raid the Atlantic trade routes. That was certainly the
most practical way to employ their strength; there is no room
for sentiment in warfare, particularly in naval warfare,
although occasionally chivalry is shown.

However, apart from knowing the *Bismarck*'s intentions,
Ultra played no significant part in the sea battle. Up till this
stage not enough was known about German naval Enigma
for its signals to be read concurrently. That situation was on
the point of being remedied but, however quickly an intercepted Ultra message was read, it could rarely, if ever, have
any influence on a battle which was already taking place. By
the time the intercept had been decrypted, encrypted again
for those requiring that particular piece of information,
decrypted again on receipt and delivered in clear, the battle
scene would probably have changed so much that the intercept would be out of date and useless.

June 1941 was a month of mixed fortunes for Britain. Crete
was lost but Iraq was now firmly under British control and the
Syrian campaign was beginning well. Wavell had made a
remarkable recovery from his setbacks in Greece and now,
urged by Churchill, had decided to carry the fight back to
Rommel. This, it was hoped, would drive the latter away
from Tobruk, which he had been besieging since March. The
code name for this campaign was 'Operation Battleaxe'. It
was doomed to failure. After initial successes Wavell's forces
were themselves driven back. Rommel had demonstrated
that he was not nicknamed 'the desert fox' for nothing. His
technique was to appear to attack, then to think better of it
and retreat. As his tanks fell back the jubilant British
armoured units would dash forward to pursue. Within a few

minutes there would come the terrible realisation that they had been led into a trap. The German retreat had lured the British tanks into the field of fire of the deadly 88 mm guns, which could blow any tank to pieces. The fearsome 88s had originally been designed as anti-aircraft guns, but had also been converted to other rôles, not least that of anti-tank guns. The British 3.7, which had also started out as an anti-aircraft gun, would have been even more effective as an anti-tank gun, but the War Office resolutely set its face against its ever being used in that rôle. The Germans were always alert to tactics of luring the unwary into traps, but after a few experiences the British too were on their guard against them. A cautious policy was necessary even on those occasions when Rommel's tanks were forced to retreat but had no ambush ready.

Even more disturbing for Wavell's forces was the realisation that the new Panzer IV tanks which had a 50 mm gun were more than a match for their British counterparts. Nevertheless a number of Panzers were disabled or destroyed during the fighting and one Panzer IV was captured virtually complete. It was shipped back to England for examination by technical experts, but the latter failed to notice that the tank was equipped with extra, face-hardened armour plates. At this time British tanks were equipped with two-pounder guns, in which the War Office had great faith but which were quite incapable of penetrating the armour of the Panzer IVs. This diagnostic failure by the technical branch accounted for many British deaths and much ill-feeling in the higher command.

After the 'Battleaxe' humiliation, Churchill decided that Wavell must now be replaced by another general. He chose General Sir Claude Auchinleck, who was probably the best general of the war. Owing to the failure of technical intelligence, Auchinleck's task was made almost impossible. It had first failed to identify what proportion of the Panzer IIIs and Panzer IVs had been fitted with the extra plates, and not until the following March did it discover that the plates on the Panzer IV were case-hardened.

The results of this were disastrous. When Auchinleck took the offensive against Rommel in November 1941, he had much the same experience as Wavell in Battleaxe – initial successes and subsequent failure. To Churchill and the Cabinet this seemed inexplicable. On paper the two armies were evenly matched; the British had marginally more tanks (455 to 412) but the Germans had more anti-tank guns (194 to 72). What those not on the scene failed to appreciate was that the German anti-tank guns had a much longer range than the British, and the British Matilda tanks were no match for the Panzers with their 50 mm and 75 mm guns. Ultimately this led to Churchill being disillusioned with Auchinleck's leadership and the latter's replacement by Montgomery. Auchinleck, the realist, had told Churchill in early 1942 that it would be suicidal for the British to embark on a further offensive unless they had a superiority of at least 50 per cent in tanks: in view of the difference in quality between the tanks of each side, nothing else was viable. Churchill, unaware of the technical inferiority, felt that Wavell had been incompetent (although he himself had shorn Wavell of some of his best troops for the Greek fiasco) and that Auchinleck was over-cautious.

Ironically, Churchill's judgement was further distorted by the Ultra decrypts. Rommel, as might be expected of any commander well-removed from the main centre of operations, felt he must plead hard and often if he was to receive a fair share of his country's military resources. The accounts he sent to Army Headquarters in Berlin painted a woeful picture of the state of his force and their equipment. It was clear from these reports that unless Rommel received a continuing supply of the latest equipment as well as well-trained reinforcements his position would be catastrophic and could lead to the total elimination of German and Italian forces from North Africa. His Higher Command, which was not unfamiliar with Rommel's tactics for getting a fair share of the equipment cake, received these dismal reports with some scepticism. Unfortunately, when they appeared in Ultra decrypts and were presented to Churchill, he believed them implicitly. Why, he asked, if Rommel's forces were in such a poor state, could Auchinleck dare to ask for a 50 per cent superiority in tanks? Eventually, when Montgomery, who had replaced Auchinleck as Commander-in-Chief

Middle East, went into battle at Alamein in October 1942, he had a two-to-one supremacy in men, in aircraft, in guns and in tanks, and the tanks included 300 Shermans which were more than a match for the best of the Panzers. But that would not occur for another 15 months, and the war would have taken a different shape by then.

In Britain, air raids killed slightly less civilians in 1941 than they had done in the previous year. The figures were 19,918 killed and 21,163 injured in 1941, against 22,069 killed and 28,240 seriously injured in 1940. By 1941 the British defence was stronger, shelters were much improved, and the population had learnt to react more quickly to emergencies. However, most of the bombs used in 1941 were larger. In 1940, 500 pounds had seemed (as it is) a very large bomb, but in 1941 it was often outclassed by 1000- and 2000-pound bombs and a particularly lethal object called a land-mine. A land-mine was a sea-mine which came down by parachute and could contain up to a ton of explosives. Whereas earlier bombs had demolished houses in ones and twos, these later monsters could, and did, demolish whole streets. Some bombs caused horrendous damage. One which landed on Balham Underground station in London went through the roof and burst a water main: in consequence the 600 sheltering there who were not killed by the explosion were drowned in the flooded tunnel. Several time bombs fell on Buckingham Palace, which the Royal Family refused to leave. Another example of the fact that no one, whatever his rank or station in life, was safe occurred when a bomb fell on the *Café de Paris* in Leicester Square, London and exploded on the dance floor.

In spite of the dislocation of the raids and the need to work in factories, which did little for their appearance, women made an impressive attempt to look their best. Hats virtually disappeared but were replaced by head scarves, once the traditional wear of Lancashire mill girls. Clothes rationing came in in June 1941, but by this time shortages had caused most women to adapt themselves to 'make do and mend', to improvising, to painting legs to simulate stockings, and to manufacturing substitute cosmetics. Most people had begun the war with a few old garments they thought they could never wear again, but were now glad to do so; for those who had had their homes and possessions destroyed by bombs the situation was particularly bleak.

German civilians were more accustomed to shortages. In the period of German rearmament they had been called upon to make many sacrifices. 'Guns before butter' had been a slogan, though not a particularly popular one. German ingenuity had produced numerous substitutes and the word *ersatz* (substitute) became a byword for an inferior version of the real thing. There was *ersatz* tea and *ersatz* coffee, *ersatz* cloth and *ersatz* rubber. Some *ersatz* products, such as atebrin and mepacrine were better than the original quinine for which they were substitutes. Some of Germany's shortages had been eased when their armies overran neighbouring countries, but very few of the benefits were seen by civilians and there were worse shortages to come.

5
HITLER INVADES RUSSIA: THE WAR WIDENS FURTHER

On 22 June 1941, Germany attacked her ally Russia, without warning or a declaration of war. Although this event, code-named 'Barbarossa', caused a shock throughout the English-speaking world, it came as no surprise to the British Cabinet, which had been anticipating it since the fall of France. The invasion of Russia could not be anything but welcome news for Britain, for in spite of Hitler's frequent affirmations that he admired the British empire and had no designs on it, the realistic view was that if he wished to preserve it intact it was merely because he wished to transform it into the German empire with the minimum of dislocation. Similarly, the Soviets, although proclaiming that they had no ambitions outside their own territories, were supporting terrorist and subversive groups everywhere from India to Iceland and Hongkong to the West Indies. However, in spite of British distrust of the long-term policies of the Soviet Union, it earnestly desired to have better relations with that country and had no wish to see her collapse under an unexpected German assault. In consequence, although the British government had been dismayed by the Russo-German pact in 1939, it had made a number of attempts to improve British relations with the Soviet Union.

One part of those efforts had been to give Russia a series of warnings about the fate which was probably in store for her. The British Ambassador to Russia, Sir Stafford Cripps, who conveyed some of these warnings, observed that the Russians were already greatly apprehensive about being attacked by both Germany and Japan. Cripps was an inspired choice as ambassador. An upper-class socialist intellectual, a barrister, a product of Winchester College which seemed to have a talent for nurturing embryonic socialists, a vegetarian of ascetic appearance, Cripps' sincerity was doubted by no one, whether conservative or communist. However, this did not extend to his being trusted with the Ultra information. Some of his warnings to Russia, which he was delivering from the beginning of 1941, seem to have been based on information he gleaned from the American embassy in Moscow. There were, of course, other sources of information about the impending attack which did not involve Ultra. Local agents disclosed that the German Air Force was rapidly constructing a huge complex of airfields and ancillary accommodation in its eastern territories, including Poland. In spite of the claims of other fronts, such as the Balkans, the number of divisions facing Russia was nearly doubled in the first five months of 1941. There were numerous reports of increased rail traffic in eastern Germany. These preparations did not, however, necessarily prove that Germany was planning to attack Russia. They may have been made to ward off a possible Russian attack on Germany, which was highly probable if Germany attacked Turkey and then made a drive to capture the Iranian oilfields. Such a threat would open up a German route to India. It would, however, pose a threat to the Soviet Union which it could not ignore.

Although the picture of German intentions was still obscure in spring 1941, some light was shed on it by American information gained from reading Japanese top-secret ciphers. These indicated that Germany had decided to abandon all idea of invading Britain for the time being and intended to make her next move elsewhere. Germany had also suggested that Japan might now attack Singapore. When Hess arrived in Britain in May it was hoped he might be able to shed further light on German plans, but this he failed to do.

During the 40 years since World War II ended there have been numerous claims that Britain frequently warned Russia of an impending attack by Germany during 1941, but Russia resolutely failed to believe that this was the German intention. Britain was alleged to have received the information from Ultra, but was unable to explain this to Stalin for fear of compromising the source. In fact Germany kept her intentions secret until 4 June when Hitler disclosed his plans to the Japanese ambassador in Berlin. Hitler told the ambassador that communist Russia must be eliminated immediately, before the task became more difficult. Within days Ultra was able to confirm that the attack would come soon after 13 June; most of their information came from Enigma readings of instructions to aircraft. Cripps believed that Russia would not be able to hold out for more than a month if Germany attacked, and his view was supported by the Allied Chiefs of Staff, whose opinions seem to have been based on nothing stronger than guesswork about the state of the Russian armed forces. To this was added the speculation that a German invasion of Britain might follow later in the year, because Polish sources had informed SIS that further German troop movements into France were imminent.

All these doubts and guesses were resolved on 22 June when Hitler launched an unannounced invasion of Russia by 165 divisions. It was the greatest invasion force yet seen and its power was enhanced by the German Air Force. The total involved numbered two and a half million men, and, as this was approximately half the strength of the German armed forces it meant a considerable depletion of garrisons in the territories overrun in the previous year. These, however, were able to reassure themselves by the speed of Hitler's previous victories: the campaign would not last long, and in six weeks at the outside Moscow would be in German hands.

There were several reasons why this optimistic forecast was incorrect. The Russians had 170 divisions on their western frontier and a sizeable air component. The strength of the army was approximately 800 divisions, a total of some 12 million men. This was twice the number the Germans would be able to mobilize. Furthermore, apart from keeping a watchful eye on their eastern front, where the Japanese looked to be increasingly belligerent, the Soviets could use the majority of their army against the Germans, who already had heavy commitments far removed from the Russian front.

But, as we have seen already, numbers are not everything, even though these figures make the 10 divisions Britain put into France in 1939 seem remarkably puny. In quality the two

forces were ill-matched. The German army was well equipped with modern tanks, being able to deploy over 3,000,
although many of these lacked the 50 mm gun which had
created such havoc in the desert war. Their training and
experience, gained in battles in Poland, Norway, France and
the desert, gave the Germans enormous confidence.

The Russians had many more tanks; it is estimated that
there were at least 20,000 but most of them were old and
likely to break down. Their army was still disorganised after
the recent purges and, although the new, more adventurous,
commanders would in time produce good results, the army
was a cumbrous and badly-organised machine. The Russians
were surprised by the German attack but not totally unprepared for it; unwisely they had concentrated many of their
divisions close to the frontier which was 2,000 miles long. In
consequence, the Germans had no difficulty in infiltrating
and isolating many Russian units which should have been
deployed in depth. The Russians had made a bad tactical
mistake in not letting the Germans penetrate deep into
Russia before they encircled them; as it was, it was the
Russians who were encircled. It was said that the Russians
were reluctant to face facts even when they were obvious. A
German communist who had escaped from Berlin, where his
unit was being briefed about its part in the invasion, and
made his way to Russia, was not believed even after a lengthy
interrogation. On Stalin's orders he was shot, the execution
being carried out after the invasion actually began.

Even so the Germans did not have everything to their
liking. Many of the roads marked on the Russian maps they
had acquired did not exist; they had not progressed past the
planning stage. In consequence there was considerable dis-
tortion in the German tactical moves. Nevertheless, within
10 days the Germans claimed to have taken 150,000 prisoners
and captured 1,200 tanks and 600 guns. Ten days later their
leading units had reached Smolensk and were a mere 100
miles from Moscow. Much of the Russian Air Force appeared
to have been destroyed, some of it while still on the ground.

On 15 July, the Germans found that instead of collapsing,
the opposition now seemed to be stiffening. Smolensk was
vigorously defended; the Russians appeared to be using a

new type of mortar, the Katyusha. This was simple to use, man-portable, and had a range of approximately 800 yards. It was one of a range of mortars which the Russians used with increasing effect. Mortars have a particularly disturbing effect, because it is impossible to take effective shelter from them unless one retreats underground, which is obviously impossible for an attacking infantryman. As a soldier advances towards the enemy he can take advantage of cover, behind bushes, hillocks, walls or other features, but the mortar bomb, wobbling through the air with disconcerting accuracy, comes over the top of his cover and explodes near or on top of him. The Germans were, of course, experts on mortars themselves; they had used them with great effect in the trench warfare of World War I, but here they found that the Russians were experts too, and they did not like it. The Russian soldiers were remarkably tough and resilient. Heat, wet, or cold seemed to make no difference to them. Generals or senior officers who lost battles were summarily court-martialled and executed. There was no administrative clutter: if a patrol of 10 men lost half its number, five more soldiers would be sent to make up their strength; they were not five more names but merely five more soldiers. Any welfare comforts the Russians acquired would have to be taken from the enemy. If anyone deserted or showed cowardice, the remainder of the platoon were liable to be shot, and probably were.

At the end of July 1941 Hitler made another of his interferences in the conduct of this campaign which cumulatively cost Germany the war. He had become uneasy about the deep penetration by the Panzers and felt they should take steps to encircle some of the Russian troops they had bypassed. Instead of allowing the forward units to press home the attack on Smolensk, he ordered that they should swing south-west and meet a similar thrust coming up from the outskirts of Kiev. This was a sensible tactical move for any campaign except this one. Until Leningrad, Moscow, Kharkov and Rostov were taken – and perhaps even after that – the Russians would have ample space to fall back, to make the Germans fight in the open, and to extend their already perilously long lines of communication; even if

Moscow fell, the Germans would only have penetrated into one-eighth of Russian territory. In August Hitler decided that all objectives could not be reached simultaneously and that one, or perhaps two, should have priority. Leningrad, with its industrial potential, must certainly be one, but should Moscow, with its prestige value, take precedence over Kiev and the great grain resources of the Ukraine? His decision would have been easier if the Russian resistance had now been crumbling fast, as anticipated; instead it was stiffening. He decided that Kiev and the Ukraine would be the next target. This would seize the great coal-mining and industrial asset of the Donetz basin, cut off the Russians from their oil supplies in the Caucasus, and produce vast quantities of food.

And at first Hitler seemed to have been right. Kiev fell on 18 September and even the great Timoshenko could not prevent the surrender of 665,000 Russians. There was nothing now to interfere with a German drive to Moscow.

It was a matter of considerable unease to the German Staff that the German forces were widely dispersed, deep in Russian territory. The early successes had been dazzling, but there were still several million Russian soldiers to be reckoned with, neither Moscow nor Leningrad had been taken, and ... it was October. Winter comes early in Russia: Moscow often sees the first snow at the end of August. Although von Runstedt had now overrun the Crimea, with the exception of Sebastopol, and should have troops to spare for the Moscow front, it would take time before they could be deployed where they were most needed. The good news was that von Bock was now within 30 miles of Moscow. Everything the Germans needed had to be transported over hundreds of miles of broken roads, most of which had been made almost impassable by bomb craters; the retreating Russians had been told to destroy everything which could be of the remotest possible use to the Germans and had done so thoroughly. This was known as the 'scorched earth' policy, and its name described it well. There were other unpleasant facts for the German Staff to ponder. The Russians had adopted some of the German tactics and were using them with a particularly disconcerting tank – the T-34. As mentioned earlier, the Russians and Germans had co-operated closely over tank design until Hitler came to power, so the Germans might have expected something unusual ten years later. The T-34 was very skilfully designed with sloping armour which deflected enemy shells. The Panzer IVs could only knock out T-34s if they hit them from behind, and the T-34s rarely allowed that opportunity. Russian tank design was going to give the Germans many problems in the future.

By the time the Germans were ready to press home the attack on Moscow, the Russian winter had set in. The Russians were prepared for it, although that did not make it much easier; the Germans were not, and suffered accordingly. First came mud, then snow. At night the engines of tanks and vehicles froze, and there was insufficient anti-freeze. Guns which had their mechanisms frozen failed to absorb the recoil as they should have done, and the results were disastrous. Tanks were immobilized by the weather faster than Russian gunfire could ever have achieved. German clothing was quite useless at keeping out the bitter cold which brought with it all the ailments associated with low temperatures and exposure. In spite of this the Germans launched an offensive on 15 November; it ground to a halt on 6 December in the Moscow suburbs in sub-zero temperatures. Like his considerably more able predecessor Napoleon, Hitler had miscalculated the delaying effect of the Russian terrain and the effect of the Russian winter. By now the German army had lost 200,000 men killed in this campaign and 8,000 of them were officers. There were four times as many wounded or otherwise incapacitated.

At that moment the Russians, commanded by Marshal Zhukov, launched a huge counter-attack. In temperatures which were now between 30 and 40 degrees centigrade below zero, the Germans were unable to use much of their equipment. Hitler insisted that they should not retreat an inch, but that was impossible. They were driven back, but not far. On the way in, they had been particularly ruthless with the inhabitants of the territory they had overrun. Now, here and there, the Russians took their revenge. Hitler decided that the stalemate was due to incompetence at the highest level and dismissed several of his generals. Among them were Guderian and von Brauchitsch. Hitler announced that from now on he himself would be commander-in-chief in Russia and insisted that no retreat would be allowed: positions must be held and the following spring the offensive would be renewed. To implement this policy he brought in contingents from Hungary, Italy, Roumania and Finland. Only the last had the sort of equipment needed in Russia.

But by 15 December, when the Germans were beginning the long agony of the Russian winter, the conflict had widened again. This time it was truly world war. Japan had unwisely attacked America without warning on 7 December and at the same time launched herself against the British and Dutch colonies in south-east Asia. As the Japanese rushed forward on a tide of apparently unstoppable success, they were not to know that in that same month plans were being made for manufacturing the weapon which would ultimately crush them, the atomic bomb.

Until the late nineteenth century the atom was thought to be the smallest, indivisible part of an element, and its state was considered to be unalterable. Subsequently physicists realised that an atom was energy, compressed into a very small area. Under suitable treatment, which meant bombardment by alpha particles and high-velocity electronic beams, it could release vast amounts of light and energy into the surrounding atmosphere. This description is, of course, a highly simplified version of an extremely complex process, which was developed by physicists of many nationalities. An Italian named Enrico Fermi, who escaped from Mussolini's Italy, realised that a neutron which collided with a uranium nucleus could set free other neutrons which would then collide with neighbouring atoms and produce further neutrons. This process was known as a chain reaction. At one time it was thought that if and when this process started it would be unstoppable and the entire universe would rapidly disintegrate. Instead it was found that the process could be controlled by deuterium and used to create an atomic bomb. Research on this project took place in England during the early days of the war under the code name of 'Tube Alloys'. In 1940 two French scientists brought to Britain 44 gallons of heavy water, which contains deuterium instead of hydrogen (hence the name). Subsequently both British and American scientists conducted further research, but at first each group seemed unwilling to share its vital discoveries with the other. This situation was resolved by discussions between Churchill and Roosevelt. In December 1941 the American Corps of Engineers of the Manhattan Distict was created to start production of an atomic bomb. It was allotted 78 square miles of land in the Tennessee Valley and the 'Manhattan Project' was born.

But much more research and experiment was needed before a usable atomic bomb could be created. There was, of course, a great sense of urgency. It was known that the Germans were also working to the same end. There were four possible ways of attaining success in splitting the fissionable U-235 isotope in the uranium. Any one of the methods might lead to success and, as it was not known which method the Nazi scientists were using, the Manhattan Project decided to use them all. In fact the Germans had decided to concentrate on working with heavy water, instead of experimenting with some of the alternatives. Their chief source of heavy water was Norway and that source was sabotaged in 1943. When the Germans had made the Norwegian plant work again, they decided that it would be advisable to transfer existing stocks of heavy water to Germany. As described above these were sunk by saboteurs in 1943 in a Norwegian lake and at that point Germany abandoned all attempts to make an atomic bomb.

Meanwhile the Manhattan Project forged ahead and on 16 July 1945 successfully exploded the first atomic bomb in the New Mexico desert. While the Manhattan Project was being launched, Japan created an empire which stretched to the coast of Australia and the frontiers of India. In the following years the Japanese were rolled back from most of their empire to the position of defending their own homeland. However, that in itself would not have caused them to surrender. It needed the shock of realising that they were the target of atomic bombs, and the command of their emperor to make them do that, as we see later.

The thought that Japan might ever lose the war they started on 7 December 1941 could never have occurred to the members of the Japanese armed forces. The campaign was easier than they had imagined in their most optimistic flights of fancy. Japan had been at war since 1931, and since 1937 had been locked in a hard, indecisive, struggle with China. However, the United States had long felt it had a 'special relationship' with China, not least because she feared Japanese aggression and was happy to see that country exhausting herself in an apparently interminable struggle on the Chinese mainland. The 'special relationship' extended to supplying the Chinese with goods via Indo-China, and over the Burma road which linked Lashio in Burma to Chungking in China. When, on 21 July 1941, the Vichy government in France was coerced by the Japanese to allow them to occupy Indo-China 'temporarily', Roosevelt was very angry. He responded by freezing Japanese assets in America, which were worth over 30 million pounds. Britain also froze Japanese assets and broke off all commercial trade as well. The Dutch government in exile, which still had a huge, rich stake in the East Indies, did likewise. Unfortunately for Britain, Japan's acquisition of air bases in Indo-China had put her aircraft within easy flying distance of Malaya.

The Japanese were clearly bent on war but could, and did, claim that they had been forced into that position by historical events. In the 1630s the Japanese had decided that their country and religion were being corrupted by outside influences and adopted a policy of total seclusion from foreigners. Japan contains a high proportion of volcanic mountains and only one-sixth of the terrain is cultivatable, but the Japanese were expert agriculturists and able fishermen and could survive in isolation. Population growth, which could have led to economic disaster, was controlled by abortion and infanticide. The period of isolation, which left a mark on the Japanese national character, ended in 1853, when Commodore Perry of the United States Navy arrived with four ships and demanded that the Japanese should open ports to America for trade and subsequently sign treaties. The Japanese, having observed the inability of the Chinese to resist Western arms and Western penetration, bowed to the inevitable and opened two ports. Subsequently the Japanese adopted some Western practices. The abolition of former methods of birth control soon produced a rapidly expanding population. In spite of emigration and the wars with China, in the 1930s the Japanese population had reached 99 million by 1939 and was expanding at the rate of five million a year. Japan had managed to expand her territories by acquiring Taiwan (Formosa) and Korea, and had been granted the administration of a few Pacific islands after World War I; but this fell far short of satisfying her real or imagined needs. When France collapsed, Holland was overrun, and Britain was besieged, Japan looked thoughtfully at all their Asian colonies: they now seemed extremely vulnerable and highly desirable.

Japan's major problem seemed to lie with America, which was unlikely to let the Japanese rampage through south-east Asia and build up an extremely powerful empire without taking some steps to restrain her. The most profitable step would be to give open assistance to the British and Dutch to preserve their colonies (much though the US disliked the idea of colonies); the US was, of course, already assisting China. The simple answer for the Japanese was to cripple the American Pacific fleet with a supreme blow, acquire the British colonies while the Americans were trying to rebuild their fleet, and then negotiate from a position of strength. Five thousand miles of ocean separated Japan from the United States, but halfway between the two countries lay the Hawaiian islands where the US Pacific fleet was based. If that could be eliminated, any threat from the United States would be relegated to the distant future, when it could easily be met, if ever it materialized.

At dawn on 7 December 1941, Japanese carrier-borne aircraft attacked the US Pacific Fleet while it lay at anchor in Pearl Harbor, and at the same time bombed Wheeler and Hickman airfields. Although the attack came as a total surprise to the Americans, they managed to fight back sufficiently well to bring down 29 Japanese aircraft and to sink five midget submarines. But meanwhile the Japanese had sunk three battleships, capsized yet another, and damaged four more. Considerable damage was inflicted on three cruisers and three destroyers. 188 American aircraft were destroyed and the total casualties amounted to 3,389. It was all over within 15 minutes.

The shock and dismay which was created in America was unprecedented. At the time, negotiations were in progress between the US and Japan to settle economic and other differences. The Pearl Harbor attack, a brilliant and carefully planned operation, was launched before a declaration of war, although the Japanese subsequently claimed that this was only a technicality due to the difference in time zones. Nothing less than such a calculated act of treachery could have stirred the US into such immediate action and long-term resentment. Years after the Pearl Harbor raid, the memory was sufficient for it to make a battle-cry for the US with 'Avenge Pearl Harbor!'.

The 'victory' was greeted with jubilation in Japan, which would soon have others to add to it. But the Pearl Harbor raid had been a partial failure for Japan, for it had failed to destroy the US carriers, all four of which were at sea; the war which was now beginning in the Pacific would rely heavily on aircraft carriers. But far worse for the Japanese was the fact that they had now brought the United States into the war, and a United States which would spare no efforts to avenge the unprovoked attack. It meant also that America was now ranged against Germany (for Hitler rather surprisingly declared war on the United States on 11 December 1941) and Italy, and was on the same side as Russia, whose intentions towards Japan were unpredictable. However, in December 1941 it did not seem as if Russia was going to be much trouble to anyone, with Moscow and Leningrad besieged and German armies deep in her territory. But, as the Japanese would find, wars cannot be won by attacks which last 15 minutes, however much damage they may do in that time.

While the Japanese launched their attack on Pearl Harbor they were also en route to invade Malaya and Hongkong. Here too their attacks came without warning: both attacks had been in preparation for a long time.

Hongkong stood no chance at all and could only hold out for three weeks. Malaya was in slightly better case but not much. As long ago as September of the previous year the Japanese had learnt that their task would be comparatively easy. In that month the Japanese had received an intelligence windfall which took their breath away. A short time earlier the GOC Malaya, then Lieutenant-General Sir Lionel Bond, had submitted to the British Chiefs of Staff his requirements for holding Malaya if Japan attacked. He required four divisions, two tank regiments, anti-tank guns and some 600 modern fighter aircraft. The Chiefs of Staff drafted a reply saying that Bond's requirements could not be met; Britain hoped to keep Japan quiet by mild appeasement, as Malaya's sea, air and land defences were totally inadequate. This reply was sent on a merchant ship, the *Autonedan*, which set off from Birkenhead in September 1940. Its total armament consisted of one small, stern-mounted gun. In the Indian Ocean it encountered a heavily armed German raider, sailing under false colours. The *Autonedan* tried to fight, but all the officers were immediately killed and the crippled ship was boarded. In the strong room the Germans found many confidential papers, including the Chiefs of Staff reply to Bond. This being of no special interest to Germany, it was sent to Japan as a symbol of good will. The Japanese could hardly believe what they read, but once they did, realised that Singapore and the Netherlands East Indies were theirs for the taking. The only real problem they might encounter would be from the United States, although that did not seem very likely. Nevertheless, if America did range herself with the Allies, the situation would be very difficult. The Japanese did not take long to decide that in the preliminary stages of this war the United States must be hit so hard she would be unable, or at least unwilling, to take any further part. Her colony in the Philippines would also be added to the empire of the Rising Sun without difficulty, for she was already at the point of granting it independence.

The Japanese prepared for their conquests with ingenuity and thoroughness. They were expert photographers and as 'tourists' took innumerable photographs of every feature which might have a military value. Malaya, Burma, the East Indies and the Philippines were so immersed in a dream that war could never come their way, that the Japanese 'tourists' were able to roam as much as they pleased. They noted all the jungle paths, crossroads and potential landing beaches, and set up commercial photographic studios where soldiers and sailors could have their photographs taken cheaply. The

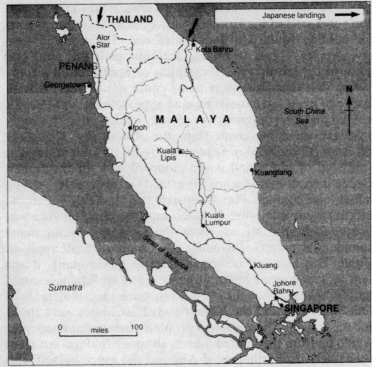

Japanese Invasion Points Dec 8 1941

Japanese did not fail to note the units to which servicemen belonged: subsequently it transpired that a number of Japanese officers had been engaged in the work. The Japanese made excellent maps; it was said that when the Malayan volunteer forces held an exercise in 1940 they were surprised to see that their maps bore the inscription, 'Printed in Tokyo'. Cafés and other places of recreation such as dance halls and massage parlours contained a number of highly intelligent Japanese women, who usually described themselves as Chinese, Burmese or Thai.

There were various assumptions about Malaya and Singapore which would all be proved to be untrue. One was that the island of Singapore, which lay at the south end of the 500-mile-long peninsula, was heavily fortified and, in any case, could only be attacked from the sea. Its 15-inch guns

were therefore mainly mounted on the southern side.
Secondly, if Singapore should by any chance be attacked
from the mainland, the attackers would have to come along
a single road because the jungle was said to be pathless and
impenetrable. Thirdly, in time of crisis Malaya would be
reinforced by naval units capable of protecting the shores
and a substantial number of fighter aircraft would be provided for dealing with the Japanese, who were known to
have at least 2,600 aircraft available. Fourthly, Malaya was
believed to contain adequate quantities of well-trained
fighting troops. Fifthly, the complaisant attitude of the civil
and military authorities which neglected to build proper
defences in spite of dire warnings, would be found to be at
fault. Malaya at that time was producing one-third of the
world supply of natural rubber and half the world's supply
of tin. In addition there were other products such as palm
oil, and Singapore was a very busy commercial port: the
official attitude to making contingency preparations was
that to do so would alarm the civilian population, disrupt
the labour force which was working in the plantations and
the mines, and generally interfere with production of essential goods.

The army in Malaya, which consisted of three under-
strength divisions and some ancillary troops, numbered
approximately 40,000 men, a figure to be borne in mind
later. Two of the divisions were Indian Army, with a sprink-
ling of British troops, the third was Australian. None had
any previous experience of war, and few soldiers had more
than minimal training. There were no tanks. There were
very few automatic weapons and the general assumption of
this small force which was strung out over 500 miles was that
it would be able to fight, if necessary, on ground of its own
choosing, strongly supported by the Royal Air Force.

Unfortunately the RAF was in no better case. Its aircraft
were old and slow; when the Japanese attacked, many of
them were destroyed on the ground. Two days after the
Japanese landed on the north of the peninsula (they also
came through Thailand) the greatest naval disaster of the
war stunned the Allies. The new battleship *Prince of Wales*
and the battle-cruiser *Repulse* were sunk effortlessly by

Japanese torpedo bombers from Indo-China; they were totally without air cover.

From then onwards the Japanese had complete control of the sea and air and could land troops along the peninsula when and where they wished. When army units contrived to hold the experienced Japanese divisions who attacked them, they were frequently ordered to fall back and take up positions further south; it was said that otherwise they would be encircled by landings from the sea or by infiltration to the rear (from the impenetrable jungle). At one point, Kampar, troops of 11th Division had actually forced the Japanese to retreat when the order came to fall back once more. Subsequently, Japanese sources disclosed that if the British had held Kampar and counter-attacked, the Japanese army would have been thrown into chaos and made a hasty retreat. They were running short of ammunition and in this area at least could have been routed, but it was not to be.

The GOC, General Percival, though personally brave, had clearly lost all understanding and control of the battles. In February 1942 the remaining troops were brought back to Singapore island, which was separated from the mainland by a narrow strip of water. Singapore, which had a population of approximately a million and a quarter of mixed races, was then subjected to an artillery and aerial bombardment which killed civilians in their thousands. Once again there were no prepared defences and the Japanese crossed the water, though not without difficulty. After a week, with unburied bodies lying everywhere and the water supplies in the hands of the Japanese, Percival surrendered.

In the final days of the campaign a desert-trained division had been landed on the island, though many of its weapons had been sunk on the way in, and this helped to swell the number of prisoners. A few weeks earlier two brigades of half-trained inexperienced Indian troops had been landed, but had been quickly routed by the Japanese. For the Japanese the campaign was a brilliant triumph; for the British government, and for Churchill in particular, it was an incredible disaster; to those who had been trying to make a fight of it the whole campaign had been a major exercise in frustration. The final insult was that the world blithely accepted the Japanese figures for the numbers who had surrendered, and the absurdly inflated figure of 130,000 passed into history. In fact, the British, Indian and Australian troops had been outnumbered throughout the campaign, and even the introduction of 22,000 more at the last moment, when the battle was lost, did not bring the true figure to above 60,000; this was a fifth of those who had been lucky enough to be evacuated from Dunkirk. There was no escape from Singapore on the last day of the fighting: the Japanese navy was all around, even if an undersized boat capable of sailing the 2,000 miles to Australia could have been found.

Of the prisoners taken, thousands died in captivity from starvation and disease and overwork. But that was still to come and in February 1942 the Japanese were driving ahead on other paths of conquest. There seemed to be no prospect of stopping them. With an army of six-and-a-half million men, every one of whom was convinced that the highest fulfilment of his life would be to die in battle winning victory for his Emperor, the Son of Heaven, with an air force of 3,000, mostly equipped with very modern aircraft, and a navy which contained ten fast carriers as well as a host of other formidable craft, Japan posed a threat to Australia, to India, perhaps to the United States itself.

On 19 January 1942 Japanese armies had invaded Burma, and having once more caught the British unprepared and under-equipped, pushed them back 1,300 miles to the frontiers of India. Even if there had been no opposition, that journey through the Burmese terrain would have been a formidable task. When the conquest was completed in May 1942 the Japanese looked forward to entering India. However, they needed time to re-group first. Other territories, such as Borneo, with its rich oil prize, Sumatra and Java (the rich Dutch colonies in the East Indies) and isolated Pacific islands, were in turn swept into the Japanese orbit. The Philippines gave them rather more trouble. General Douglas MacArthur, who was the overall commander, had long tried to warn his countrymen about the probability of a Japanese attack. MacArthur had 200 aircraft of good quality, 19,000 American troops and 11,000 Philippine Scouts. There was a Philippine army, but it was not yet properly trained.

Burma

The Allied leaders of 1940: *(from left to right)* General Sir William Ironside CIGS; Winston Churchill; General Gamelin, C-in-C, French army; Viscount Gort, C-in-C, British Expeditionary Force; General Georges, French army.

September 1940. Air raid damage to London.

The blitz on London's St Paul's Cathedral, 1940.
Sherman tanks advancing across the desert in 1942.

Churchill and the famous cigar.

The evacuation of Dunkirk, 1940. British and French troops await their return to England.

The return of British troops to Normandy, 1944.

General Dwight D. Eisenhower.

General Douglas MacArthur and his corncob pipe.

The U.S.S. *California* sinking in Pearl Harbor after being bombed by the Japanese on December 7, 1941.

American marines storm up the beach of Guadalcanal Island unopposed.

Aftermath of a kamikaze attack on U.S.S. *Bunker Hill*, 1945.

The Allied leaders at Yalta, 1945. Front row *(from left to right)* Churchill, President Roosevelt and Marshal Stalin. Behind are Lord Leathers, Mr Eden, Mr Stettinius, Sir Alexander Cadogan, M. Molotov and Mr Averill Harriman, U.S. Ambassador to U.S.S.R.

Suspected Russian partisans caught and summarily executed by Germans in 1943.

Nagasaki.

After the war German camp officials are made to dispose of the bodies of Russians, Poles, Frenchmen and Jews who had been starved and burned in the concentration camps.

The Philippines group contains over 7,000 islands, but the vital one was Luzon in the north, as this contained Manila, Corregidor and Bataan.

Luzon had been attacked three days after Pearl Harbor in 1941, and the Americans had insufficient forces in the Philippines to prevent the Japanese destroying most of their aircraft and making landings on the north and east coasts. Manila was declared an 'open' city, but soon suffered the same fate as other 'open' cities in this war.

In January 1942, MacArthur's hopes of defending the island much longer had disappeared, so he withdrew all available troops to the Bataan peninsula, which projects 25 miles into the sea of Luzon. Here they held out until the end of March. The survivors were then sent on the notorious Bataan death march of 700 miles; many of them died on the way. Subsequently the Japanese claimed that they believed that honourable men always died in battle rather than surrender (even though ordered to do so) and that this justified bestial cruelty such as bayoneting those who fell whilst on forced marches in the tropics. As they also bayoneted women and children, this argument did not prove particularly convincing, when produced at later trials of war criminals. In February, when the American position was clearly hopeless, MacArthur was ordered to Australia. Before he left, he assured the inhabitants of the Philippines, 'I will be back'. Few believed him at the time. Lieutenant General Wainwright held out in the ancient fortress of Corregidor until 6 May. Subsequently the treatment of Wainwright and his troops showed little of the Samurai warrior chivalry on which the Japanese prided themselves.

America was more deeply shocked than Britain by events in the Pacific, although the British took years to reconcile themselves to the loss of the *Prince of Wales* and the *Repulse*. The British had always considered the defence of the Far Eastern colonies to be impossible if the Japanese attacked when all the British troops and generals were engaged elsewhere. These had all been sent to the Middle East. But MacArthur was an outstanding general and a legendary figure in American military circles, so if he could not hold off the Japanese the situation looked ominous indeed. Meanwhile the Japanese swept triumphantly on until they reached New Guinea, virtually on the borders of Australia. Some senior Japanese officers were now beginning to worry about the very long lines of communication, from Japan to India and to Australia, but the possession of a first-class navy, an excellent air force and sky-high morale soothed any momentary flutters of alarm. Some, perhaps, wondered how much trouble Admiral Nimitz, appointed C.-in-C. Pacific in late December, would be able to give. But overall the outlook seemed very good indeed for the Japanese. They appeared to have complete control of the seas from Hawaii to India, for on 4 April 1941 they had sunk three British warships in the Bay of Bengal. India was threatened not merely from the frontier with Burma but also along her long eastern coastline. If, as it appeared, the Japanese navy was now roaming freely in the Bay of Bengal, there seemed every chance that Madagascar and the east coast of Africa could be its next objective. Madagascar was a French colony at this time and, in order to forestall the Japanese landing and taking control, a British force invaded on 5 May 1942. Although Madagascar does not look very impressive against its huge neighbour, it is in fact the fourth largest island in the world.

At the beginning of the summer of 1942 it seemed that the war as a whole might have stabilized after the recent series of disasters for the Allies. The Germans were still attacking in Russia, but here and there the Red Army was holding them and occasionally driving them back. The United States extended the Lend-Lease agreement, and a British convoy reached Russia in spite of heavy air attacks. There was enormous good will for Russia in Britain and when the factories declared a 'Tanks for Russia' week production was higher than it had been for the supply of British forces. Germany had just begun the Baedeker raids on Britain. Karl Baedeker was an early nineteenth-century German publisher who produced a series of European guide books, all of which emphasised the beauty of historic towns. When therefore German aircraft began bombing cities such as Exeter and Bath, the raids were given this ironic description. In May the RAF retaliated with a massive raid on Cologne, which was an industrial city, but carefully avoided bombing the cathedral.

On 31 May, Czech patriots assassinated the local Nazi official, Reinhard Heydrich. The German response was one of the worst atrocities of the war, for they destroyed the entire Czech village of Lidice. All men over the age of 16 were shot, and women sent to the concentration camp at Ravensbrueck, and all children to the concentration camp at Gneisenau.

In the Middle East the offensive which Rommel had begun in mid-May was alarmingly successful. He captured Tobruk and caused the British troops to fall back to the Egyptian frontier. 230 British tanks were lost in the desert fighting and as he pressed on to El Alamein it seemed as if nothing would stop him reaching Alexandria. Fortunately for the British, General Auchinleck, who was now Commander-in-Chief, Middle East, decided to take over command of the battle himself. After several weeks of hard fighting, Rommel realised that he was not going to reach Alexandria after all and fell back. Subsequently there were two other battles at El Alamein, of which the third (October 1942) became the most famous. Nevertheless the battle which Auchinleck had fought with infinite skill in July had undoubtedly been the most critical.

May and June 1942 offered the first signs that the Japanese had reached their limit in the Pacific and that the war might now turn against them. The first of these events occurred in the Coral Sea, which lies between New Guinea, the Solomon Islands, and Australia. At the beginning of May the Japanese landed on Tulagi, an island in the Solomon group, and began to convert it into a seaplane base. Decrypts from the American version of Ultra, code-named 'Magic', indicated that the Japanese were now beginning to concentrate a formidable fleet in the area. This was the first occasion when code-breaking enabled the US navy to take a definite step in reversing the string of defeats the Japanese had inflicted on all those who tried to oppose them.

Although less well-known than the European Ultra, the American code-breaking operation in the Pacific was equally effective. Unfortunately it has never received full credit for its achievements, even inside America itself. The reason for this is twofold. Immediately after Pearl Harbor there was much recrimination over the fact that a disaster of this magnitude had not been anticipated. The American Intelligence service was blamed but could not defend itself by disclosing what it could and could not achieve. Although the American code-breakers were reading the Japanese diplomatic signals, these gave no indication that the Pearl Harbor attack was about to be launched. Such information could only have come from decrypting Japanese navy signals, with which the United States had not made sufficient progress at the time. The Americans had bought one of the early Enigma machines and by 1940 had developed decrypting skills which were sufficiently advanced for them to decipher Japanese diplomatic codes. This development had been given the code name of 'Magic', while the Japanese version of the Enigma machine was known as 'Purple'.

However, the machine codes used by Enigma and Purple were far from being the only ones in use. There were dozens of others. American Intelligence had worked assiduously to penetrate as many of their codes as possible and eventually acquired the ability to decrypt a wide range of military and naval signals. Somewhat confusingly this part of the American code-breaking system was also given the name of Ultra, and is sometimes referred to as 'the other Ultra'. Eventually the combination of information acquired from reading the diplomatic signals via 'Magic' and the other signals read through 'the other Ultra' enabled the United States to acquire vital knowledge of Japanese shipping movements. Although therefore the US Intelligence service had been surprised by the Japanese attack on Pearl Harbor, it was the Japanese turn to be surprised when, exactly five months after the Pearl Harbor attack, their warships in the Coral Sea were intercepted and battered by aircraft from American carriers. On that occasion the Japanese sank the most shipping, but lost more aircraft. However, the essential importance of the battle was that the damage done to the Japanese fleet caused their Admiral to call off his intended attack on Port Moresby, New Guinea, and return to his base in Rabaul. Australia had therefore been saved by a naval battle conducted entirely by aircraft. This was a turning point in naval history, but it was an event which would soon be repeated.

While the battle of the Coral Sea was taking place Japanese Imperial Headquarters, full of confidence for the future, had issued instructions that Midway Island and the Western Aleutians should be occupied. Midway Island lies just to the east of the International Date Line (which runs approximately through the central part of the Pacific Ocean). The Aleutian group lies almost directly north of Midway (so called from its position in the Pacific) and is to the south of the Bering Sea. Possession of both groups of islands would give the Japanese an enormous advantage in carrying the war further to America, beginning perhaps with an invasion of Hawaii. Even if that far-reaching prospect did not materialise, possession of these two forward bases would secure the Pacific outposts of the recent Japanese conquests, and at the same time enable them to bomb out of existence any attempt by America to collect together a large attacking fleet.

For this ambitious and complex operation the Japanese assembled a huge naval force. 162 warships were deployed in five groups, each with specific tasks. The advance force consisted of 16 submarines; the force detailed to immobilize Pearl Harbor consisted of four large, fast carriers; the main body, which was the centre of Admiral Yamamoto's command, consisted of seven battleships; and the Midway occupation force and the Northern Area force both included heavy cruisers and transports. The northern force also included two carriers.

Against this formidable army of seapower, Admiral Nimitz could muster a total of less than half, 76 in all. He had three carriers only, and one was the *Yorktown*, which had been badly damaged in the battle of the Coral Sea. The Japanese were amazed that the *Yorktown*, which they had estimated as needing several months to repair, was now back in action against them. It was a portent for the future. Not only would America be able to produce new ships at a rate greatly exceeding that of Japan, but she would also be able to repair damaged ones at undreamt-of speed.

Difficult though Nimitz's task was, he had the advantage of knowing Yamamoto's battle plans. This he owed to 'Magic', which was reading codes which the Japanese thought were secure.

Yamamoto's northern group began proceedings by bombing Dutch Harbour and capturing Attu and Kiska in the Aleutians. While this was happening, four fast carriers, commanded by Admiral Nagumo, were heading for Midway, to clear a way for the occupation force. The Americans had insufficient fighters to protect the Midway airfield, but by good luck none were put out of action by the Japanese air attack. In this the Japanese lost some 35 aircraft, whereas American losses only totalled 15. American aircraft from Midway now joined in the battle. At this moment Admiral Nagumo was informed that ten American warships were now coming towards him from the north-east. He found the information incredible but was forced to believe it when aircraft from American carriers attacked his ships.

The first round of the ensuing Battle of Midway was entirely a Japanese victory: the Americans sustained heavy losses against Japanese fighters and anti-aircraft fire without succeeding in making a single hit on the Japanese carriers. Then, just as the Japanese were priding themselves on their devastating victory, they were hit by another wave of American bombers. This time the Americans made no mistake. Nagumo's flagship, the *Agaki*, was hit and set on fire, and the *Kaga* suffered a similar fate. Another Japanese carrier, the *Soryu*, was crippled, and later sunk by a submarine, leaving one carrier afloat of the four which had been the pride of the Japanese navy. The fourth was the *Hiryu*. This succeeded in getting off sufficient aircraft to put three bombs and two torpedoes into the *Yorktown*, settling the fate of that gallant ship, but revenge was taken swiftly on the *Hiryu* by a squadron of American dive bombers: four direct hits sent her to the bottom. The Japanese had now lost four fast carriers, 250 aircraft and 2,200 men. By comparison Nimitz's force had lost the *Yorktown* and 147 aircraft. The end of this vital sea battle was almost farcical. Desperate to save face, Yamamoto despatched cruisers and battleships to bombard Midway, which there was now no hope of occupying. This order merely resulted in the loss of a cruiser which had collided with another when both were trying to avoid an American submarine. As the two cruisers limped out of action, they were attacked by American aircraft and one of them, the *Mikura*, was sunk.

It had been an occasion of enormous importance and significance. For the second time a great naval battle had been fought without the surface ships coming nearer than 250 miles from each other. The era of the battleship was seemingly over, although nations would still continue to find reasons for building them. The Japanese had now lost half their carrier force and, although they had six more either being built or being repaired, there was no possibility that they could increase this number to match the 13 the Americans were rapidly building, with scores more to follow. The most humiliating feature of Midway for the Japanese was that they had been annihilated by a force which was not merely inferior in total numbers but inferior in number of carriers. At the end of the battle, America had two out of three of her carriers still afloat: the Japanese had none. Undoubtedly the ability to read the Japanese signals had been of great value to the Americans, in that it enabled them to be in the right place at the right time. But once the battle began, codes and decrypts were of no significance. All that mattered was courage, determination and skilful flying. In defeating their opponents – who had greater numbers – the Americans demonstrated that they were superior in all departments.

6
DECEPTION AND DIRTY TRICKS

In mid-1942 the war was approximately at the half-way point for Britain and Germany, effectively finished for France, a year old for the Russians and barely six months old for the Americans and Japanese. Up till then there had been ominous signs that Germany, Italy and Japan would emerge the victors: Europe, from Norway to the Mediterranean, was under their control; German armies were deep in Russia; in the Far East the Japanese roamed freely over an area stretching from Japan's northern isles to Australia and from India to half-way across the Pacific. But 1942 was the year when the tide turned in favour of the Allies. There was much still to be done; somehow the aggressors must be ejected from the vast territories they had overrun, and while the Allies attempted to accomplish that task the tide might suddenly turn against them again. On several occasions it seemed that that was about to happen. There were several points when the outcome of the war was delicately poised at this time.

Perhaps the most important was the battle of the Atlantic. As long as the sea lanes were open, supplies from America could reach Britain and some be sent on, many by Arctic convoys in conditions of great hardship, to the northern coast of Russia. But if that lifeline were broken, Britain's very survival would be in doubt, for with much of the Royal Navy at the bottom of the sea, German thoughts could once more turn to invasion.

Secondly, the narrow superiority which Allied land forces might now begin to develop against the forces ranged against them would quickly disappear if the secret of their code-breaking was disclosed: this would cause Germany and Japan to make changes which might mean that their codes would never be deciphered. There was always a danger that this could happen through a deliberate betrayal by one of the traitors working inside the British and American governments, or by a careless mistake, or by an investigating journalist. The latter breach did occur in America, but miraculously was not noted by either the Germans or the Japanese. In 1942 America was not so security conscious as she later became. Thousands of men and women worked in American Intelligence, many of them concerned with codebreaking, but it seems that the vital importance of secrecy was never stressed to the same degree that it was among the British code-breakers at Bletchley Park. Americans have always prided themselves on their right to know what their government is doing, which all stems from the original constitution, emphasising the rights of the individual citizen. Unfortunately the drafters of the constitution of the United States could not anticipate the days when the fate of the nation might depend on the preservation of one of its technical secrets.

Immediately after the Midway battle, the American High Command was shocked and infuriated to read a report in the *Chicago Tribune* which said that the Midway battle had been won because American naval circles had known of the Japanese plans in advance, even to the extent of the number and armament of the ships involved. The information had come from a war correspondent who had been travelling on a transport after the battle of the Coral Sea. This transport was part of the US Pacific Fleet and had therefore received a copy of Nimitz's signal, sent out several days before the Midway battle began. The fault on this occasion lay less with the correspondent, who was a war correspondent doing his professional job, than with the looseness of the organisation which allowed vital secret information to be so widely distributed. After the battle the correspondent had sent in his story, apparently unaware that by doing so he was putting at risk the entire 'Magic' code-breaking system as well as thousands of American lives. The owner of the *Chicago Tribune*, which blazoned the news across the front page, was the notorious Colonel Robert McCormick, hater of Britain, fervent isolationist, and critic of Roosevelt and all that he did. The report was also published by two other papers, both owned by McCormick's relations. It was not the first, nor would it be the last time that McCormick behaved with breath-taking irresponsibility. Subsequently both McCormick and his paper tried to claim that the correspondent had written the despatch from deductions based on his knowledge of naval warfare. This assertion was demonstrably untrue, for the despatch followed the Nimitz signal word for word, even to the extent of repeating a mistake in it. Whether the correspondent had been naive, devious, or simply wildly greedy and irresponsible was less to the point than the fact that there were many others who would send off a despatch without enquiring too closely into the implications of doing so, and that newspapers would print secret information without caring for the consequences. It was said that American code-breakers were facing two deadly enemies, the Japanese and their own journalists, who would stop at nothing in order to obtain a 'scoop'. In this the latter were sometimes aided and abetted by politicians.

In 1944, when a presidential election was impending, Thomas Dewey, the Republican candidate, planned to accuse his opponent, President Roosevelt, of disastrous negligence and thus to lose him votes. Dewey's plan was to disclose the fact that Roosevelt had been in possession of top-secret information, derived from reading Japanese and German codes, several days before the Japanese attacked Pearl Harbor. This disclosure, thought Dewey, would lay the blame for the Pearl Harbor disaster firmly on his rival. Fortunately Dewey was stopped before he could cause the catastrophic damage that such a disclosure would have caused to the Allies' war effort.

Mercifully for the Allies, the Japanese did not take the *Chicago Tribune*'s disclosure seriously. They felt that American newspapers were full of idle boasts and that their navy had merely been unlucky in the Midway battle. They did, in fact, make some changes in their coding two months later, and thereby caused much alarm in Allied circles, but this was apparently routine, and not an emergency measure.

The changes were not large enough to give the American code-breakers much trouble and the State Department decided that to try McCormick for anti-American activities in the courts would merely draw attention to a subject best left to suffer the normal fate of yesterday's news.

Valuable though 'Magic' was for the American naval operations against the Japanese, it was even more vital for the overall progress of the Allies in the war. The Japanese Ambassador in Berlin, Baron Oshima, enjoyed Hitler's confidence and, in a series of interviews, was given full information about German achievements and intentions. Accounts of these interviews, as well as those with other leading German personalities and his own comments and observations, were sent in a steady stream to Tokyo. The subject matter was very wide-ranging. Hitler noted with glee the great success his submarines had had in sinking Allied craft off the eastern seaboard of the United States. This had been made possible because the doomed ships all carried lights, the coast was not blacked-out, and the hulls could be seen clearly in silhouette against the blaze of light behind. Another useful area of information was in the field of German aircraft production. Tokyo was particularly anxious to know what progress Germany was making towards the production of jet-propelled aircraft: Oshima obtained this information and the Allies were grateful. Oshima's own observations on the state of German war production and defence were invaluable. Paradoxically, he was also the Allies' best source of information about certain aspects of the Russian war effort. Russia and Japan were not at war, although they were both allied to countries which were. In consequence, Japanese could travel to Moscow through regions which would have been impossible for even the most skilful SOE agent. From this the Allies learnt much about Russian intentions in the Far East.

One of the greatest bonuses from Oshima was the report he sent to Tokyo of the German defences on the French coast. This gave a full description, based partly on official sources and partly on the observations of a Japanese officer, not merely of the defences themselves, but the depth of the defence zones, the siting of the guns and their calibre, the

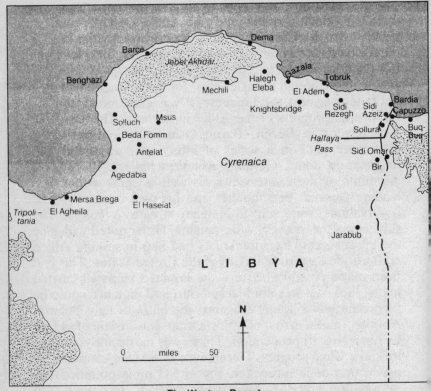

The Western Desert

number and disposition of divisions and even the troop rotations currently in use. The information was, of course, priceless. It is not clear why Hitler was so free with highly confidential information to an ally whom he did not rate very highly, but the fact that he was enabled the Allies to arrange deception plans which fitted in very well with what Hitler wished to believe. But the story of the 'Magic' intercepts is not one of unblemished success. There were occasions when senior commanders, distrustful of all intelligence, even that from the highest level, felt instinctively that they knew best. This could be a costly delusion.

Although Midway suggested that the Japanese had reached the end of their expensive programme for the moment, any conclusion that danger from that source had

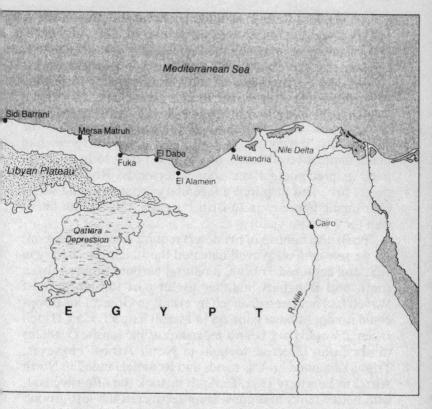

now passed its peak would have been premature. The Japanese presence in Burma constituted a threat to India and if ever they managed to break into that country in the north, there was a strong possibility that they would use their naval power to make landings further south. Whatever their setbacks in the Pacific, their navy was still a dominant force in the Bay of Bengal. However, it was felt that the Japanese needed time to digest their gains and that the threat to India was not immediate.

The war against Germany looked less stable. Sebastopol had fallen on 1 July, Rostov on 23 July, and by early August German armies were en route to the Caucasus. They would be halted at Stalingrad at the beginning of September, but few would have forecast that fact in the summer.

The Middle East now occupied the attention of the Allies. Before Auchinleck checked him in the July battles at Alamein, Rommel seemed set fair to break through to Cairo, to seize the Suez Canal and to make a thrust towards the Middle East oilfields. If the German troops in Russia then came south, this would form a great pincer movement and virtually end the war. Churchill was very worried about the dangers posed by Rommel and could not understand the reason why, during the past two years, British forces had made impressive advances in the desert only to have to fall back in precipitate haste soon afterwards. Rommel, 'the desert fox', had acquired a legendary reputation and was a charismatic figure even to British troops; this did not augur well for a British victory.

The British failures in the desert require some explanation. As we saw earlier, Wavell defeated the Italians decisively in 1941 and captured Tobruk, a natural harbour on the Libyan coast, and Benghazi, another useful port further west. If Wavell had not been diverted by events in Greece, his troops could no doubt have gone on to assault Tripoli. Had Tripoli fallen, it would have been almost impossible for the Germans to obtain an effective toehold in North Africa. However, Tripoli remained in Axis hands and Rommel landed in North Africa in February 1941. In April he took the offensive and, with better tanks and guns, soon recovered the lost ground and besieged Tobruk. This, it will be recalled, was underway when Rashid Ali launched his revolt in Iraq, but the main reason for Rommel's success was the fact that most of the RAF had been diverted to Greece in a vain attempt to stop the Germans there. Tobruk would have made a very useful forward base for Rommel, so Wavell decided that it must not be given up. The ensuing siege of Tobruk became a minor legend, with a strong appeal to the British who felt kinship with the town because their own country was also under siege. Another place destined to become famous for its siege was Malta. Malta was in easy air-striking distance of Italian and North African airfields but its own aircraft also represented a great threat to Axis supply routes in the Mediterranean.

By June 1941 Wavell felt that the general situation had

stabilized enough for him to be able to launch an offensive against Rommel. Code-named 'Battleaxe' this began on 15 June and was aimed at relieving Tobruk. It was over in two days, as the Panzer IVs and 88 mm guns showed their complete superiority to the British armour. As mentioned earlier, this was when the British forces managed to capture the Panzer IV tank which was then shipped to England for examination. The findings of that examination eventually were that the German tanks had armour which was resistant to the existing British anti-tank guns. It also had a 50 mm gun which could penetrate British tank armour. The failure of the War Office to take this information into account was one of the most damaging lapses in the war. Subsequently, it was suggested that Wavell had moved too quickly to take the offensive, having been prodded by Churchill to do so, but as neither had any conception of the superiority of the German guns and tanks at the time, any criticism of the timing seems unjustified. However, the defeat was blamed entirely on Wavell, who was then replaced by General Sir Claude Auchinleck, at that time serving as Commander-in-Chief, India. Wavell went to India as Viceroy.

Auchinleck decided that an offensive against Rommel would be feasible in the following November and in consequence launched one on the 18th. The British 8th Army was now commanded by Lt-General Sir Alan Cunningham, of whom Auchinleck had formed a high opinion. Cunningham had the misfortune to encounter Rommel in one of his more brilliant moods and was completely out-flanked and out-fought. The battle seemed to be lost, but Auchinleck decided otherwise. He replaced Cunningham with Major-General N. M. Ritchie, who managed to reintroduce some stability into the British position. The 8th Army went on the attack again, relieved Tobruk, and took 36,500 Axis prisoners.

The siege of Tobruk had, by this time, become something of an epic story. Rommel had needed Tobruk badly as a forward base and supply port and had constantly pressed home the attack. The garrison commander at this time, an Australian, Major-General M. J. Morshead known as 'Ming the Merciless', had ordered that life for the besiegers must be made as near intolerable as possible, and his garrison took him at his word. Constant attacks and sallies by night and day inflicted heavy casualties on the surrounding German and Italian troops, who must have been as relieved to see the end of the siege as the 8th Army was.

In January 1942 Auchinleck should have received a substantial reinforcement in the shape of 18th Division. 18th Division mustered over 20,000 and would have given Auchinleck the numerical superiority he needed to out-fight Rommel's superior equipment. However, as we saw earlier, 18th Division was diverted from the Middle East to take part in the battle for Singapore. It was a disastrous decision. The division, which contained no experienced jungle fighters, and was unacclimatised to the tropics, arrived in Singapore when the battle was already lost. It had been attacked by Japanese aircraft as it came towards the island and in consequence lost much vital equipment. It was too late to have any effect on the battle, and its arrival merely presented 20,000 troops to the Japanese for use as slave labour. There was considerable bitterness over the wastage of such a valuable asset as an entire division, but no one was picked out for censure.

In January Rommel, having been reinforced, attacked again and drove the 8th Army back to a line running from Gazala to Bir Hakim. Here the front was stabilized. By this time both sides were too exhausted to continue fighting and there was therefore a lull of four months, while both made plans for a successful and decisive offensive at a suitable time in the near future. By now both commanders were well aware that electronics might soon begin to play a decisive rôle. In 1941 the RAF had fitted a bomber with devices for jamming Rommel's tactical communications, but the experiment had been short-lived, as the Germans had shot it down.

Auchinleck had been informed by the War Cabinet that he must open another offensive in May or, at the very latest, in June. He had decided on the latter month but his decision was pre-empted by Rommel on 26 May. Rommel was a specialist in 'hook' tactics. These had been used since warfare began, but usually on a much smaller scale and more slowly. In previous wars the main body, mostly infantry, would be in the centre, with cavalry on the flanks. When such tactics were

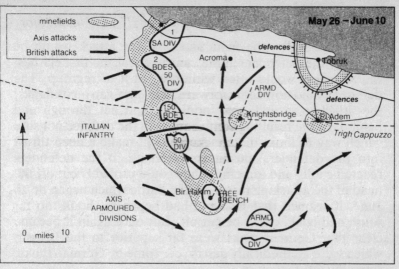

May 26 – June 10

minefields
Axis attacks
British attacks

1 SA DIV
2 BDES 50 DIV
Acroma
defences
Tobruk
ARMD DIV
150 BDE
defences
N
Knightsbridge
El Adem
ITALIAN INFANTRY
Trigh Cappuzzo
50 DIV
Bir Hakim
FREE FRENCH
AXIS ARMOURED DIVISIONS
ARMD
DIV
0 miles 10

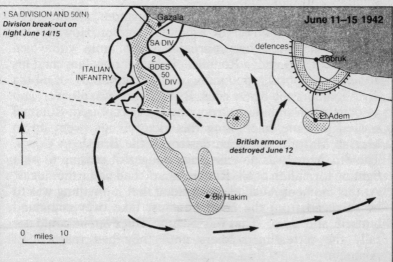

June 11–15 1942

1 SA DIVISION AND 50(N)
Division break-out on night June 14/15

Gazala
1 SA DIV
2 BDES 50 DIV
defences
Tobruk
ITALIAN INFANTRY
El Adem
N
British armour destroyed June 12
Bir Hakim
0 miles 10

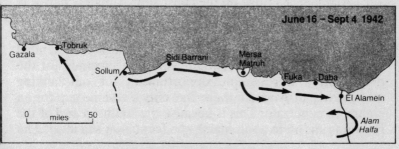

June 16 – Sept 4 1942

Gazala
Tobruk
Sidi Barrani
Mersa Matruh
Sollum
Fuka
Daba
El Alamein
Alam Halfa
0 miles 50

The War in the Western Desert 1942

used successfully, the main shock of the attack would be taken by the defenders in the centre. After the first clashes, the attackers would often withdraw, as if to regroup. The defence would now come forward, leaving a gap on its flanks; the attackers would now 'hook' in and get through and behind. In the resulting confusion, with the defence not sure which way to look, the attackers might make a deep thrust into the defenders' positions. However, if the defenders reacted coolly and forcefully they could probably cut off the head of the attacking thrust. In the battle which began on 26 June, it seemed that Rommel had begun his hook too far south and could easily be cut off. But once again it became clear that German tanks were far superior to the British, which were methodically destroyed, some by German tanks, some by anti-tank guns.

General Ritchie, the 8th Army commander, attempted to stabilize the position on the Egyptian frontier. However, by this time the British had approximately 70 tanks with which to confront 160 under Rommel. Rommel now launched his attack on Tobruk, pounding it with hundreds of Stuka dive-bombers and heavy guns. By 22 June it was all over, and 33,000 British and Indian troops had been captured. Rommel wasted no time celebrating this victory, but swept on to Mersah Matruh, where he destroyed the British 13 Corps. The 8th Army was now in grave danger of ceasing to be a fighting formation at all. Ritchie clearly had no further ideas. At this moment Auchinleck decided that if anything was to be salvaged from the ruins he must take over command himself, and did so. That was 25 June. But even he could not rally the retreating soldiers until they had reached El Alamein.

El Alamein is a ridge on the coast approximately half-way between Mersa Matruh and Alexandria. A road and a railway run along the coast; there is a small railway station which bears the name El Alamein. The name soon extended to the whole position for, whereas in the remainder of the desert there were ample opportunities for out-flanking movements, at Alamein there was only a 28-mile gap for an enemy to penetrate. This is because the southern end of the position runs on to a salt marsh 500 feet below sea level. The marsh is known as the Qattara Depression and, although light vehicles have been known to cross it, it is impossible for normal military traffic. There is no possibility of skirting around the Qattara Depression, for to the south-west it links with the Great Sand Sea. The defensive value of the Alamein position had been recognised for many years and it had been discussed at the Staff College, Camberley in the context of the unlikely event of a threat coming from the west towards Alexandria in a future war. There had of course been desert skirmishes with Turks and their Arab supporters in that area during the previous war.

The main enemy threat was likely to come in the north of the position, in the sector known as the Alamein box. Here the desert surface was well capable of supporting tanks. The word 'desert' now needs some amplification: it covers a wide variety of surfaces from soft, shifting sand to bare rock. It also includes gravel, salt marsh or hard sand. Wherever the men were in the desert, they were certain to be tormented by sand and flies. Sand penetrated everywhere: it made a fine layer on food, had to be skimmed off tea, combed out of hair, picked out of ears, cleaned off guns and engines, and shaken out of clothes before it chafed the skin into soreness. At times it would blow up into a storm and blot out everything; when it settled many landmarks would have disappeared or been altered. The opportunities for being lost were unlimited. In order to keep as much sand as possible out of clothing, normal conventions of uniform were discarded. To keep it out of the shirt a neckerchief was worn, this often being a coloured cravat. Battle dress or khaki drill trousers were less comfortable than corduroys, suede boots were quieter, more comfortable and kept out sand better than army issue footwear. Eau de Cologne helped to keep soldiers fresher and cooler when washing was seldom possible through shortage of water. All this gave a superficially dandy look to the desert army, but there was nothing soft or effeminate about it when it came to fighting. Solar topees and pith helmets, once thought to be essential if sunstroke was to be avoided, had soon been discarded in favour of a beret or an Australian bush hat, and in action most men fought stripped to the waist. Cameraderie had developed between officers and men which would have been unthinkable in a peacetime army, but it is impossible to travel in a tank and eat, sleep, suffer and often die together maintaining a barrier of rank or social status. Everyone and everything was interdependent.

The worst torment was flies, which seemed to appear immediately in the most remote parts of the desert. They formed a black cluster on wounds, sores or ulcers; they crawled around eyelids and lips, and over hands; they settled on food as a man conveyed it to his mouth and would often get inside with it; they drowned in the tea he was drinking, but he fished them out and drank it just the same.

And yet. Men grew to love the desert. They were baked by the midday sun, and often nearly frozen at night, but they liked its vastness, its sweeping lines, and the feeling that they were close to unspoilt nature. Parts of it did not remain unspoilt for long, for they became the dumping ground for broken trucks, burnt-out tanks, empty oil drums, old tins, spent ammunition and, of course, bodies and shallow graves.

Rommel's thrust at the Alamein box received such a hammering from the South African brigade in its path that his leading troops turned and retreated in disorder. Elsewhere, wherever he tried to penetrate, he was checked by a swift thrust ordered by Auchinleck. It was an unusual situation for a commander-in-chief to be directing a desperate defensive battle in the field, and few could have done it. Eventually Rommel had to face the fact that he had been out-fought by a better tactical commander, who had anticipated his moves and pre-empted them. In his subsequent despatch he wrote: 'Although the British losses in the Alamein fighting had been higher than ours, yet the price to Auchinleck had not been excessive, for the thing that mattered to him was to halt our offensive and that unfortunately, he had done.' Privately he added, 'I could weep.'

Unfortunately for Auchinleck, his magnificent victory did him no good at all, for the War Cabinet had decided that the 'Gazala gallops' or 'Benghazi handicaps', as the troops described the surges back and forth, must now be ended. For this, they felt, a change of command was needed. Auchinleck had freed Tobruk, then lost it again. Large numbers of men and much equipment had been sent to the Middle East, which had been given priority over all the other theatres of war, and now the 8th Army was back in its defensive position, after huge losses, and the Germans were still within striking distance of Alexandria. Churchill felt that, with the German thrust exhausted, this must be a good moment for a counter-attack. It was presumably what Rommel would have done. But when he asked Auchinleck how quickly he could go on to the offensive, Auchinleck replied, 'Six weeks'. Churchill was appalled. But Auchinleck knew the ways of 'the desert fox' and Churchill did not. Auchinleck respected Churchill, but he did not intend to risk everything in a politicians' war.

What nobody realised at the time was that Rommel knew as much about British intentions, strength and resources in the desert as GHQ Cairo did. In fact the British had occasionally learnt about the position of their own units by intercepting German signals. As was discovered later, there had been considerable carelessness in the desert over radio security. Once when a German battle headquarters was captured it was found to contain comprehensive transcripts of intercepted conversations between British units. Those guilty of security lapses could scarcely believe their own foolishness when they read them. Even more serious was the fact that Rommel had been receiving more and better supplies than had been expected; the German Higher Command had not turned an entirely deaf ear to his pleas.

In the desert, as in other battle areas, information from intercepts was of varying value. This was because a commander might state his intention to higher authority but then change it at the last minute. On the ground the situation changed so rapidly that much intercept information was out of date by the time it was received; all too often the British learnt what Rommel intended to do when he had already done it, as they knew to their cost. Nevertheless, every scrap of information derived from enemy sources can be valuable.

In addition to the leakages from carelessness in radio transmissions there was a perpetual problem from enemy agents. Cairo and Alexandria, which were full of troops entering or leaving the battle zone, employed in head-quarters, or seeking recreation, also contained a large temporary population of attractive women, many from Syria, who made loving companions for soldiers, sailors or airmen. So loving were they that they enquired assiduously about the serviceman's welfare – when did he expect to return, where was he going, what dangers might he encounter, and how did he propose to avoid them? Information about the arrival or departure of ships was particularly valuable. Cairo, it was said, was 'as leaky as a sieve'.

By August Churchill had already decided to replace Auchinleck with Alexander, and to give command of the 8th Army to 'Strafer' Gott. This plan was upset when Gott was killed in an air crash. On Auchinleck's recommendation, Montgomery was then brought out from England to take over the 8th Army. He repaid his benefactor ill for this service, for once he had taken over he proceeded to criticise everything which Auchinleck had done or was supposed to be doing. This malevolent attitude, which Montgomery maintained right up to the end of the war, was, in fact, a deliberate policy to remove from Auchinleck, who was senior, any possibility of taking command of the land forces when the day came to invade Europe. It succeeded. When Auchinleck's name was being considered by the Chiefs of Staff for another active command, Montgomery's criticisms effectively sabotaged his chances. Auchinleck was reappointed C.-in-C. India, but never again commanded troops in the field. However, his work in organising the war effort in India probably could not have been achieved by anyone less respected in that country.

Montgomery introduced a very different style of leadership to the Middle East, constantly assuring the officers and soldiers of the 8th Army that they would never retreat again. At the end of August Rommel attacked once again in the south of the Alamein position at Alam el Halfa. The area had been heavily mined under Auchinleck's instructions and Montgomery met Rommel's thrust with deep defence. Rommel's options were limited by the fact that the RAF destroyed many of his petrol supply lines.

Although Churchill had been pressing for a desert offensive at the earliest possible moment, he accepted Montgomery's statement that it could not be mounted until sufficient supplies had been accumulated. These eventually amounted to 220,000 men against Rommel's 108,000, and twice the number of tanks, guns and aircraft that he commanded. Montgomery's greatest asset was 300 Sherman tanks, which were more than a match for the German PzIVs. Shermans were tanks of a British design which had been adopted by the American army, but production had only just begun; the first models were now available for distribution to units but Roosevelt, in response to an appeal by Churchill, sent them to the 8th Army instead. This was a magnificent gesture, even though the American army did not yet need them for battle.

Montgomery chose 23 October as the most suitable date to launch a major assault on Rommel, who was now well dug in close up to the Alamein position. By this time Ultra was sending a continuous supply of information to GHQ Middle East, enabling the RAF to sink 52 per cent of the supplies destined for the Afrika Korps. German staff officers, not suspecting that Ultra was reading their codes, assumed that the British had a reliable network of agents in Italian ports. Unaware that the Germans had formed this view, the British resorted to elaborate subterfuges in order to conceal the fact that they were reading the German codes. Usually, if a German ship was known to be on its way to Rommel, it would be 'accidentally' sighted by a reconnaissance aircraft before being sunk by larger forces. During the weeks before the final battle of Alamein, when Montgomery's supplies were increasing dramatically, Rommel's were diminishing. The latter's long line of land communications from Benghazi and Tobruk was extremely vulnerable to RAF and SAS attacks, but the sea route would have been even more perilous. His requests to the German Higher Command now had truth and urgency in them: at one point he had fuel for only eight days fighting and ammunition for only 14. But that eight days could still win a battle. Although Montgomery was building up to a two-to-one all round superiority, it was not overlooked that for an attack against prepared positions to be reasonably certain of success, a three-to-one superiority is usually required.

Not least of the 8th Army's assets was an elaborate

deception plan. World War II abounded in attempts to mislead the enemy, and most of them relied for success on persuading the enemy to believe in his own theories and Alamein was one of them. Knowing that Rommel was certain that an attack would be coming in the near future, and that he would be prepared for it, Montgomery had a complicated deception plan, aimed at making Rommel think that the main thrust would be in the south. An enormous concentration of guns, dumps, pipelines, tanks and vehicles was made in the southern sector of the Alamein line, but it was an army of canvas, wood, paint and inflatables. Constructing such an army was not easy, and well-known conjurors and experts in stage deception were brought into the army to advise and organise. Nothing could be left to chance; an extensive, complex system of bogus radio traffic had to be organised to make the German and Italian operators believe that everything was genuine. There was no room for mistakes, unless these were part of the general ruse. If a German airman saw lines of camouflage netting covering what appeared from their shapes to be 25-pounder guns, he might possibly suspect that the camouflage was a little too perfect to be genuine. If, however, he saw what appeared to be an artillery piece, or a tank, imperfectly concealed, he would assume he was observing a genuine article, exposed by someone's carelessness. The deception plan was successful and Rommel extended and weakened his defences in consequence.

However, the deception plan could not have succeeded if the German Air Force had been able to fly low over the 8th Army assembly areas: the RAF ensured that it did not. In the four days before the battle began, the RAF kept the Luftwaffe out of the area where the 8th Army was making the final preparations.

Rommel himself was not in the battle zone when the British attack began; he suffered from recurrent stomach trouble and had just departed on sick leave. His deputy, General Stumme, died of heart failure in the first 24 hours of the battle and was replaced by General von Thoma. Rommel returned in haste when the battle was two days old. Already progress was slower than the 8th Army had hoped for, and casualties were higher than had been expected. Rommel decided that his best policy was to use most of his reserves to drive the British back from the positions they had won. His attack was only partially successful, so he renewed it the next day, this time committing the remainder of his reserves. His principal target was the Australian 9th Division, which was moving up the coast in a diversionary movement. The Australians posed a grave threat to a weakened sector of his line, but when attacked stood firm. Rommel, who now had only 90 tanks to face 800 British tanks, decided he must retreat; he began his withdrawal on 3 November. Hitler, on learning of Rommel's intentions, expressly forbade any retreat. Rommel stopped, and was hammered relentlessly by British attacks. Hitler, having been told that Rommel's army was now being completely destroyed, changed his order. It was almost, but not quite, too late. When the 8th Army broke through on 4 November, Rommel had already taken advantage of the metalled road behind him to get much of his equipment away. At this moment he had an unexpected stroke of luck. Torrential rain began to fall and bogged down many units of the 8th Army as they were concentrating in order to implement 'Operation Supercharge', the code name for the pursuit and destruction of Rommel's army after the battle. But the order for 'Supercharge' should have been given earlier: a great opportunity had been lost. This was not the last time that Montgomery would be blamed for reacting too cautiously to an opportunity.

But it had been a great and invaluable victory: 30,000 of Rommel's troops had been taken prisoner, and a probable 10,000 killed or wounded. For the first time it looked as if Axis power in the desert had been really broken. The effect on morale at home was enormous. As Churchill put it, not quite accurately: 'Before Alamein we never had a victory. After Alamein we never had a defeat.' There was, however, more hard fighting to come before the Germans and Italians were finally cleared from North Africa.

Although Ultra had been unable to give tactical warning of Rommel's counter-attack on 27 November, which was held off by British shelling and bombing, it gave valuable information about the state of his fuel, ammunition and tank reserves. These were dwindling fast, and when Rommel was informed that both the supply ships on which he was relying for fuel and supplies had been sunk by the RAF, he realised that his only hope of saving his army was to retreat rapidly. If the two supply ships had not been sunk, he would have rallied his forces and made a stand at Fuka. Instead, he fell back to El Agheila in Tripolitania, where he was not attacked until 14 December. On two occasions he could have been cut off if the 8th Army had moved more quickly. It is, of course, easy to be wise after the event, but if the 8th Army had been able to move a little faster – and it probably could have done if it had been encouraged to do so – Rommel would not have been able to take such a large part in the defence of Tunisia. But, as the 8th Army knew well enough, cornering 'the desert fox' was a highly unpredictable process: there was a strong chance that he would slip out of the tightest net and inflict considerable damage while doing so.

In the meantime another dramatic development had occurred in North Africa. With the aim of seizing the ports of Casablanca, Oran and Algiers, and then crushing Rommel between two armies, another invasion force had been landed on the night of 8th November. This time it was a joint Anglo-American force and for that reason alone it was a decisive step forward in Allied co-operation. Command had been given to an obscure American officer, who had never commanded soldiers in battle, or even been in action himself. His name was Dwight D. Eisenhower. At the beginning of the war he had been a lieutenant-colonel; at the end of it he was in command of the largest assembly of land forces the West had ever seen.

The territories which the Anglo-American force was now invading was under the control of Vichy France, but the Allies hoped that the French in North Africa would see them as a force liberating them from the danger of German control and therefore offer no resistance. These hopes were not fulfilled. Although secret negotiations with local French leaders had taken place before the landings, the Vichy forces proved to be hostile and intractable. Having jealously guarded the integrity of their territories from occupation by German troops, they now invited them in, though not in time to prevent the Anglo-American force establishing itself. This invasion, code-named 'Torch', never caught the public attention as other landings – Sicily, Anzio, Salerno, Southern France – did. It was not, of course, on the same scale as the Normandy landings, but the fact that the invasion force had to sail from Britain through waters infested with Axis submarines made it a remarkable achievement.

The landings had taken place on 8 November. By 11 November the Allies had occupied Casablanca, Algiers and Oran. Events were proceeding well for the Allies when they received yet another stroke of good fortune. On 11 November Admiral Darlan, who was in Algiers at the time, surrendered the Vichy forces to the Allies and invited the French fleet to join them; his price for this was to be recognised as Governor of French North Africa. This move meant that Vichy forces, which had been bitter opponents of the Allies in Syria as well as in North Africa, would now be allies instead of enemies. The Germans were infuriated, and lost no time in occupying the remainder of France, which so far they had left under Vichy control, provided it did not impede the German war effort in any way. The Germans, rightly suspecting that resistance was being fomented in Vichy France, had several times thought of occupying that part of French territory, but had hesitated to do so because that would immobilize 10 divisions. Germany was beginning to realise that conquering territory might be less of a problem than holding it. By now Hitler had his armies distributed over Scandinavia, France, Greece, Crete, the Greek Islands, Tripolitania and, not least, Yugoslavia, which alone would account for twenty divisions. Even when supplemented by Poles, Roumanians, Hungarians, and other 'volunteers' the German pool of manpower was not inexhaustible, as Hitler was now beginning to realise. Nevertheless, this act of 'treachery' in an area which was meant to be under Pétain's influence could not go unpunished. The move would have the advantage of putting France's Mediterranean ports and shipping under German control, it was thought, but now Hitler was frustrated once more. Darlan's appeal resulted in some French ships joining the Allies and the main fleet at Toulon being scuttled; among the ships sunk were the battle cruisers *Dunkerque* and *Strasbourg*.

Eisenhower was criticised for making an ex-Vichy minister political chief in North Africa, but in this instance his compromise of principles seems to have been a wise move militarily. Fortunately for his own reputation, he was able to escape too much recrimination due to the fact that Darlan was assassinated by a patriotic young Frenchman in December, leaving the way for General Giraud, a man with an excellent record in both world wars, to be appointed in his place.

The German High Command was now worried that unless checked Allied forces, numbering 185,000, would quickly clear the remaining Axis forces from North Africa and then be ready to begin a thrust north through the Balkans into what Churchill used to refer to as 'the soft underbelly of Germany'. In spite of the needs of the Russian front, Germany now withdrew 400 aircraft from it and began pouring troops into North Africa at the rate of 1,000 a day, together with guns and tanks. This rapid reinforcement, combined with the seasonal rains, produced deadlock from December 1942 until February 1943. Hitler was now becoming disenchanted with Rommel, who had once been his favourite general. The Afrika Korps had retreated all the way from Alamein to Tripolitania, but Rommel said that his position there was untenable and that he should be allowed to retire as far as Tunisia. His realistic assessment was not well received by the German Higher Command, which commented that it was fortunate that he did not possess enough petrol to enable him to do so. They observed that Rommel, who had failed in his effort to reach Cairo, was now voicing doubts about German strategic plans for North Africa; this marked him as a potential danger, not yet a liability, but a man to be watched carefully.

But Rommel was by no means at the end of his resources. He had a strong army facing Montgomery in a former French frontier area known as the Mareth Line. In February, when he realised that two American divisions were now threatening his links with his fellow general, von Arnim, in Tunisia, he broke through them, inflicting a shattering defeat at the Kasserine Pass. The inexperienced American troops there learnt the bitter lesson the 8th Army had had earlier: when the Germans appeared to have retreated in disorder they are merely luring their enemies on to well-concealed anti-tank guns. It was clear that the desert fox was not going to be trapped yet awhile, and the war in North Africa was likely to be prolonged well beyond the optimistic forecasts of the Allies.

In March the Allies took the initiative again, breaking through the Mareth Line, and pressing on to El Hamma. Rommel was now recalled to Germany and his command given to the Italian General Messe. In May the Allies captured Tunis and Bizerta and followed this up by thrusting into the heart of Tunisia. On the 13th Messe surrendered: 250,000 German and Italian soldiers became prisoners-of-war. A year earlier Rommel had been threatening Cairo; now the German effort in Africa had all been in vain, and the Allies had made the first of their many huge captures of Axis prisoners.

One part of the war, that in the desert, was now over, but it would live on in the memories of the survivors. To those who had not experienced the desert it was almost incomprehensible – the desert did not involve civilians and the battles were fought with chivalry. It was said that Rommel was better known and more respected by the British than their own generals were.

By this stage in the war the flow of intelligence from Ultra was invaluable. This makes the relative performance of generals difficult to assess. The commanders in the earlier campaigns in France, Norway, and the desert, had had little guidance about the enemy's intentions, strengths and weaknesses: Gort, Mackesy, Wavell and Auchinleck were not merely short of essential equipment, they were also without the priceless information which Ultra provided later. Montgomery was a very competent general, but his performance on the battlefield might have been very different if he had not known where his enemy was weak and where strong. Until the disclosure of Ultra in 1974, Montgomery had been able to claim a form of extra-sensory intuition. 'I kept a photograph of Rommel in my caravan,' he told an audience at Sandhurst in the late 1940s, 'and by looking at it carefully I was able to work out what he was likely to do.' It was something less than the truth. He was also able to look at intelligence reports from Ultra which told him exactly what his opponent was likely to do.

Although in terms of numbers the Middle East was a minor theatre, its importance was enormous. If Germany had captured Egypt and advanced to the Persian Gulf, they would have won the war, irrespective of what was happening in Russia. In wars, as in battles, it is possession of the key points which makes the difference between victory and defeat. A well-tried military maxim stresses the importance of 'maintenance of the objective'. Whenever commanders have forgotten that maxim, and been tempted into diversion, the results have usually been very unsatisfactory for them. Hindsight tells us that Hitler would have been wiser to concentrate on the Middle East rather than allowing his huge armies to flounder in Russia.

Already, by the autumn of 1942, Hitler had learnt that the Russian campaign was going to take longer and be more difficult than he had anticipated. He had been frustrated at Leningrad and Moscow, though he still hoped for eventual success in those areas, but when his 6th and 4th Panzer armies were halted at Stalingrad on 6 September 1942, he decided that the fault must be one of generalship. He therefore dismissed Field-Marshals List and Halder, and took command of Army Group 'A' himself. It must by now have been clear to the German High Command that the dictator was mad: he was commanding an Army Group from 700 miles behind the front. But even if he had been on the outskirts of Stalingrad, there was nothing Hitler could have done to alter the trend of events. The German army was now extended far beyond the limits of ordinary prudence, and for the conquest of a city which was not an essential strategic objective. It was an unusual target for it stretched for 25 miles along the west bank of the River Volga, but at no point was it more than three miles wide. This meant that even if the Germans broke through at one point, there would still be uncaptured areas on each side. And everywhere the Germans tried to penetrate they found Russians grimly clinging to every shattered building, often to emerge at night to deprive the Germans of their gains of the previous day.

Soldiers on both sides fought with the desperation of the doomed, as they often were. When they were fighting inside the larger buildings, these often changed hands several times. The Luftwaffe, which had been the mainstay of previous German attacks, had now suffered so many losses that its strength was cut by one third. And while the Germans were locked in battle at the end of their long line of communication, the Russians could still mass troops on the far side of the river and then launch attacks from the flanks. It was the classical tactical situation: hold your opponent in the centre and then, as he puts in his last desperate thrust, encircle him with attacks from the flanks.

In November the German army was caught, quite literally, in this trap. The divisions which failed to hold the Russian flank attacks were Roumanians who were not the most willing combatants in Hitler's armies. The enveloping wings pressed on until they joined forces at Kaluch, encircling 250,000 German troops. Von Paulus, the German commander of 6th Army, could go neither forward nor back, and his supply line was cut. Realising that his position was hopeless, he asked Hitler for permission to surrender; it was refused. Goering had assured von Paulus that the Luftwaffe would give him all the supplies and support he needed, but it was clearly an empty promise. The army froze, rations were cut, and ammunition was running low. Meanwhile the Russians pressed home their attacks relentlessly. Von Manstein tried to break through the Russian line with Army Group 'B'; he was hoping that von Paulus would help by coming east to meet him. But von Paulus had orders to stay where he was, and von Manstein's attempt came to nothing.

By Christmas the plight of von Paulus's army had passed the limits of endurance, but there was no relief. The meagre bread ration was cut by half; dead horses were dug up where the frozen ground allowed and made into vile stews. Aircraft tyres froze to the runways, ice blocked the apertures of tanks; there was no petrol to enable vehicles to move, many guns could not be used because their recoil systems were frozen up; frostbite was widespread and the living envied the dead, who now numbered over 60,000.

All along the broad front over which the Germans had

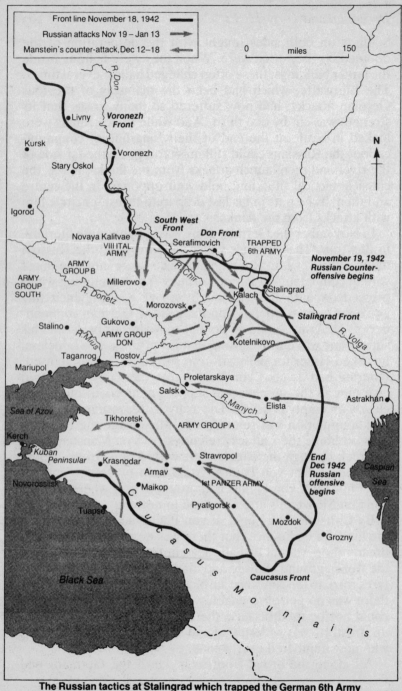

The Russian tactics at Stalingrad which trapped the German 6th Army

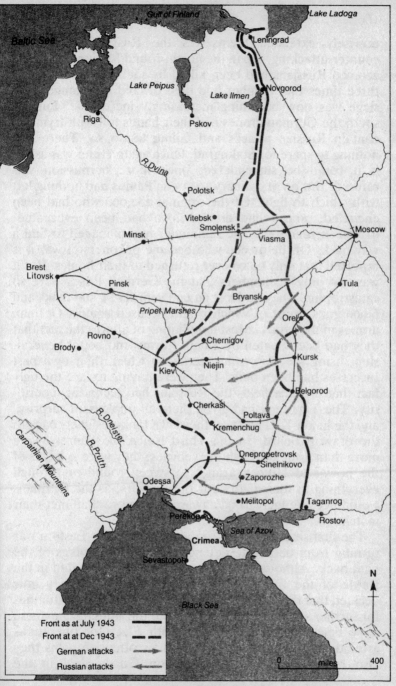

The Campaign in Russia in 1943

unwisely extended themselves the Russians were now counter-attacking. Up in the north, round Leningrad, where 200,000 Russians had been killed by shells and bombs and three times that number had died of cold and hunger, the siege was now becoming increasingly ineffective. Further south the German armies had their hands full with trying to contain Russian attacks and failing to do so. There was nothing to spare for Stalingrad. Once again Hitler was asked if it could be surrendered: once more permission was refused. But on 31 January 1943 von Paulus had nothing left with which to fight. Of the original 280,000 who had been encircled, 70,000 had died, 42,000 had been evacuated; 91,000 surrendered. The remainder had managed to find a way back. Of the 91,000 who became prisoners of war it is reported that only 6,000 ever returned to their homes. But it was not only in numbers that the German losses were so catastrophic. They had lost 60,000 vehicles, 1,500 tanks and 6,000 guns, most of which would be used against German armies in the future. Most humiliating of all was the fact that they had been beaten by a better army and better general-ship, using the very same tactics on which their own past successes had been built. They were having to face the ugly fact that in some fields the Russians had technical superio-rity. The T-34 tank had given them an unpleasant surprise, and the heavy KVI had sent their own tank-designers back to the drawing-board. In the Third Reich the Panzers were more than armoured fighting vehicles: they were symbols of the power of Hitler's armies to sweep round or through everything in their path. But the Panzers, as the Germans would become increasingly aware, had more than met their match.

The first six months of 1943 also saw the Far Eastern war turning from desperate defence into the beginnings of the fight back. Although the Japanese had been defeated in the Battle of the Coral Sea in the previous year, they now decided that the south Pacific still offered good opportunities for further advances. In consequence the Imperial Japanese navy began to assemble a new 8th Fleet for operations around New Guinea. As part of their offensive plans they also began building an airfield on Guadalcanal in the

Solomon Islands. Tulagi was already being turned into a strong base, mainly for seaplanes.

Capturing Guadalcanal and denying the Japanese the use of an airfield there was obviously a priority. Unfortunately the Americans had had no experience of amphibious landings and lacked some of the necessary equipment. However, surprise was a formidable ally and the 2,000 Japanese on the island retreated swiftly into the jungle, abandoning the airstrip, which was renamed 'Henderson Field'. But capturing this essential point seemed easier than holding it, as there then followed a murderous jungle campaign in which numbers were evenly matched. Both sides urgently needed reinforcements and, equally, each navy was straining to prevent any relief getting through to the other side. This situation produced some fierce naval and land battles later in the year.

Burma had also seen the beginnings of a fight back in December 1942 when the British launched an offensive in the Arakan: this did little more than show the Japanese that the war there was not now running entirely in their favour. In the spring of 1943 a new and somewhat charismatic figure appeared on the Burma scene. This was Brigadier Orde Wingate, a British officer who had much of the appearance and manner of an Old Testament prophet. Wingate was a specialist in unorthodox and guerrilla operations, which he had practised with some skill in Palestine and Ethiopia. He put forward a plea for upsetting Japanese communications by means of a Long Range Penetration Group; he aimed also at destroying the reputation of the Japanese for being invincible jungle fighters. His LRPGs were later given the name of 'Chindits', after the models of lions (*chinthés*), which the Burmese put outside their temples as spiritual guardians. The LRPG which set out in February 1943 comprised 3,000 men, travelling on foot with mule transport. This expedition cut the railway line between Mandalay and Myitkyina in many places and undoubtedly gave a shock to the Japanese, who found their units were harassed by an elusive enemy appearing where no enemy could be expected to be. However, this blow to Japanese morale was achieved at prohibitive cost. Eight hundred men of the original expedition failed to return; a badly wounded man could not be evacuated and would be left in the jungle to die or be killed by the Japanese, unless he was fortunate enough to be helped by a Burmese villager. The survivors, who had spent four months in the jungle, were mostly so affected by malaria, ulcers, or intestinal parasites, that they were unfit for further service. This was in sharp contrast to the SAS in the desert in the previous year, for there casualties had been extremely light while results had been considerable.

However, Wingate's Chindits had drawn attention to the sort of problems which would be encountered when men fought for long periods in the jungle. Familiarization with the terrain meant not merely learning to move unobtrusively and not get lost, but also to ward off – as best one could – the diseases which were endemic. For every soldier wounded, 120 had to be evacuated as sick. In one division one-third of the soldiers, some 5,000, were too ill to fight. General Slim, the 14th Army commander, reported that this was a new dimension of warfare, in which insect-borne infections could be more lethal than the Japanese. Many of the hardships of jungle warfare were mitigated by an extremely effective form of casualty evacuation by light aircraft, but the task was difficult and hazardous. When the Japanese came under pressure later in the war they lacked similar resources and unknown thousands died in the jungle.

Although 1943 had begun well in Russia, in the desert, and in the Far East, the Battle of the Atlantic was by no means as satisfactory. The British people were unaware how great the threat to their survival was. To them victory appeared to be in sight, even if at some distance. Casualties among civilians had dropped enormously, 2,372 were killed in 1943, as compared with 22,069 in 1940, and 19,918 in 1941; this seemed to show that the threat from the air was now almost negligible. A rude awakening was in store: late 1944 would be worse than ever.

Faith in the ability of the Royal Navy to protect the lifelines and shores of the British Isles had never wavered, even though there had been some unpleasant shocks, such as the losses of the *Hood*, *Ark Royal*, *Repulse* and *Prince of Wales*. The more important threat to merchant shipping was hardly appreciated, except by those with maritime links. In February 1942 the *Scharnhorst* and *Gneisenau* had slipped through the English Channel without being observed by either the Royal Navy or the Royal Air Force, and this had given rise to doubts about the British belief that the danger of invasion was past.

In fact the naval position was far more delicate than even Churchill would have cared to admit. At the beginning of World War II the Royal Navy was smaller than it had been in 1914; it was still larger than the German fleet but most of its ships and guns were obsolescent if not actually obsolete: one-third of its 150 destroyers had been built for the 1914–18 war. In spite of the experiences of 1917, the Admiralty had reported (in 1936) that modern scientific developments had made the convoy system obsolete and that it would not be used in future. Convoys required many escort ships, used up a lot of valuable fuel, and were slow. It was assumed that anti-sumbarine devices, such as ASDIC, would suffice for destroying U-boats, and that the mastery of the seas would be achieved by huge naval battles between giant battleships. Naval manoeuvres which involved attack by aircraft had always found the surface fleet more than a match for the bombers; the final defeat of that naive assumption would cost Britain the *Prince of Wales* and *Repulse* in December 1941. And attempts to hunt down submarines in the wide waters of the Atlantic had been a costly procedure. The result was that by January 1943 German submarines had sunk an average of three British ships every day of the war. Whereas the average British citizen believed (as he had been told) that the German war effort would collapse rapidly and ignominiously from lack of oil, it was the British economy which was in greater danger. By December 1942 Britain was reduced to a mere two months reserve of oil.

Surprisingly this damage had been caused by many less U-boats than was thought to have been responsible. In 1939 the German navy had 56 U-boats, many of pre-1918 design, far less than Admiral Doenitz had said would be required for a major war. Even by 1945 they only had 434. If Hitler had waited till 1944, instead of precipitating the nation into war in 1939, there could have been a very different outcome.

By 1943 the Royal Navy had agreed a strategy for winning a war which, against the odds, they looked like losing. It was as well that they did so, for the progress of the land and air battles were now bringing a series of invasions into prospect, and for a successful invasion naval supremacy was absolutely essential. By this time the American navy had joined in the war, but it lacked both experience and modern shipping; furthermore the Pacific must be the American navy's top priority until Japan was finally defeated.

To gain command of the seas the Allies organised their resources more economically and wisely. Different classes of ships were allotted to specific rôles. Aircraft carriers were mainly to be used for escort duties, although on occasions, as in the Coral Sea and Midway, they would assume the rôle of battleships. Destroyers would also be used for escort duties. Cruisers were to be used to keep open longer sea communications, and battleships drawn in to help if cruisers ran into superior forces. Submarines would be countered by convoys and the extensive use of radar. Convoys were not as effective as might have been hoped. 97 ships were sunk in three weeks in March 1943 and over 60 of them were in convoy; a more effective method was to use information derived from code-breaking to know when U-boats would be on the surface. Aircraft and surface ships could then be sent to the appropriate areas and, having pinpointed by radar the exact position of the enemy submarine, would sink it. Improved radar and accurate intelligence made a substantial contribution. U-boats had to rise to the surface frequently. Their underwater speed was only two to nine knots, and this used up the power in their storage batteries: on the surface they could manage 25 knots. They could not remain submerged for more than 48 hours, and normally could not be at sea for more than 42 days.

In view of the fact that the Germans came close to winning both world wars by means of U-boats, it is remarkable to consider how inefficient these were. High motivation was essential, for they were badly ventilated and the crews were always breathing in fumes from battery gases and diesels. The temperature was either too hot or too cold, and the humidity at either extreme was excessive. Washing facilities were limited and fresh meat and vegetables never available after the first few days. Some two hundred U-boats were lost during the war. Strangely, the most effective U-boats were those of the small World War I design: Germany's efforts to build larger U-boats were not as successful as had been hoped. The hundred submarines the Germans gained from the Italian navy were not considered worth having unless crewed by Germans. When one contemplates the research that went into the design of German tanks and aircraft, the money spent on submarines seems totally inadequate in relation to their cost effectiveness.

Up till 1943 the German navy had an invaluable asset in being able to read the Allied Combined Convoy cipher. This was intercepted by B-Dienst (Beobachtung-Dienst), which therefore knew the numbers, varieties, locations, departure dates and changes of direction of all Allied convoys. The Allies did not change this system to a totally secure one until November 1943. If a U-boat was lost, both it and its crew would be replaced twice as fast as its Allied counterpart.

Yet after May 1943 the war against the U-boats turned irreversibly in favour of the Allies. Mass-produced ships were coming from US shipyards faster than any U-boat could find and sink them. With the Allied convoys there was not merely an air patrol, but every device the scientists could muster. Among them were microwave radar, improved sonar, multiple depth charges, magnetic detectors and sono-radio buoys. The war at sea was being won, not by courage and determination in the Atlantic, but by patient scientists in engineering laboratories.

The combined efforts of cryptographers and scientists enabled Britain to know the names of every U-boat commander and his crew, and their state of readiness. It also enabled British scientists to begin designing countermeasures to new German weapons before these were actually brought into service. This introduced yet another form of deception warfare. When the Germans introduced the acoustic torpedo, Britain had a counter measure ready which caused the torpedo to explode short of its target. Britain then reported that ships were sunk by them and the

Germans continued to manufacture and use these expensive weapons, although they were quite useless.

Although the Allies were well aware that U-boat crews were dedicated and courageous men who lived uncomfortable lives and often died slowly and in agony, this did not make them any the less hated. Too many unarmed ships had been sunk, too many non-combatants left to drown because rescue ships had themselves been torpedoed, for U-boats to be regarded as honest opponents.

Two important lessons were learnt from the campaign against the U-boats. The first was that the U-boat dominance in the Atlantic was not ended until electronic warfare and cryptography combined to bring it about. This was revealed by messages from U-boats themselves in which they noted their increasing vulnerability to attack from radar-guided aircraft, and commented that this had a bad effect on the morale of the crews; they no longer felt protected by the obscurity of the seas. The second was that submarines were probably the most cost-effective of the weapons of war. At least thirty warships were occupied in attending to every U-boat, and the proportion of men engaged in this aspect of warfare was 800,000 hunters to 39,000 in the U-boat crews. There is a further lesson to be learnt from the fact that although the British and US navies were allies there was sometimes a rivalry between them which did no good to, anyone except the enemy. The US navy was the first to realise that the U-boats were reading British ciphers and thus knew all the future movements of convoys, but the British were reluctant to accept this information from a source that they felt must be inferior to their own. Almost as damaging was the fact that the US navy knew that the British had vast experience of anti-submarine warfare but were not prepared to accept advice until made to do so by bitter experience.

Although the naval war was never easy, its unpleasantness varied according to the oceans or seas on which it was being fought. In tropical waters survivors were liable to be eaten by sharks, if in the water, or die of heat or thirst if on boats or rafts. Ships operating in the Mediterranean were attacked by submarines or aircraft, those in the Atlantic mainly by submarines, but those on the Arctic convoys were subjected to such unpleasant weather conditions that attacks by aircraft or submarines seemed one of their lesser misfortunes. The Arctic convoys which delivered supplies to Russia were within easy reach of German shore-based aircraft operating from Norway. As Hitler had a constant fear that the Allies intended to invade and recapture Norway at the earliest possible opportunity, there were always a number of large warships based in Norwegian waters. Losses on the earlier convoys were so high that at times they became unacceptable, but eventually there was a very high success rate. Many of the cargoes consisted of American vehicles which were vital to keeping Russian armies supplied in the field, but the Russians showed so little gratitude for the enormous effort and risk of delivering them that the navy became extremely angry. The reception of the ships which limped into Murmansk contained more suspicion than gratitude, making a sharp contrast to that accorded to those which managed to run cargoes into beleaguered Malta.

Doenitz, who had begun the war as commander of the German submarine fleet and in 1943 succeeded to the overall command of the German navy, did not limit his predatory activities to the North Sea or the Atlantic. His U-boats hovered off Cape Town or looked for likely targets in the Indian Ocean. Tactics varied, sometimes U-boats would operate singly and at other times in teams up to 40 strong – the renowned 'wolf packs'. Doenitz stepped up production, armed the U-boats with more powerful anti-aircraft guns and equipped them with 'Schnorkel' breathing tubes which enabled them to recharge their batteries when submerged. He built heavily-fortified 'pens' in their bases and although these were bombed by the Allies in spring 1943, using 11,000 tons of high explosive and 8,000 tons of incendiaries, not a single U-boat was put out of action.

An unpopular but successful tactic was to disguise warships as innocent merchantmen. Such ships did great damage in the Indian Ocean, where they would approach unsuspecting cargo ships until within close range, then demand surrender. The outcome was usually the sinking of the out-gunned victim. This, inevitably, produced counter-measures in that the innocent merchantman was not all it seemed and, when

when the German raider approached and made its demands, would open fire with devastating effect.

Although there were some extremely unpleasant incidents in the war at sea, such as boatloads of survivors being machine-gunned, or rescue ships themselves being sunk, the opposing navies usually fought with chivalry and conformed to accepted codes of behaviour.

7
DIEPPE AND OTHER
LANDINGS

The second half of 1943 saw the Allies begin a series of offensives which met with varying success. Nobody believed invasion would be easy and for that reason in the previous August an attempt to gain some experience of the problems had been made at Dieppe. It had been a costly experiment.

At dawn on 19 August 1943 Dieppe was attacked by a force of 6,000, with accompanying aircraft and naval forces. The aim of the raid was to discover whether a force of this size could get ashore, seize a number of strongpoints and secure the entry of a larger force which would then drive inland. The lesson that it could not do this was learnt very clearly. Before the raid it had been thought that an essential preliminary to a successful invasion would be the capture of a port with facilities for handling heavy vehicles. Dieppe showed that in France at least, the chances of doing this from the sea were negligible.

The attacking force included elements from three commando regiments, Phantom Regiment, and some 5,000 Canadians from their 2nd Division. Of these, over 3,000 were eventually killed, wounded or missing. Although the raid had been planned carefully, the strength of the opposition had been underrated. Dieppe was very well defended, with batteries of heavy guns commanding the entrance to the harbour. The beach, which is of shingle, is steep enough to be a formidable obstacle for tanks and landing craft; behind it was wire and carefully constructed defences. The cliffs, on which further defences were mounted, were steep and heavily wired. Only one of the raiding parties reached its objective, which was the coast defence battery at Varengeville. When the raiding party went in, most of the defences were intact, for the Royal Navy had been unwilling to risk their larger ships in a venture which might easily result in their loss, thus leaving the country at greater risk than before. In the event the raid cost a destroyer and a number of landing craft. 106 aircraft were lost against 48 German. The Germans lost a mere 591 men.

Apart from discovering the feasibility of capturing a port by means of a raid from the sea, Dieppe was meant to demonstrate to Stalin that the Western Allies were taking serious steps towards the opening of a 'Second Front'. A frequent request from the Russians was that the Western Powers should open a second front by invading the continent. This would cause the Germans to withdraw troops and aircraft from their Eastern Front. In fact there had been a second front in North Africa long before the Russians became involved in the war and, as we saw earlier, at the time of the 'Torch' landings substantial numbers of German aircraft had been withdrawn from the Russian front and sent to Tunisia. Dieppe proved that an attempt to invade France without long and complicated preparations would undoubtedly end in disaster for all concerned. A bungled invasion would not merely be a catastrophe for the Western Allies, but it would also enable the Germans to withdraw from France many of the troops they kept there and to despatch them to fight in Russia. There were at this time numbers of ill-informed and perhaps politically motivated people in Britain who wrote up on walls 'Open the Second Front in the West now!': they did not however append their names as volunteers for a spearhead attack. Faint traces of this graffiti may still be seen today.

With the experience of Dieppe firmly in mind, an assault was planned for Sicily in mid-July 1943. Although the Allies were aware that the Germans were now at some point expecting an invasion on the northern shores of the Mediterranean, they realised that there was considerable scope for deception over the exact spot. Every German and Italian soldier and airman who could be decoyed away from Sicily to guard some other potential invasion point would mean one less to oppose the Allied landings. Deception was practised by means of 'turned' spies who would confidently report Allied intentions. As we shall see later, every German spy who was sent to Britain was either caught and executed, or decided to act for the Allies while still pretending to serve his German controller. However, reports by spies were considered useful but not infallible; the integrity of the spy was not suspected but information which clashed with the opinions of the German Higher Command tended to be treated with reserve. The Allies had had great success in disguising the 'Torch' invasion which had been rumoured to be aimed at the Azores or the south of France and, as a result, had found the Germans with no aircraft or submarines conveniently situated to counter it. Undoubtedly as a result the Germans would be highly suspicious of Allied intentions and therefore an elaborate series of deceptions was arranged to confuse them.

The first was that of 'The Man who Never Was'. This involved a confidential letter written as from General Nye, the British Deputy Chief of Staff, to the British General (Alexander) commanding the British forces in North Africa. The letter explained Eisenhower's alleged intentions for the next stage of the war. This was to be an invasion of Sardinia, but in order to deceive the Germans there would be a diversionary attack on Sicily, aimed purely at concealing Eisenhower's real intentions. When the Germans saw a copy of this letter, as it was planned they should, they would realise that the attack on Sicily was not a serious venture and would not let it interfere with their disposition of troops for the defence of Sardinia and other regions west. To ensure that the Germans would see this bogus letter a macabre plot was devised. A corpse was dressed up to appear to be a drowned Royal Marine officer, and given identification papers which could not be faulted. The corpse had actually died of pneumonia, but except to an expert pathologist would appear to be that of a man who had been drowned. It was deposited in the sea off the Spanish coast, wearing a life-jacket, and this seemed to be that of someone who had tried to escape from a shot-down aircraft. The Spanish authorities, who at that time were very friendly with the Germans, found the corpse, extracted the letter from its special envelope, photographed it and replaced it, before handing the body over to the British authorities. The Germans never suspected a hoax and made their tactical dispositions accordingly.

In case the bogus letter plan did not work, there were several other deception plans as well. The volume of Signals traffic to and from Eisenhower's headquarters would obviously indicate to the enemy that something important was pending, so his real headquarters, near the invasion point, was given a very low profile and traffic kept to the minimum; meanwhile a simulated headquarters at Oran was flooded with bogus Signals traffic, including much passing between there and Washington. As the invasion force was made up of contingents from Egypt, Malta, Tunisia and Britain, separate sets of deception plans were concocted. The British force was issued with English/French phrasebooks, supplied with French currency, and shown models of the coast near Biscay. The other groups, being already in the area, were supplied with vaguer but supporting plans, some of which, it was conjectured, would fall into the hands of known enemy agents. Numerous rumours were also spread around.

The invasion of Sicily was code-named 'Husky'. It was hoped that if it met with rapid success the Italian people would see this as an opportune moment to revolt against the fascist regime, depose Mussolini and make a separate peace with the Allies before the latter set foot on the Italian mainland. Unfortunately, at the Casablanca Conference in January 1943, the Allies had stated that the war would continue until the Axis powers made an unconditional surrender. This bleak prospect seems to have suggested to many Italians that the known oppression of Mussolini's fascism might be preferable to Allied domination, particularly if the Russians had a hand in it. The policy of demanding 'Unconditional Surrender' seems, in hindsight, to have been a mistaken one, for if a less demanding peace treaty had been made it seems likely that the fascist regimes in Germany and Italy, though not perhaps in Japan, might not have lasted much longer.

The island of Sicily is a triangular rock with useful airfields and good ports at Palermo, Catania, Syracuse, Messina and Augusta. It was heavily garrisoned, containing 75,000

Germans and 275,000 Italians. The beaches were wired and fortified but not considered to be impassable. Rather more effective defence was expected inland. Some 60 miles south of Sicily is the island of Pantellaria. Before the war this had been considered to be a formidable, perhaps impregnable, island, but in the event Pantellaria succumbed quickly when the Allies bombed it, and its 11,000 Italian soldiers were all taken prisoner.

The Allied invasion force was made up of the US 7th Army, commanded by General Patton, and the British 8th Army commanded by General Montgomery. Patton's army contained two-and-a-half divisions, Montgomery's four-and-a-half. This was in fact a larger force than would land in France on D Day. A greater contrast in commanders could not have been found: both were flamboyant but Patton believed that a thrusting policy would always bring successful results, while Montgomery was equally certain that rapid, hastily prepared moves were a recipe for disaster. Furthermore the two men regarded each other with dislike bordering on contempt.

Although the North African 'Torch' had been a successful landing, this was largely due to the fact that it was both unexpected and lightly resisted; Sicily was clearly going to be more difficult, more complicated and required a larger concentration of shipping. However, on 10 July 1943 Montgomery's army invaded in the south-east of Sicily, and Patton on the south. The operation had its share of disasters, mainly caused by lack of experience. The British glider regiment had practised over dry land only and did not appreciate that, as the sea cools more quickly at night, the thermals which kept their gliders airborne would be weaker; in consequence many of them came down prematurely into the sea. The Americans fared even worse, some of their airborne troops being shot down by their own aircraft. Many of the parachutists who got through landed far away from their destined areas and had to make their way to them belatedly on foot. This was mainly on account of the weather; however, if the weather had not been so bad the garrison on the island would have been much more alert to the possibility of an attack. The beach assaults were very successful and the speed with which the landing was accomplished alarmed Hitler so much that he ordered his generals to withdraw some troops from the Russian front and send them to bolster the remaining defences of Sicily. Stiff resistance was encountered when the British reached the lower slopes of Mount Etna. Here and elsewhere the aim of the Germans was to delay the Allied advance as much as possible while the bulk of the Axis troops were evacuated to Italy via the Straits of Messina. In this they met considerable success for 60,000 got away to the Italian mainland, but overall the invasion had been an Allied triumph. For a loss of 31,000 killed, wounded or missing, they had removed nearly 160,000 Axis troops from the battlefield, mostly as prisoners of war. The whole campaign had taken less than six weeks.

Although 'Husky' was a successful operation, it could have been infinitely more so. If, as Churchill wished, the Allies had invaded in June or even as early as May, they would have found Sicily very thinly defended. In spite of the success of the deception plans, a good number of reinforcements were sent to the island in the months following the defeat of the Germans in Africa. Secondly, Patton should have been allowed to land near Palermo, as originally planned: if he had done so he could have reached Messina and prevented the evacuation of those three divisions which were such a useful addition to the German defensive strength on the mainland. The presence of Patton's army moving across the north of Sicily, and threatening their rear, would also have reduced the effectiveness of the troops holding up the Allied advance in the central region.

The fact that the British and American troops were competing against each other to be the first to reach Messina might have led to disaster through impetuosity, but in the event it did not. Patton distinguished himself during this campaign, but not as he would have wished. When visiting a hospital he encountered a soldier who appeared to him to be an obvious malingerer because he had no visible scars of battle. Patton hit him across the face and told him not to be a coward but to get back to his unit. Unfortunately for Patton the man had some easily diagnosable disease which made him unfit for combat. Eisenhower was forced to order Patton to make a very public apology, not merely to the soldier, but also to the staff of the hospital concerned. In view of the fact that he, an officer, had struck an enlisted man in hospital, this might well have terminated Patton's military career there and then. He did not become a reformed character but he did his best subsequently to show that Eisenhower's clemency had been justified.

In the event there *was* a form of revolution in Italy. On 25 July 1943 Mussolini was deposed by what he had thought were his closest supporters; the King of Italy, King Victor Emmanuel III, then appointed Marshal Badoglio in his place. Theoretically Badoglio was still co-operating with the Germans, but in practice he was already negotiating with the Allies to sign an armistice. Meanwhile Mussolini was imprisoned in what was considered a virtually inaccessible hotel in the Gran Sasso mountains. The armistice was signed at Syracuse on the very day that the Allies landed at Reggio.

However, for some months the Germans had realised that the Italians would make peace with the Allies at the earliest possible moment, if they were allowed to do so. They acted promptly and seized Rome, nearly capturing both Badoglio and the King in the process. However, they could not prevent a substantial part of the Italian fleet sailing to Malta and joining the Allies. As this included four battleships and six cruisers, it was a welcome addition to the Allied strength in the Mediterranean. Although the Italian fleet had come off worst in most of its encounters with the Allies, it had had a considerable nuisance value. Not least of the accomplishments of Italian sailors had been that of the frogmen who had managed to attach limpet mines to two British warships and sank them while they imagined they were safe in Alexandria harbour 1941; in the event valuable ships were badly damaged at minimum cost to the Italians. (This success caused the Allies to establish special forces for similar operations. Men were trained to approach targets under-water and attach explosive charges known as limpet-mines to the hulls. British Marines paddled canoes in the dark up the Gironde Estuary to sink two Axis ships in Bordeaux Harbour in 1942 and in 1944 British frogmen damaged the German battleship *Tirpitz* as she lay in a Norwegian fjord. Midget submarines or semi-submarine canoes were usually

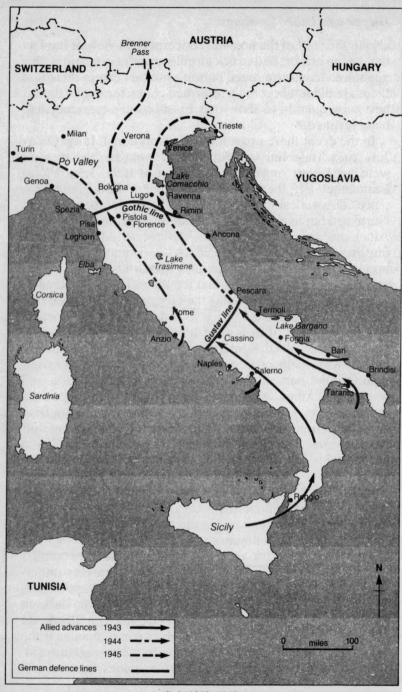

Italy 1943–1945

employed on these missions. British and Australian frogmen sank 40,000 tons of Japanese shipping in Singapore Harbour in 1943. American frogmen had many successes in demolishing Japanese defences in the Pacific.)

There was now a general impression that the remainder of Italy would fall into Allied hands without further difficulty. That view was greatly mistaken. The Germans had 15 divisions in Italy, as well as substantial numbers of aircraft; furthermore they had made sound tactical plans against this event. When, on 9 September 1943 General Mark Clark's 5th US Army landed at Salerno, five of those divisions were sent to resist the invasion force, and two days later the Salerno beachhead looked like being the scene of a hasty evacuation of Allied troops. Fortunately for the Allies, they were able to call on massive air support, and the disaster was averted. A new electronic development appeared at Salerno, this time in the hands of the Germans. Using radar-controlled rocket bombs, the Luftwaffe scored direct hits on the British battleship *Warspite* and two American cruisers. The two invasion forces linked up on 16 September, some 40 miles south-east of Salerno. The British then moved up the east coast to Bari, which fell on 22 September, and to Foggia, with its valuable airfield, five days later. After Commandos had captured Termoli, the German 16th Panzer Division counter-attacked with great vigour, but the town was held. However, when the British pushed on from Termoli and the Americans moved north from Naples, they met formidable opposition along what became known as the Gustav Line. Here. along the River Garigliano, Kesselring had 10 divisions; he had three more in reserve and a further two were stationed in northern Italy to ensure there was no trouble in that quarter.

However by this time, December 1943, planning was well advanced for the much more important invasion of France, which would take place within approximately six months. As a result Eisenhower, Montgomery and Air Chief Marshal Tedder were taken from the Italian front and brought back to Britain. Eisenhower's post in Italy was taken by General Sir Henry Maitland-Wilson. Lieutenant-General Alexander was commanding 15th Army Group, which comprised 8th and 5th Armies. He was also Deputy Supreme Commander.

Lieutenant-General Oliver Leese took command of the 8th Army, replacing Montgomery. After several British and American formations had also been sent to Europe to add weight to the D Day invasion force, the 8th Army consisted of a mere seven divisions, all from the Commonwealth. General Mark Clark's 5th US Army was larger, containing five American divisions, five British, two French, and one Polish division in reserve.

The Allied assault which became known as the battle of the Garigliano began on 17 January 1944, but made slow progress. Three days later, another Allied seaborne landing took place, this time at Anzio. 50,000 men were landed but instead of pushing ahead to cut the German communications they stayed and dug in on the beachhead. Doubtless the commander's wish was to avoid all possibility of being pushed back into the sea again, but this cautious policy completely nullified the purpose of the landing. Churchill referred sardonically to it as 'a stranded whale'. However, both Salerno and Anzio provided useful lessons for the D Day planners. Unless overwhelming strength was brought to bear at the invasion point the defence could rally and even threaten to push back the invaders. This did not, of course, happen on D Day but there were moments when it seemed within the bounds of possibility.

The battle along the Gustav (Garigliano) Line now settled into a stalemate. When by February the Allies had failed to capture Cassino, the part played by the ancient abbey was called into question. Although the Germans protested that they were not making use of the building, which provided observation over the entire battlefield, the Allies were not convinced: the abbey at Cassino seemed too important a tactical point to be left intact in German hands. On 15 February, after warning all monks and civilians to leave, Allied bombers reduced the abbey to rubble; the only two places to escape damage were the cell and the tomb of St Benedict.

Although the Germans denied using any part of the abbey precincts for military purposes, there seemed to be some evidence that they had used certain places for observation points. But the destruction of the monastery resulted in no military advantage to the Allies and was widely condemned. The gainers were the Germans who established strongpoints in the rubble and successfully resisted any attempts to eject them. The hill remained in German hands until 17 May. By then it had been out-flanked, but was only captured by heroic action from the Polish Corps. But before following the Italian campaign further, it is necessary to look at what had been happening in other theatres since the invasion of Sicily had begun.

In February 1943 the Americans had finally cleared Guadalcanal of Japanese by resolute fighting. In consequence the Japanese decided they must strengthen their foothold in New Guinea. They therefore sent a convoy of reinforcements, numbering 7,000 troops, from Rabaul in the Bismarck Archipelago. It set out on 1 March and on 3 March was intercepted by 336 American and Australian aircraft from New Guinea. For a loss of five aircraft, they sank seven of the eight Japanese transports and four destroyers. The last of the eight transports was sunk by a torpedo boat and half the Japanese soldiers were killed or drowned. An even worse disaster hit the Japanese in April. Their most famous admiral, Yamamoto, was killed when his aircraft was shot down between Rabaul and the Solomon Islands. Decoded messages had given his exact itinerary and he was intercepted by a squadron of American aircraft. It was a severe blow to Japanese morale, but they still did not suspect that their codes were being read. Yamamoto had been the master mind behind the Pearl Harbor attack, so his death was a matter of no slight satisfaction to the United States forces.

MacArthur was now ready to begin the return which he had promised to a somewhat sceptical audience before he left the Philippines. His first move was to eject the Japanese from the Solomon group and establish his own troops in their place. This involved tactical hopping from island to island, capturing essential airfields or making new ones. He managed to establish a substantial force on Bougainville before the Japanese could concentrate their garrison of 60,000 to prevent him. This move was seen by the Japanese as a preliminary to an assault on Rabaul in New Britain, where they had a garrison of 100,000, but instead MacArthur

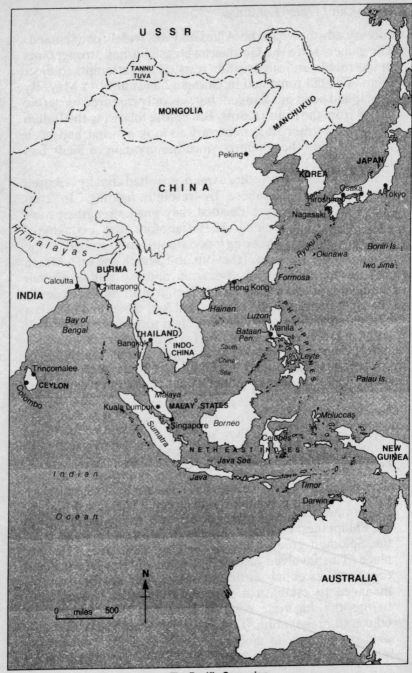

The Pacific Campaign

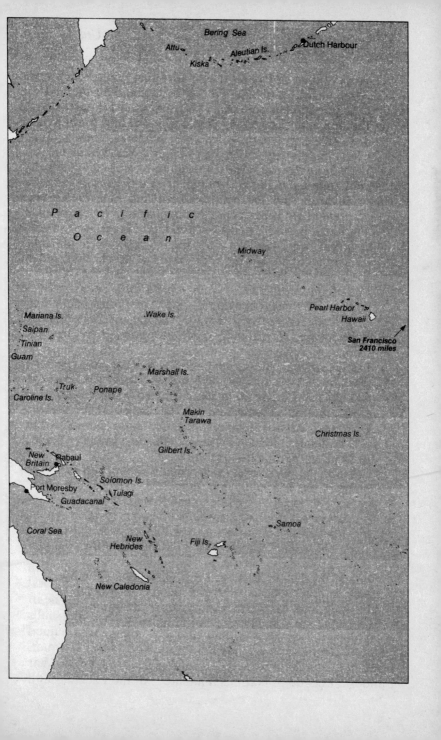

took Manus Island, which had a magnificent harbour at Seeadler. Each new conquest brought MacArthur a step nearer Japan and would eventually bring that country within range of his formidable fleet of bombers. This method was infinitely quicker and easier than trying to follow the route the Japanese expected he would take and which would have involved lengthy battles for Java, Sumatra, Malaya, Indo-China and perhaps Formosa (Taiwan). MacArthur's island-hopping technique required local naval and air superiority. In theory it was possible to pulverise any local defences by massive air and sea bombardment and then land troops without incurring casualties. In practice this never happened. The initial bombardments were certainly devastating, but the Japanese were usually well dug in, and were so highly motivated that, in the early stages at least, they fought literally to the last man. Sometimes Japanese forces retreated into deep fortifications from which they could only be removed by flame-throwers. The Americans might have respected them for their courage, had they not been sickened by evidence of revolting cruelties practised by Japanese troops on civilians and prisoners of war. When the Japanese had launched their attacks in the Far East they had claimed it was to establish 'The South-East Asia Co-Prosperity Sphere', and for a while this attracted some co-operation from the inhabitants of the territories they overran. However, when it became clear that 'co-prosperity' meant plundering the conquered lands of their goods the 'subject peoples' became sullenly resentful.

While the Americans were forging ahead with their conquest of the Solomons they were also engaged in a similar operation in the Gilbert and Marshalls Group. This operation was directed by Admiral Nimitz. The Gilberts had been a British colony before the Japanese seized them in 1942. The capital Tarawa was a prosperous town on a coral atoll; it would soon become renowned for being the scene of one of the firecest battles of the Pacific War. The Marshalls had originally been explored by an Englishman named Captain John Marshall, had subsequently become German, and had been administered by the Japanese after World War I under a League of Nations mandate. All the Pacific island groups contained a large number of islands, some very small and uninhabitable. Even after heavy bombardment, taking Tarawa was a formidable task. One thousand US Marines were killed in the battle for it, and over 2,000 were wounded. The Japanese lost nearly 9,000.

The Marshalls were no less formidable. Most of the islands are the coral tops of dormant volcanoes, which rise a mile from the ocean bed; some of them scarcely break the surface, others have been pushed up to 18,000 feet. American troops captured Kwajalein and the key position of Eniwetok in February 1944. The Marshalls subsequently achieved another form of fame, for early experiments with atomic bombs took place at Bikini, as well as Eniwetok.

The acquisition of bases on the Marshalls enabled the Americans to destroy the important Japanese bases at Ponape and Truk in the Caroline Islands; Ponape was knocked out on 16 February 1944, exactly two years after the Japanese had begun to celebrate their conquest of Singapore. Recapturing Singapore did not even interest the Allies. Two days after putting Ponape out of action, the American carrier fleet unleashed a storm on Truk, the best known and most powerful base in the Pacific. By 18 February 275 Japanese aircraft, two destroyers and a variety of merchant shipping had been destroyed, and the base rendered useless. The war was still a long way from Japan, but the Allied forces in the Pacific, which, of course, included Australians and New Zealanders as well as Americans, were pressing inexorably forward. The next move would be to the Marianas, 1,000 miles north of the Marshalls, where the Japanese had a garrison of over 50,000.

By this time both sides had evolved a special technique for the Pacific battles. The Japanese constructed deep bunkers, often linked by tunnels. At this stage in the war they usually continued fighting until every soldier was dead. The American technique was that of the production line. The target area was bombed by aircraft and then bombarded from the sea. The landing parties, mostly consisting of Marines, were conveyed in boats which came up to the beaches then opened at the front. From the bow doors emerged tanks, vehicles and men. By this time the beach assault was also being covered by heavy bombardments of points further inland.

All over the United States ships, tanks, guns, ammunition, equipment, supplies of every variety were designed, manufactured and despatched to the appropriate destinations. In the shipyards new methods of welding had been introduced so that women could replace men at this vital task. Almost everything manufactured was regarded as expendable. A ship was made to last for one voyage, even though subsequently it might be capable of hundreds. Men were conscripted from one end of the country to the other, trained, equipped and then sent to the point at which they would kill or be killed, either on the sea, in the air, or on land.

And it was not only the Japanese who fought with fierce, ideological patriotism. America was at war and on whatever front her servicemen fought they realised fully that they were fighting for their country as well as for the elimination of fascist tyrants. In the years since World War II ended, patriotism has become an unfashionable virtue, often being mocked at by pseudo-intellectuals who deride it as being old-fashioned, as if that were a reason to condemn it. What is not understood by these people is that they owe their liberty to express their thoughts, however unpatriotic, disloyal and inappropriate, to the earlier generation who endured much to preserve liberty of speech.

By May 1944 America and its naval forces had established themselves on latitude 10. This line runs through the Carolines and Marshalls, through the centre of the Philippines, north of Borneo and Malaya, and touches the tip of Indo-China. It is less than 3,000 miles from Japan. But having followed the Pacific war to this point, we must take a look at what was happening on the other fronts.

8

BY AIR TO BATTLE

By 1944 the complexity and sophistication of World War II had increased to a point which could scarcely have been envisaged in 1939. It was now truly a world war with China, Japan, Russia, the Pacific, India, Africa, Europe and North America all committed. There were battle fronts in the Far East, the Middle East, Europe, Russia and the Atlantic. It was also a war of scientists unobtrusively experimenting with new ways of killing men or preventing them being killed, a war of electronics, a war of psychologists who advised on the best ways to motivate one's own people and to destroy the enemy's will to resist, it was a war between strategists who might or might not be military leaders, it was a war fought by the medical services against death by wounds, disease, exposure and exhaustion. On some fronts men went into battle with each other in thousands; on others they fought completely alone. It was a war in which natural leaders strove to inspire their fellow-countrymen; Churchill with his defiant speeches, Roosevelt with his cosy style, Stalin with his revival of past Russian glories, all won before communism had been invented.

In some fields the competition was obvious. Germany and Russia had both begun the war with good tanks, Britain with poor ones and America with virtually none. By the middle of the war an entirely different picture had emerged. By 1943 the more realistic German and Japanese leaders knew that they could never match Allied war production. In spite of losing a substantial part of her terrain to the German invaders, Russia was still producing enormous numbers of tanks, guns and motivated soldiers. Britain was producing a wide variety of highly complicated weapons, Canada, Australia, New Zealand, South Africa were doing likewise, and America was manufacturing enough for her own needs and for most of her allies too.

There was a battle for the hearts and minds of neutrals, who might adjust their neutrality to favour one side or the other; there was also a propaganda battle, often fought over the radio waves. William Joyce, a disappointed Irishman, had become a German citizen soon after the war began and broadcast nightly messages of impending doom to the British people. His jeering, affected accent caused him to be nicknamed 'Lord Haw-Haw' by his audience; although most of the time he amused, sometimes he struck a chill. 'Tokyo Rose', who warned American troops in the Pacific of the appalling fate awaiting them unless they all went home at once, also enjoyed little success. Ironically, the song chosen by the German army to boost the morale of their soldiers in the Middle East was enthusiastically adopted by the British army and given different words. 'Lili Marlene' was probably even more popular with the British than the Germans.

Parts of the propaganda war were very clever; others somewhat unsubtle. The British leaflet 'raids' over Germany accomplished nothing. Later in the war both sides tried to undermine the morale of the opposing soldiers by alleging that while they were suffering and being killed, others were enjoying the favours of their wives. Sadly this was sometimes true: many young men had married hastily before joining the services, and then departed overseas for years on end. Their wives, who during air raids might well have been in greater danger than their husbands in uniform, were bored and unhappy and often found solace with Allied troops, Canadians, Australians, and especially Americans who were well paid, better clothed, and a novelty. Americans had the added attraction of goods from their well-stocked PX (the forces shop) and the ability to obtain nylon stockings, then an unbelievable, newly invented, luxury. Pre-war, infidelity would have been considered socially and morally unacceptable to many people, but with the danger of being killed by a bomb, with the thought that a husband might never return and had probably not remained faithful anyway, and that a lover could meet his death in the invasion of Europe, the temptation to let go was too much for many, though not, it should be emphasised, for all.

The aerial battlefield was dominated by the Axis forces until 1942. The RAF had made sporadic bombing raids on Germany in the earlier years without much effect: its greatest contribution had been inflicting unacceptable casualties on the Luftwaffe in 1940 and therefore deterring Hitler from invading Britain. The Japanese Air Force had enjoyed complete air superiority during its earlier conquests, and it was only when the Japanese naval air arm met the American pilots in the battles of the Coral Sea and Midway that they realised that the honeymoon was over. The Luftwaffe had excellent aircraft in large numbers; this enabled it to dominate the skies during the invasion of Russia, but just when the German army was in most need of Luftwaffe help for transporting supplies, as well as attacking targets, the Luftwaffe was prevented by bad weather from giving that vital assistance.

Pre-war fears that soon after the outbreak of war whole countries would be devastated by massive gas and chemical warfare attacks proved to be unfounded. Much despondency had been caused by the predictions of scientists such as J. B. S. Haldane. Haldane's motives in writing alarming accounts of the effect of gas, in which he said that the population of a city of 50,000 could be exterminated by one small bomb, may have been political. He must have known that these claims were wildly exaggerated, but, being an ardent communist, he may have thought that this prediction would deter the West, with its concentrated manufacturing resources, from waging war against the Soviet Union, where industry was much more widely dispersed. Nevertheless, although neither side employed its huge stocks of poison gas, they were never far from the front line. The major restraining influence was fear of retaliation and ignorance of the long-term effects. Surprisingly, many German citizens had no form of protection against gas attacks, so it would have been unwise for the Luftwaffe to have provoked a retaliatory strike. In contrast, everyone in Britain was provided with a gas mask and was encouraged to carry it wherever he or she went. The civilian version was held in a small box, about half the size of a shoe box, giving the impression, when slung from a shoulder string, of being a sandwich-container. These were all too easily left behind in shops, pubs, cinemas and railway carriages. Superior versions in haversack containers were issued to the services and certain government employees: these were rarely lost but, like the civilian respirators (the official term) would have been useless against the forms of gas the Germans would probably have used. Nerve gases were being produced as early as 1942. The main use of a gas mask was to bolster morale: everyone felt protected. Where ignorance is bliss, 'tis folly to be wise. In 1941 Britain learnt that both Germany and the Soviet Union were experimenting with germ warfare, both chemical and bacteriological. Britain therefore developed an anthrax bomb and tested it on Gruinard Island, off the coast of Scotland. In consequence, Gruinard was considered to be unfit for humans for the next 50 years. However, in 1987 tests established that it was sufficiently clear for a flock of sheep to be allowed to graze there. If they suffered no ill effects, it was thought that it would soon be fit for human occupation once more.

However, the most profitable use of the bomber, in the view of all the belligerents in World War II, was to drop high explosive and incendiary bombs on suitable targets. Britain began the war with a very small bomber command, but, nevertheless, it made two vital contributions to her survival. On 24 August 1940 some Luftwaffe bombers, which had lost their way, dropped their bombs on Central London *by mistake*. The RAF promptly ordered a retaliatory raid on Berlin, using 80 bombers. This act of open defiance so enraged Hitler that he commanded that London must be made to suffer severely in return. In consequence, the Luftwaffe was diverted from destroying airfields in south-east England and instead ordered to use its resources to terrorize London. The decision gave the airfields, which were on the point of becoming unusable, time to recover – and to prepare to win the September battles. During this period Bomber Command was also inflicting considerable damage on the fleet of invasion barges which the Germans were assembling along the French coast preparatory to invading Britain.

On 23 February 1942 Air-Marshal Sir Arthur Harris took over Bomber Command. His entire force consisted of less than 400 bombers, of which the majority were medium and light. Only 200 new aircraft were being delivered each month at that stage, so any casualties represented a serious loss in striking power. Although America was now in the war, no help could be expected from that source for many months; British production was, of course, increasing rapidly. Nevertheless Harris directed his force wisely. He used 236 of his aircraft in March against Lubeck and destroyed half of its manufacturing potential for the loss of 13 aircraft. He lost another 12 against Rostock, which produced the deadly Heinkel aircraft. In May he used every available bomber to launch the first of what were called the 'Thousand Bomber Raids'. On this occasion he had 1,074 bombers and 25 fighters. Cologne was the target, and the entire industrial complex was devastated for the loss of 39 aircraft.

Harris continued to build up the strength of his bombers and in future years asserted that they had done more than anyone or anything to win the war. He supported this claim by pointing out that after his 'strategic bombing' began the Luftwaffe had to divert an increasing portion of its strength to home defence, that German aircraft production was being reduced by attacks on the factories, that German submarines and surface ships were prevented from going to sea by attacks on docks and repair yards, and that large numbers of 88 mm guns, which would have been invaluable as anti-tank weapons on the Russian front, were being retained in Germany to fulfil their primary function of anti-aircraft weapons. His claims were disputed by the other services, which felt that his bombers could have been employed more profitably in other rôles, such as close support of ground troops. However, Harris' claims seem well based. Whatever one may feel about the effects of strategic bombing on the war, its cost in terms of British casualties should not be overlooked. Bomber crews flew tours of 27 missions, by the end of which their original number had been greatly reduced. Casualties among bomber crews, a total of 55,573, exceeded the number of all British officers killed in World War I.

The loss of nearly 60,000 of its most intelligent, venturesome and courageous young men was certain to leave its mark on generations to come. One must not forget that many others of equal quality, in Fighter Command or in the navy or army, were also being killed at the same time. Clearly it takes years for a nation to recover from the loss of so many of its leaders.

Harris justified the losses of Bomber Command by saying that they produced far greater casualties elsewhere. It is arguable that if Bomber Command had not been seen to be inflicting enormous damage on Germany, Britain would have been forced to attempt the invasion of Europe in 1943 instead of 1944. The Americans favoured the earlier date, but although they were gaining experience of invading Pacific islands, this was not comparable with the problems likely to be encountered in Europe. The difficulties met in invading Sicily in 1943 indicated that similar, but worse, hazards would be inevitable in France. There would certainly have been losses on an even greater scale than those at Dieppe.

Although there is a tendency to think of the RAF as an essentially British service, it must be remembered that 37 per cent of its pilots came from outside Britain. There were Canadians, Australians, New Zealanders, South Africans and, by no means least, Poles, Czechs and French.

As with tanks, Britain was slow to develop the formidable monsters which could travel the required distance with the appropriate firepower. However, Britain was first in the field with a bomber capable of taking the huge bombs created by Barnes Wallis. These aircraft were four-engined Lancasters and they could carry the 22,000-pound, 'Grand Slam' bombs. In comparison with modern aircraft Lancasters were painfully slow, with a cruising speed of 216 m.p.h.; consequently they took four hours to reach Berlin and, what somehow seemed worse to the crews, nearly as long to return, if return they did. There are certain forms of noise which will never be forgotten by anyone who was old enough to recognise them in World War II. One was the grinding roar of a heavy bomber, another was the purposely desynchronised engines of the Luftwaffe as it probed the night sky over Britain in 1940, another was the rhythmic pumping of the Bofors 40 mm anti-aircraft gun. Although the Bofors was a product of neutral Sweden, it was the most widely used 'ack-ack' gun of the war.

In the early years of the war a major bombing problem had been finding the target. Once there, courage and skill could ensure that the right (military or industrial) areas were bombed, and historical buildings and civilian quarters were avoided. Shortage of navigators of the required degree of skill led to the creation of the Pathfinder Force. This could be relied on to take the bombers to the right target. Sometimes they would draw off the enemy fighters by 'marking' a 'target' with incendiaries a pre-arranged distance from the real one. The bombers would therefore be able to unload their cargoes without molestation by fighters which were hovering around the wrong area.

1943 brought the full force of the bomber offensive to bear on the Ruhr. Essen, which was the site of the vast Krupps armament factory, was attacked by 442 aircraft in March 1943 and much damage was done. Other attacks followed and, among other towns, Duisburg, Bochum, Krefeld, Munster, Wuppertal, Düsseldorf and Cologne were heavily bombed. Krupps, which had supplied arms to many countries as well as Germany itself, was frequently bombed but was too vast to be put out of action completely. Ironically its quietus came in 1987 from bureaucrats rather than bombers, for in that year the European Economic Committee decided that Krupps was surplus to Europe's steel requirements and must cease production in the interests of rationalization.

Hamburg was an obvious target and in July 1943 was devasted by a mixture of 4,000-pound bombs and incendiaries. This created what was known as a firestorm, an enormous blaze with temperatures of up to 1000 degrees at the centre. 40,000 people were killed, a similar number injured, and the town's shipbuilding and repair yards completely destroyed. Over 70,000 tons of bombs was used in the consecutive raids which obliterated Hamburg. This demonstration of destructive air power convinced most leading Germans that the war was now lost and it would be folly to try to continue. Unfortunately Hitler was not among them, and the war was therefore destined to drag on in Europe for almost another two years.

After Hamburg, it was Berlin's turn once more but, although some 75,000 people were killed, the city was not devastated to the same extent as Hamburg. As we saw earlier, these raids took a heavy toll on Bomber Command. The German radar defences had been disrupted at Hamburg by 'Window'. This consisted of dropping thousands of strips of metal foil. However, the Luftwaffe night fighters had many successes and their anti-aircraft fire, known as flak (*Fl*uga*bwehrk*anone) accounted for an unknown number of aircraft. Probably one of the most important raids was that on Peenemünde. Spies had reported that the Germans were working on a secret weapon on a remote island in the Baltic. Photographic reconnaissance indicated that there was certainly something unusual taking place, and in consequence Peenemünde was bombed by 600 aircraft. The German rocket programme was considerably delayed and as a result the first V1 did not fall on Britain until one week *after* D Day. Had V1s begun falling earlier, on the troops being assembled in southern England, on Southampton, or on the D Day beaches themselves after the landings, the war might have taken a very different course.

Another extremely important raid was that of 'the Dambusters'. This was another form of attack on the industry of the Ruhr. On the night of 16 May 1943 the Möhne and Eder dams were both breached by special 'bouncing' bombs, again designed by Barnes Wallis. The Möhne dam let out 130,000,000 gallons of water, the Eder let out 202,000,000 gallons. The disruption caused to German war industry was enormous. The bombs, weighing a total of 9,250 pounds, of which 6,600 was underwater explosive, were delivered by 19 Lancasters. Navigating to the exact spot, releasing the ricocheting bombs at exactly the right moment, and at the same time coping with a very active defence, made this one of the most effective and spectacular feats of the war.

Although US aircraft were distinguishing themselves in the Pacific, their early ventures in Europe were disastrous. Unfortunately, the possession of the new 'Flying Fortresses', as their heavy bombers were known, had given unjustified confidence that they could fly high enough and fast enough to carry out missions in daylight without fighter escort. Daylight bombing was likely to be more accurate than night-time bombing, but was, of course, infinitely more hazardous. Owing to their shorter range, the earlier fighters could not accompany the bombers for more than a part of the journey. When therefore 291 'Forts' set off to bomb the very important German ball-bearing factory at Schweinfurt on 14 October, their escorts were unable to accompany them to their targets. Sixty fortresses were shot down by German fighters; 130 were damaged but managed to limp home. Fortunately for the Americans, they had the remedy to hand. This was the P.51 Mustang, a long-range fighter which, three years earlier, had been rejected as being underpowered. Now re-equipped with a Rolls Royce Merlin engine it proved to be one of the great success stories of the war.

As the war grew more scientific, some of the night targets were almost as well lit as in daytime. It suited the incoming bombers to illuminate their targets by dropping flares and at the same time it suited the German fighters to climb above the bombers and drop parachute flares among them. The bombers had the worst of this game of illuminating the target, for the searchlights below, instead of trying to pick out individual aircraft, concentrated on silhouetting the whole flight against clouds. In spite of the enormous damage done by British and American bombers, the German fighter defence was never completely beaten.

Perhaps the most remarkable aircraft of the war was the De Havilland 'Mosquito'. This all-wooden fuselage had been designed as early as 1938 but did not go into production until July 1941. With a range of 3,500 miles, a cruising speed of 315 m.p.h. a top speed of 425 m.p.h. and a ceiling of 36,000 feet, it was obviously ideal for photographic reconnaissance but it also had the advantage of being able to carry four 500-pound bombs. The Mosquito fully justified its name: it could fly out of range, then come in suddenly and attack in an undefended spot. At the outbreak of the war no one would have predicted that the most successful aircraft at the end of it would be a wooden one.

The full effect of strategic bombing was not readily observable until the final year of the war. From June 1944 German oil production, which had now come within range, was attacked relentlessly. This included both refineries and synthetic-fuel plants. Within eight months German oil production fell from 650,000 tons to 80,000 tons. In consequence, training flights were suspended, operational fighters were grounded, vehicles were abandoned, and many tanks could not even reach the destination to which they had been ordered.

One of the sadder casualties of strategic bombing was the town of Dresden. Its destruction in February 1945 has been described as an act of brutal vandalism, for it was a town of great beauty and at the time contained 630,000 people, one-third of whom were refugees from the Eastern Front. One-third of these inhabitants were killed in the 800 bomber raid.

Dresden was not, however, merely a peaceful residential city, threatening no one. It was an important industrial centre and a nodal point for several important roads and railways. At that particular time it was the centre of communications for the German armies fighting on the Eastern Front. Usually belligerents try to avoid destroying historic or beautiful towns, and thus Paris, Rome and Oxford were spared, but if a town becomes strategically vital, it is unlikely to survive intact.

The most disturbing fact for the advocates of strategic bombing to swallow was that, in spite of the great success achieved by Bomber Command and the US Air Force, German industrial production increased throughout 1943 and 1944. Only in 1945, when Germany was actually being invaded, did it begin to fall away.

Not surprisingly, the war in the air relied less on the skill and courage of aircrew, although that was vital too, than on scientists and electronics experts. Some of these were helping to design faster and more powerful aircraft but a more important element was concerned with radar and its offshoots.

This battle too had begun some years before the war and grown in intensity after hostilities began. After 1940 both sides had highly sophisticated radar defences and were constantly trying to improve them. Radar would doubtless have been invented sooner or later, but wartime needs gave the development urgency; in consequence, travel has been made infinitely safer and easier for millions of post-war travellers on land and in the air.

Earlier in this book the work of R. V. Jones in countering the German guidance system was mentioned. In spite of the hazards contrived by Jones for the German beams, they continued to be used and to proliferate. Obviously it was very difficult to intercept every beam, particularly those from the small transmitting stations along the French, Dutch and Belgian coasts. These were often used to guide German pilots who had become lost after bombing raids or reconnaissance flights. Flying over unfamiliar enemy territory, avoiding fighters, anti-aircraft defence and the balloon barrages (wires held up by balloons around major towns), pilots could easily become lost. Several German pilots landed in Britain under the impression they were in France. Similarly one British navigator returning from a bombing mission in which considerable evasive action had become necessary found himself over Spain rather than Norfolk, as he had intended. The Luftwaffe was usually guided home by direction beams sent out on agreed frequencies. A British unit, No. 80 Wing, learnt all the frequencies used and arranged for powerful post office transmitters to jam or over-transmit false signals on the same frequency. A pilot deviating slightly from an agreed frequency, which was being jammed, would be reassured to come across the required beam running closely alongside the jammed line. Unfortunately for him, he would now be on a British beam and not a German one. This process was known as 'meaconing'; this British beam would then take the German pilot on a course which was extremely unhealthy for him.

Patiently collecting all the necessary information about German codes, call signs, times of transmissions, frequencies and conventions was the vital Y Service, formed from highly skilled operators from all three services. They were a very special body of men and women who lived isolated, lonely lives, constantly alert to the tiniest sound or change in their earphones. In Britain they worked in the innocuous-sounding Home Defence Units, a title designed to appear no less secret than the Home Guard, with which it was often confused if people ever heard of it. Operators from Royal Signals were not allowed to share messes with their fellow-soldiers, and were usually given some bland cover story to disguise their activities. Often they worked in foreign countries, or enemy-held territory, in conditions of great danger. They knew too much to be allowed to come back into the mainstream and receive the promotion they merited and had earned. Their families had no idea of their true whereabouts, and even when the war was over they were bound by their oath of security from disclosing the fact that they had held one of the most vital jobs in the war; because of it, they were probably holding the same rank as the one in which they had begun.

The main intercepts for Enigma were made at Chicksands in Bedfordshire, where 100 sets were perpetually tuned in to German transmissions, but most of the Y operators lived in considerably less supportive conditions.

Detecting a new device which was being used by the enemy did not necessarily mean it could be countered quickly, if at all. When the Germans were using an élite Luftwaffe unit, KGR 100, as a Pathfinder Force, there was no easy solution to the problem of preventing some of its aircraft finding a target, illuminating it with incendiaries, and then drawing off the fighter defences as the heavy bombers came in. The appropriate counter-measure was found to be, not in electronic measures, but by old-fashioned deception. As soon as intercepts revealed that KGR 100 was on its way, a series of dummy targets were illuminated. These were mock cities constructed in open fields or heathland; those living near those areas protested, but in vain. In one area the German guidance system was so complex that it could not be unravelled. The only solution was to make a Commando descent on the transmitting station responsible: this was the Bruneval raid, and its purpose was to acquire pieces of apparatus whose importance would only be recognised by an accompanying expert.

In addition to the Y Service, there were sophisticated

monitoring systems run by the services themselves: NID 9 in the navy, M 18 in the army, and A 14 in the RAF. All worked in close co-operation. The greatest bonus the listener could have was to hear a frustrated enemy pilot who had lost patience, or panicked, and who asked for instructions in clear (uncoded). The fact that the pilot was unfamiliar with the system and was thus confused, probably meant that he was trying to operate a new and complicated system; in a few intense moments the entire secret of it could be revealed when the intercept was passed back to Bletchley.

Electronic warfare was a world of its own and developed its own special detective skills. Operators knew all the 'fists' of their opposites. The 'fist' is the particular style of sending morse and is as recognisable to an operator as is handwriting. Apart from individual characteristics, such as the rhythm in sending single letters or figures, there is a natural style which helps identify a sender. The most dangerous situations could occur when regimental operators in front-line units began to establish a form of rapport. 'Get off my frequency, Fritz.' 'Your frequency! You're using mine.' Remarks about favourite football teams could lead to possible identification of an operator's regiment. In the Far East, where there were numerous Japanese who had lived in America, front-line chit-chat became so dangerous that the United States used Navajo Indians as front-line operators; the Japanese found their dialect quite impossible to penetrate.

Even the most harmless-sounding intercept could prove valuable. Any distress calls from either side indicated that some form of battle had taken place and that survivors were hoping to be picked up. The nearest units would race to the scene, one to pick up an aircrew for interrogation, the other to rescue their own men to fight again. Skilled aircrew were a valuable commodity. The damaged aircraft or ship might also be of great value to an enemy, for apart from its design it would probably still contain papers and code books which the crew had not had time to destroy.

Co-operation between Britain and America was very close, but the same could not, unfortunately, be said of co-operation with Russia. The Russians tended to be extremely secretive, perhaps largely because of their bureaucratic system and traditions. Although it could be said rightly enough that the Russians had good cause to be suspicious of the West, which in 1919 and 1920 had tried to prevent the formation of the USSR, there was an even stronger reason to be wary of Russia, which had signed a treaty with the arch-enemy Nazism in 1939 and only come into the war because it was attacked by the German ally. Britain and America were never certain that the Russians would not make a separate peace with Germany, as they had done in the First World War in 1917, and although the Western Allies were prepared to give the Soviets all the material help they required to prosecute the war, they dared not trust them with their most vital secrets. However, information derived from Ultra was passed to the Russians at regular intervals and found to be of very great help; the source was not given in case it should be betrayed by carelessness. The Russians gave the West little information about the course of their battles with the Germans on the Eastern Front, and most of what Britain and America knew of them came from Enigma decrypts of German reports. This was irritating but not so damaging as the fact that the Rusians often captured German Air Force codes but did not disclose them till they were too late to be of use. The situation changed for the better when, in June 1943, the Russians captured both a German naval Enigma machine and the 'Auka' code used by the German Air Force. As they did not know how to make use of either, they sought British help. Britain therefore gave the Russians a recently captured machine with instructions on how to use it.

Ultra was by no means an unbroken success story. Some codes transmitted by Enigma machines proved impossible to break; others took so long that the information they carried had ceased to be of use. Electronic warfare, whether concerned with cryptography, radar, detection, deception or any other of its many aspects, is vulnerable to what may be called 'the luck factor'. One side's good luck may be the acquisition of vital information from a shot-down aircraft, a surface ship or even captured servicemen; how far this represents an equal quantity of bad luck for the enemy is determined by the use the lucky side makes of its gains. When Britain knew or suspected that vital information had fallen into German hands, every attempt was made to downgrade its importance; the Germans were rarely deceived. Often 'bad luck' was directly due to stupid behaviour. At the beginning of the war the German Seetakt radar was superior to anything possessed by Britain or the United States, but was large and somewhat fragile: in contrast the British sets were small enough to be fitted into aircraft and were robust enough to withstand shocks. However, when Britain developed the sophisticated H 25 radar, which was devastatingly effective against U-boats, the Air Ministry noted that it would also be extremely valuable for bombers flying over Europe, as it would enable them to detect approaching German fighters at long distance. R. V. Jones advised the Vice-Chief of the Air Staff that this presented too great a risk and the sets should only be issued to the aircraft of Coastal Command. He was overruled, and when a bomber was brought down on German territory, the Germans could hardly believe their good luck. The H 25 enabled the Germans to listen to the Allied bombers while they were forming up in England prior to setting off on their missions. This was very bad for strategic bombers, but the Germans failed to realise that the machine was even more effective against submarines. They were encouraged to believe that these were being located, not by radar, but by infra-red detection. The possession of an advanced special microwave pulse radar did not necessarily mean that the new owner would be able to make use of it as efficiently as the originator. It was, of course, always easy to overrate or underrate an enemy's capacity; there were many more factors to a successful operation than one's opponents' intentions (gained from code-breaking) and his whereabouts (gained from long-distance radar). Nevertheless, ability to make use of what was known as the electro-magnetic spectrum was a vital factor in securing ultimate victory.

Looking at the war as a whole, certain features now appear extraordinary. The great cryptography battle fought between the users of the Enigma machines and the British and American decrypters was made easier for the latter, although difficult enough, because the Germans never believed their secret was known. Yet the machine had been marketed commercially as long before as 1923 and, as it had been adopted by the German services, one would have thought they would have suspected that the Allies were using it also. In fact the Allies did devise absolutely secure coding machines, the British Typex and American Sigaba, which the Germans never mastered, but this did not prevent the Germans reading a whole range of British and American lower-grade encipherings and using their knowledge to great advantage.

Radar, as we saw, was employed by both sides, Germany having adopted it in 1934 and Britain in 1935. But eventually it was the Allies who made the best use of it.

At the beginning of the war the German Air Force had formidable aircraft in large numbers. They were defeated in the Battle of Britain by Spitfires and Hurricanes which were piloted with great skill and courage. As Allied war production got into its stride, it produced excellent aircraft, but the Germans were usually able to match or excel them. However, when a Mosquito came down in German territory, the Germans were unable to build a similar aircraft because their only factory capable of producing the necessary glues had just been bombed out of existence by Harris's bombers.

This very selective account of the air and electronic war may give the impression it was a comparatively straightforward and limited matter. In fact it was a field of enormous complexity, on which subsequently much fascinating and detailed information has become available. Some of this is still in documentary form, but there is also a vast collection which may be read in some of the books listed at the end of this volume.

9
SPIES AND SABOTEURS

While the armies were battling on land, the naval forces were seeking out and destroying each other at sea and the electronics experts and scientists were assessing and countering the technical advances of the enemy, there was yet another battle, separate but closely related. This was the battle of the rival intelligence services. We have already seen how they influenced the deception plans and engaged in such bizarre exploits as 'The Man who Never Was', but there was another vast area of activity too. Each of the belligerents had a complex intelligence service with several branches. In theory the specialized branches would work closely with each other; in practice there were inter-departmental jealousies which hampered them. In addition, as we have learnt subsequently, there were traitors in the intelligence services of all countries, and some of them, such as Philby, Burgess, Maclean and Blunt in Britain, stayed in position after the war, inflicting considerable damage on their own homeland.

In Germany, the principal intelligence agency was the Abwehr, and this contained departments which in Britain came under separate organisations. The head of the Abwehr was Admiral Canaris. Extraordinary though it seems, he wished Germany to be defeated, for he was fervently anti-Nazi and believed that if Hitler was not stopped quickly he would destroy everything which Canaris and his friends valued in their country. However, Canaris had to be very careful in his attempts to assist the Allies, as the Abwehr contained many ardent Nazis who would easily become suspicious. Eventually his double rôle was realised and he was executed in 1944.

In spite of Canaris, the Abwehr had many successes against the Allies, outstanding among them being the '*Englandspiel*' (England Game) run by Colonel H. J. Giskes between 1942 and 1944. In March 1942 a Dutchman who was working for the British Special Operations Executive was caught by a German who detected his transmissions with direction-finding apparatus. The Dutchman was told he could save his life if he collaborated with his captors. SOE agents were instructed to refuse to do so at first and then be persuaded. If they collaborated too readily, this would arouse suspicion; the reluctant collaborator would then send back messages to Britain but include pre-arranged codes from which SOE headquarters would know he was now in German hands. However in this case these codes were ignored and, even when he included the word 'caught', no notice was taken. As a result, 58 other agents were dropped in Holland, all to be captured and mostly executed. In addition the Germans were given large quantities of secret radio equipment, guns, ammunition and supplies. Giskes later admitted that he was astonished at the success of his scheme and believed that some person or persons in SOE HQ must be helping him, though he had no idea of whom it could be. When *Englandspiel* was investigated after the war none of the SOE records were available and most were said to have been destroyed. The cold-blooded traitor who had sent over 50 people to their deaths had covered his traces well. A strange fact about this episode was that it only occurred in one section of the SOE division concerned with Holland. Other sectors were not affected. Giskes was also the Abwehr chief for Belgium and Northern France, but there were no similar occurrences there either.

In addition to the Abwehr, Germany also had the Gestapo (*Geheime Staatspolizei*) and the SD (*Sicherheitsdienst*). The Gestapo, the secret police, numbered 30,000 and was hated even by the Germans. It ran the concentration camps, had its own prisons, could torture and execute anyone of any rank or record; it massacred prisoners-of-war, and organised the extermination of the Jews and many other minorities. The closely-linked SD controlled information services, foreign spies, subversive activities in other countries and sabotage.

By the end of the war it had extended to controlling the Abwehr. SD numbered 6,000 agents.

In Russia there were two main intelligence organisations, the NKVD which later became the KGB, and the GRU, the Intelligence Directorate of the Soviet General Staff. The KGB (*Komitel Gosudarstvennoy Bezopasnosti*) is the Committee of State Security and previously exercised this function under earlier titles such as Cheka and OGPU. Whatever name it operated under, its range and activities were much the same. Although using every form of electronic and photographic device, the KGB was a firm believer in the value of the human factor. KGB agents were in every Russian embassy abroad and also, by subversion, often in the embassies of other countries too. In the years immediately before the outbreak of World War II, it had great success in recruiting intellectually gifted young men, usually of upper-middle-class background, who believed that they should support Marxism on the grounds that it represented a fairer system than the one in which they themselves enjoyed a privileged position. Features of the Soviet Union, such as a low standard of living, secret police, purges or travel restrictions were disregarded as being unavoidable anomalies in the development of the ideal, just state. Others were attracted to working for the KGB by hatred of German Nazism and Italian fascism, dislike of the structure of British society in which they themselves were 'have nots', or simply for money. In spite of its enormous power and range, the NKVD failed to appreciate that the Nazis were about to attack Russia in 1941. One of the most successful Russian spies was Richard Sorge, who had been born in Baku and served in the German army in World War I. After the war he took a degree in political science in Germany and became a journalist. Although a communist, he managed to join the Nazi party and soon became political adviser to the German ambassador in Tokyo. Sorge warned Stalin that the Germans were about to attack with 170 divisions on 20 June 1941 (the actual attack came two days later). The following August, Sorge reported to Moscow that the Japanese were planning to launch an attack in south-west Asia, and not in the direction of Russia as the Soviets had feared. In consequence, the Russians were able to withdraw many divisions from the Manchurian border and employ them against the German armies in the west. Two months later the Japanese arrested Sorge and a fellow agent and executed them both. In 1964 Sorge was declared a 'Hero of the Soviet Union'.

In 1939 the secret service in the United States was still in the small, neglected state to which it had been reduced after World War I. However, in July 1941 Roosevelt instructed his special envoy, Colonel William J. Donovan, to organise a department to collect and assess secret information. It was known as the OSS – Office of Strategic Services. Among Donovan's early recruits was Allen Dulles who later became head of the Central Intelligence Agency. Although Donovan obtained an Enigma machine, his department was only able to read diplomatic, not military, codes at that time, and therefore was not able to give firm warning of the attack on Pearl Harbor. However, as was shown in the course of the Pacific war, the OSS was soon reading Japanese codes and enabling US forces to anticipate Japan's every move. Among the OSS's major achievements was picking up a report on the developments at Peenemünde from a listening post established by Dulles in Switzerland. Working in close cooperation with the OSS was the FBI (Federal Bureau of Investigation). This liaison facilitated the arrest of various agents whom the Nazis had recruited in the United States.

In addition to the army of spies which were mentioned earlier as being in places all over south-east Asia in 1941, the Japanese had positioned many others in America, Canada and China. The most feared organisation in Japan was the Kempei Tai, which by the end of World War II numbered 75,000, one-third being officers. The Kempei worked closely with the Thought Police, which took careful note of potentially dangerous tendencies. Both units planted agents among the servants of any household wealthy enough to be able to employ them. Potential Marxists, defeatists, and people who had lived abroad were their special targets. One of their better known agents was Madame Nogami, a good-looking woman in her mid-thirties who acquired the nickname of 'Queen Cobra'. The Kempei were members of the army but usually worked in plain clothes. If the Kempei took an interest in anyone, even of high rank or status, it bode ill for them. The exact number of their tortures, beatings and executions is not known but was certainly enormous. They were particularly vicious during the final stages of the war, when they were combating what they believed was defeatism.

The British had no thought police, but they kept a watchful eye for potential enemies. Judging by the traitors who worked in positions of authority, they cannot have looked in all the right places. The principal branches of Military Intelligence were MI 5, which dealt with counter-intelligence, MI 6 which was concerned with overseas espionage, and MI 9, which helped overseas service personnel, such as shot-down airmen, to escape. There were equivalent branches of air and naval intelligence. Unfortunately some of the secret departments unknowingly employed spies who were passing information to the Rusians even when that country was allied to Nazi Germany. There were departments for using propaganda to undermine morale in enemy countries, and a very large organisation known as Special Operations Executive, which was referred to in relation to *Englandspiel*.

SOE was created in 1940 in response to Churchill's order 'Set Europe ablaze.' In its heyday it contained at least 10,000 employees, with a further 10,000 in loose association with it. There was some conflict between SOE, which specialized in working quietly and unobtrusively to collect intelligence and recruit resistance fighters to work later, and organisations such as the SAS and SBS (Special Boat Squadron), which concentrated on destroying vital equipment deep behind the enemy lines. When the SAS blew up a railway bridge, the Gestapo would descend on the district to interrogate (under duress) local people who were valuable sources of information and support for the SOE, much to the latter's dismay and annoyance. Section D, a branch of the SIS (Secret Intelligence Service) otherwise known as MI 6, also directed its main effort towards sabotage. The greatest triumph of SOE was undoubtedly the sinking of the heavy water on Lake Tinnisjoe in Norway, which frustrated German efforts to build an atomic bomb; there were also many smaller successes. An SOE agent was usually a man or woman who had lived for a long period in the country to which he or she was assigned, spoke the language fluently, and had nerves of steel. A captured agent was likely to meet a very unpleasant death, for torture invariably preceded execution.

Before being parachuted into the area to which they were assigned, agents would have been trained as burglars, lock-pickers, safe-blowers, demolition experts, and silent killers. As they would be working where no doctor would be readily available, they would also be given a grounding in medicine, and would be able to tackle minor surgery and dentistry. Unfortunately, many of the skills which were developed for SOE agents, as well as many of their material aids, have been used by terrorists subsequently for less creditable reasons. An SOE agent never knew whether his or her assignment would be in a jungle, mountains, town or country. Some of the areas where they were required to work were unhealthy in more ways than one. Agents relied on not being betrayed by those among whom they moved. People in occupied Europe never knew when they went to bed whether there would be a knock on the door in the middle of the night and at least one member of the household would be taken away for 'questioning'. People who were removed in this way would probably be tortured, perhaps sent to a concentration camp, or executed inside the prison. Whenever there was an act of sabotage, the local people would be very closely interrogated by the Gestapo.

Dangerous, lonely and difficult though SOE work was, there never seemed to be a shortage of volunteers. Some of the best agents, both inside and outside SOE, were women. They often acted as couriers and if caught carrying messages had no chance of bluffing their captors. That fact, however, did not save them from being tortured to extract further information. Four British women who were captured were pushed into furnaces while still alive.

As the war progressed, resistance groups grew larger and more daring, in spite of the brutalities and atrocities of the Gestapo. Many young Frenchmen joined the Maquis and lived in the woods and mountains when the Germans started deporting males of military age for work in Germany. In spite of Hitler's bland promise that his wish was to work in friendly co-operation with Britain, the Nazis had made plans to deport any male between 16 and 45 to work on the continent if Germany carried out a successful invasion.

Of the local forces who worked with SOE the best organised and most dedicated were those with strong communist or nationalist sympathies. A number of SOE agents were themselves left-wing oriented and therefore did not inform their superiors how strong this element was. But even if they had, it is not easy to see what the British govenrment could have done about it; in the middle of a desperate struggle one can hardly start asking one's helpers their political views and then refuse to accept their help if these are not orthodox. In Malaya, where the anti-Japanese group included many Chinese communists, SOE was well aware that many of the supplies parachuted to them had been spirited away for use by the communists after the war with Japan was over. Supplies of arms and ammunition which fell outside the target area were usually reported lost. Yugoslavia and Greece also presented problems, even when the war was far from over. In the former there were two main forces of resistance, the Chetniks under Mihailovich, and the partisans under Tito. Mihailovich initially inflicted considerable damage on the German army of occupation, but when he realised that they would be succeeded by Tito's partisans, ardent communists with strong Russian links, he decided that if he could reach an accommodation with the Nazis this would be the lesser of the two evils. Not unnaturally, the British government then stopped aid to Mihailovich, who soon afterwards was captured by the communists and executed. In the last year of the war and afterwards, the Allies had considerable trouble preventing Tito extending his territories into former Italian possessions. Eventually however Tito objected to being under Russian orders and broke off relations with the Soviet Union. He then became nonaligned, driving hard bargains with East and West, each of which hoped to influence him.

Greece had fought well against the Italians and the Germans, had been occupied, and was eventually liberated. The monarchy was to be restored, but this did not suit the communists. There were three conflicting groups in Greece, much to the dismay of the OSS which had been very active there. ELAS, the military wing of the National Liberation Front EAM, wanted to establish a communist government; EDES wanted a republic, but not a communist one. EDES assisted Britain and was supplied with arms to do so; ELAS, on the other hand, was using its arms to attack EDES, so Britain cut off further supplies. However ELAS now found the Germans would supply them with arms and, using these, captured parts of Athens and Piraeus. Dislodging ELAS from this area required two British divisions, which had to be withdrawn from the Italian front for the purpose. In January 1945, ELAS agreed to a truce and all but a few hard core members, who retreated to the mountains to fight on, settled under the restored monarchy.

Few SOE agents would have guessed that their training, which was mainly in weapon handling, would eventually place them in situations where diplomatic skills would be even more important. Presenting an Albanian professional bandit with a modern weapon in the hope that he would use it to kill Germans sometimes meant that he practised his skills by killing off a few enemies of his own choosing first. Discipline was not the strongest aspect of the partisan guerrilla philosophy.

At the end of the war, huge numbers of arms of all types fell into the hands of those whose inclinations were rarely peaceful. In the Far East, many Japanese soldiers handed over weapons to people likely to cause trouble to the victors; we have mentioned the communists in Malaya, where the Malayan Peoples' Anti-Japanese Army promptly changed its name to the Malayan Peoples' Anti-British Army; and there were similar situations in Indonesia, Burma, and Indo-China.

A feature of World War II was that there were apparently numerous groups all independently trying to help win the war. Sometimes these changed their function without changing their name. Thus the Long Range Desert Group, which had begun its life in 1940 with the task of obtaining information about the enemy (then Italian) in the Western Desert. It could raid and fight, but intelligence gathering was its primary function. When the Special Air Service was formed in 1941, with the primary object of destroying German aircraft on the ground, the LRDG co-operated closely with it. The two units were often confused, but were totally different. When the North African war was over, the LRDG was sent to the Adriatic to engage in guerrilla work in Albania, Yugoslavia, Italy and Greece, where desert was conspicuously absent. It had no connection with the LRPG, the Long Range Penetration Group, which was the official name of the Chindits in Burma.

The most renowned of these 'private armies', as they came to be called, was the SAS, some of whose activities have already been described. Its founder, David Stirling, was captured in North Africa, but before that he had laid down firm directions about how the regiment should be run. Its best work, destroying 350 German aircraft on the ground, was undoubtedly done in the desert, but subsequently it performed useful work in Italy, France, Belgium, Holland and Germany. Its sub-unit, the Special Boat Squadron, performed a very important task in the Greek islands, harassing the German and Italian occupation forces so consistently that the Axis powers had to keep thousands of men stationed there; those troops would have been invaluable to the Axis in Italy or France. The art of war is to make one's opponent waste his resources by dispersing them, and the SBS were ideal for doing this. Another totally separate unit also entitled 'the Special Boat Service', was a small team of canoeists which entered Bordeaux harbour in December 1942 and blew up four German ships with limpet mines. These were affectionately called 'The Cockleshell Heroes'.

World War II was a war of 'private armies' and special units. Some, like the American 'Merrill's Marauders' in Burma and the British 'Phantom' in Europe, were official, though secret, units; others, too numerous to mention, were created for special sabotage or liaison missions and vanished without trace as soon as they had succeeded – or failed. The services usually referred to special units as 'the funnies'.

Perhaps the most bizarre unit was the Twenty Committee. The Twenty (XX) implied the Double Cross, and was set up for the purpose of 'turning' German spies. Its chairman was

J. C. Masterman, an Oxford don who had been interned in Germany during World War I and knew a lot about German thought processes. He was also a superb athlete whose team usually seemed to win.

The Double Cross Committee claimed to have captured every spy who set foot in the British Isles. This may have been facilitated by Admiral Canaris, for many of the German spies had out-of-date ration cards, obviously forged passports, and inadequate radio equipment. One of the earlier spies who parachuted in had a genuine German Frankfurter sausage in his rations. Another, who had not been very well briefed, went to the public house and tried to buy a drink at 9 a.m. Arrested spies were given the option of working for their captors, or being shot: some chose the latter alternative, but most co-operated willingly. One performed so well that he was awarded a MBE by the British and an Iron Cross by the Germans, who were greatly impressed by the bogus information he had sent them.

The spies who had been turned were given bizarre code names such as 'Tricycle'. In their new rôle ingenious cover-stories were built up for them; the Germans were not unaware they might have been persuaded to change their allegiance, and their reports did not have to be too perfect. Sometimes the XX Committee recruited fictional helpers for the turned spies. Garbo, the winner of the MBE, had originally planned to be a double agent and to work from Lisbon, but soon decided to work solely for Britain. He played an important part in confirming Hitler's belief that the invasion of Europe, when it came, would be in the Pas de Calais.

The secret war was by no means one-sided: as we have seen, the Germans, the Italians and the Japanese had notable successes too. Otto 'Scarface' Skorzeny snatched Mussolini from his mountain prison in a daring operation using gliders and a Fieseler-Storch aircraft, much to the chagrin and annoyance of the Allies. On both sides men and women accomplished deeds which would previously have been thought impossible. Shot-down airmen walked their way back to their own lines under conditions which might have been thought unendurable. Two members of the SAS walked an incredible distance in the Western Desert. In 1942, David Sillito, then a private, was cut off from his unit near Tobruk. During the next seven days he walked 180 miles, drinking what dew he could find and his own urine. At night, when it was cooler, he navigated by the stars. Tom Langton led a small group 350 miles, but they did have some help from friendly Arabs on the journey. One British soldier, Denis Martin, swam 14 miles to Turkey when Leros was captured by the Germans, although he had never swum such a distance before.

Unfortunately, as we have seen, partisan activities against occupation forces often brought horrifying reprisals. In May 1942, Heydrich, head of the Nazi Secret Police and deputy head of the SS, was ambushed and killed by Czech partisans. In retaliation the Nazis destroyed the two nearby villages of Lidice and Lezaky, killed all the male inhabitants, shot thousands of hostages and sent thousands of men and women to concentration camps. The Czechs and Slovaks paid a fearful price for resistance activities; over 350,000 died in battle, by execution, or in concentration camps.

Another major atrocity was at the Vercors. The Vercors is a plateau, south of Grenoble, which had been made the headquarters of a French resistance group in 1944. It held 3,000 Maquis when it was attacked by 10,000 Germans with superior arms. The Germans then murdered all the men and raped all the women they could find. The French felt that the Allies could have done more to help and saw this as a betrayal; the Allies felt that the concentration on the Vercors had come too soon and that they could not be blamed for what had happened.

When a German company commander was shot by a sniper in Oradour-sur-Vayres, the SS descended on Oradour-sur-Glane, which was 15 miles away. The population was herded into the square, and the women and children were sent into the church. The men were all shot and the church was set on fire. Nearly 700 died. Although another explanation for this callous massacre has been put forward recently there seems no reason to accept it in place of the account given here. But even this did not stop the resistance, which was later to take a more decisive part in the war.

10

INTO THE FIFTH YEAR

By mid-1944 the war had been grinding along for nearly five years, but was still far from over. Five years is a long time. The reader will appreciate this more if he or she imagines a war breaking out today and lasting for six years, as World War II did. It has been said that war consists of short intervals of acute fear between long periods of intense boredom. This is an imperfect definition. Certainly if one was caught in a bombing attack, was heavily shelled, or was in close contact with the enemy, the tension would be acute; however, the emotion was of heightened apprehension rather than fear, which is a negative emotion. Some people lived for years in conditions which were always dangerous and at times became desperate: they included crews of bombers and fighters, sailors, soldiers on campaigns such as those in Burma or in Italy (which lasted for years without much relief), and 'loners' working in special forces, who could betray themselves by one false move. Boredom did not come from having nothing to do, although entertainments were severely restricted, but from being prevented from living a normal life. Everywhere one went there were uniforms: civilian clothing for those still able to wear it also had a uniform look, for wartime restrictions prohibited anything fancy or extravagant. Even those lucky enough to have had a large wardrobe before 1939 were in 1944 ruefully wondering how much more garments could be patched and repaired. The wartime diet in Britain was healthy but monotonous: tea, meat, butter, eggs, cheese and bacon (about one rasher a week) were all rationed, and in many homes fair distribution and consumption was assured by each member of a family having his or her individual portion for the week placed separately on the table. Although no one realised it at the time, rationing in Britain was going to continue for several years after the war. Some people were the recipients of occasional food parcels sent from abroad, from America, Canada, New Zealand, South Africa or Australia. Many familes grew vegetables on allotments, kept chickens or rabbits, and tried to brew beer. One of the problems with producing supplementary food was that it often required other heavily valued ingredients to make it possible: beer, for example, requires yeast and malt; chickens require meal as well as household scraps. In any case, most people were so careful not to waste any edible food that 'left-overs' virtually disappeared. Cautionary posters and advertisements were everywhere: one stated, 'If you waste a scrap of bread, a sailor's life is on your head.'

Food rationing gave shopkeepers an importance they had never previously experienced. But shopkeepers were not alone in enjoying their new prestige and authority. As some 15,000 minor laws were created each year of the war, petty officialdom flourished. As Shakespeare put it:

> But man, proud man
> Drest in a little brief authority . . .
> Plays such fantastic tricks before high heaven
> As makes the angels weep

Scarcities ensured that there were queues for everything. An Oxford wit remarked that if you see a queue you should join it regardless of what it might be for and until you reached the end you never know whether you will be buying a pound of potatoes or becoming a blood donor.

The BBC was the fount of wisdom, instruction, advice and entertainment. Early in the war, the news ceased to be read by an anonymous voice: instead the readers identified themselves, so that the public would become familiar with their names and voices. This was in case the Germans should ever capture a radio station and try to give out false information. In occupied countries, listening to BBC broadcasts, which at that time were regarded as models of impartiality, was forbidden. Offenders faced severe penalties.

Radio entertainment produced a new range of 'stars';
notable among them was Tommy Handley, a comedian. For
the services ENSA – the Entertainments National Service
Association – toured with teams of actors and actresses,
singers and entertainers. Some teams went very close to the
front line in places like Burma. Vera Lynn was a very popular
singer, who blended the right notes of nostalgia and hope.
Although many books had been destroyed in the blitz and
few were published during the war, reading flourished.
Novelists like Anthony Trollope, writing of peaceful cathedral cloisters, were especially popular. Paper, of course, was
rationed and so the daily newspapers became thinner and
flimsier. The shortages never seemed to affect the Ministry of
Information or Ministry of Food (which had a Director of
Tea and a Director of Sugar). The Ministry of Information
was meant to raise morale, but for many produced a cynical
chuckle. It was staffed by journalists and writers, but was
generally thought to be an enormous waste of money.

The Army Bureau of Current Affairs sent lecturers and
pamphlets to various camps and sites. It was regarded with
suspicion by some officers, as so many of the lecturers used
the opportunity to explain how much better life would be
post-war than pre-war if a Labour government was elected.
The service vote was subsequently said to be responsible for
Churchill's losing the election which took place in July 1945.
In retrospect it seems surprising that an election could have
been called when the war in the Far East was still continuing.
However, in spite of the impact made by the loss of Malaya,
Burma, Singapore, Borneo and Indonesia, the war in the Far
East never caught the public interest to the same degree as
the much closer war around the Mediterranean. The 14th
Army, which fought for year after year in Burma, referred to
itself as 'The Forgotten Army'. Far Eastern prisoners-of-war
were unable to correspond with their families at home. Some
PoWs received a few letters, others none at all; in reply they
were allowed to send two printed postcards in three and a
half years. Many were already dead when those bleak cards
were delivered to their families.

Although by 1944 the Japanese leaders could no longer
hope to avoid defeat, they intended to make the Allies pay

dearly for their victory. When the worst came to the worst, every Japanese was expected to die for the Emperor and the homeland. Similarly, many of the German leaders now thought that the Fatherland would ultimately be crushed between the Russian juggernaut and the firepower of the West, but dared not voice their opinion. Hitler, who was becoming more and more morose, had not given up hope of victory entirely, for he felt that one of his wonderful new weapons might easily turn the tables. The German army was still formidable; it was fighting a dogged battle in Italy, was making the Russians pay a price for their advances, and could even yet inflict a shattering blow on the armies of the West. Europe from Norway to central Italy and the French coast, was still in German hands. However Germany, like Britain, was beginning to run short of manpower. Britain mobilized the highest percentage of its population of all the combatants, a total of over four million, and those citizens who were not in the services were working in various forms of production for the war effort: farms, factories, mines or transport. Women, who had startled the country by becoming train drivers in World War I, were now driving the heaviest vehicles as well as piloting heavy bombers across the Atlantic. The list of reserved occupations, once very long, had been drastically reduced. Periodically the ministries and the BBC were combed for reluctant young men of military age, who to their dismay found themselves destined for the infantry.

The fortunes of the Russian front were of much greater interest than the Far East to the average member of the British public, even though he or she had little conception of the vast numbers and huge distances involved. Russian forces, now greatly strengthened by enormous shipments from America, outnumbered the Germans in some areas by two-to-one. In addition, their tanks, guns and aircraft were, with few exceptions, superior to those of the Germans. Two events had shown that the longer the war went on, the more it turned in the favour of the Russians. The first was the battle of Kursk, the second the relief of Leningrad.

Kursk, which had taken place in July 1943, was the greatest tank battle which the world had ever seen. Hitler had decided that a crushing victory in Russia was necessary for all-round morale, and therefore assembled an army which included 17 Panzer divisions. Among these were the élite names, such as Das Reich, Gross Deutschland and SS Totenkopf. The Kursk salient offered an excellent chance to break right through the Russian lines, and the new Tiger tank seemed ideal for the purpose. Unfortunately for the Germans, a great deal went wrong with their plans. The Tigers, with their massive frontal armour and 120 mm guns, broke through easily enough but then found themselves isolated; their supporting elements, smaller tanks and infantry, had been held up, mainly by mines. Although the Tigers were un-equalled at engaging targets at long distances, they had no machine-guns for dealing with close-quarter attacks. Rain and mud held up the advance in another sector. After a final, gruelling, eight-hour battle, the Panzers were withdrawn. The German generals expected there would now be a pause during which they could re-group, but it was not to be. The Russians followed up relentlessly, re-taking Kharkov and Poltava, and even crossing the Dnieper in October. The Germans were astonished at this breaching of their defences along the river which they had seen as their East Wall.

However the Russian army was still pressing on. In November 1943 it captured Kiev. In March 1944, the siege of Leningrad was finally lifted. Although at times the Germans checked the advancing Red Army, the first six months of 1944 saw an almost continuous retreat. Odessa fell in April and Sebastopol in May. By June the Russians were on the border of Finland. But the price of these contests was high. The Russians lost an average 15,000 dead every day they fought against the German army and by June 1944 that drain on manpower was beginning to tell. Even so, exhausted and weakened though their armies were, the Soviets kept up the pressure. Their generals had made numerous tactical mis-takes in the past, and had learned from them quickly or been removed. The German generals had learnt many lessons too, but were usually prevented from using their knowledge by Hitler's interference.

When the Russians once more launched an offensive on 23 June 1944, Hitler refused to allow his troops to fall back even where they had been bypassed and where it was vital to straighten the line and close the gaps. By this time the Russians had nearly 150,000 partisans behind the German lines, thus effectively ensuring that vital supplies did not reach the troops who urgently needed them. At intervals, isolated German troops were captured in pincer movements and on 3 July 1944 huge pincers closed around Minsk, inflicting another 100,000 German casualties. As the Russians pressed on, freeing Belorussia, these German casualties mounted to 350,000, though many of them were prisoners-of-war. Vilna fell on 13 July, Brest-Litovsk (the scene of the humiliating peace the Germans had imposed on Russia in World War I) fell on 28 July. The Red Army was now deep into Poland.

But even with the Russians poised to invade Germany, the war in Europe still had nearly another year to run. The war in the Far East would last even longer and then would only finish because a master weapon was used. The despair of the German people, who were bombed nightly and now knew of the approaching Russian army, did not seem to worry Hitler. His new master weapon the V1 rocket had just been brought into use and even at this late stage, he believed, would ensure that the Fatherland would emerge as the ultimate victor. By now he and his immediate entourage dared not contemplate surrender: they realised what their own fate would be when the full Nazi atrocities were revealed. If defeat became inevitable, they would all go down in the final cataclysm – a truly Wagnerian finale. But even now the Nazis still pursued their domestic policies relentlessly. Jews and prisoners of other nationalities who had worked till they could work no more were killed by the thousand in concentration camps. Many of the victims were nearly dead from starvation and brutality before being herded into the gas chambers.

A second great blow had fallen on Germany on 6 June 1944. The long-expected Allied invasion of France had begun.

II
D DAY AND AFTER

As mentioned earlier, planning for the return to Europe had begun even as the last remnants of the BEF were being evacuated from France in June 1940. As France had fallen, Russia was still Germany's ally, Mussolini had joined forces with Hitler by invading France and America was neutral, the War Office's decision to begin plans for invading Europe seems to have been somewhat optimistic. Nevertheless, it was a perfectly reasonable step to take. If Britain was to win the war one day, the continent must be invaded. Planning for that must begin, even though Britain seemed to be in imminent danger of invasion herself.

The obvious place for a landing in Europe appeared to be Calais, which had a port, was only 21 miles away from the British coast, and would be an ideal point from which to begin an offensive drive towards Berlin. However, if Calais was the obvious place, the Germans, in due course, would take appropriate steps to give an invasion force a very warm reception in that area. As the months passed, the British planners pondered how best to encourage the Germans to believe that, at some time in the future, Britain would strike back at Calais, while at the same time examining the possibility of an invasion at some other point on the French coast. For an invasion to be successful, it would be necessary to capture a port at a very early stage and thus enable the heavier guns, tanks, and other supplies to come ashore in the appropriate quantity. However, the experience of the force which raided Dieppe in 1942 showed that capturing a port from the sea was an enterprise fraught with danger and uncertainty.

In view of the disaster at Dieppe and the subsequent more satisfactory experiences in the North African and Sicily landings, it was decided that the safest approach would be over open beaches, but at a point near enough to a port to enable that desirable objective to be captured from the landward side at the earliest possible opportunity. After considerable debate, the area between the River Orne and the Vire estuary, a stretch of beach some 50 miles wide, was chosen. This point would enable half the invasion force to swing right and capture Cherbourg, while the other half swung left and captured Le Havre. This manoeuvre looked like being easier to plan than to execute. In the event Cherbourg was captured, but Le Havre held out for a long time.

During 1942 and 1943 intrepid canoeists were brought close inshore by submarine, landed, and took samples of the surfaces of the proposed landing beaches. This was to ensure that the terrain would be solid enough to take the weight of tanks and other vehicles.

Astonishingly, the secret of the invasion area was kept, although 189,000 maps had to be prepared for the day. There were several near misses. Once several maps were blown out of a window on to the pavement of St James's Square; on another occasion a truck loaded with D Day maps overturned on a road near Salisbury. All were recovered without any unauthorised person getting a glimpse of them.

The main problem of the landings was to put ashore sufficient troops to defeat the Germans confronting them, but not in such concentrations that they would strangle themselves in the bottlenecks they created, and thus form an easy target for the opposition. The second problem was to transport enough divisions to ensure that, once in France, the invasion force would not be pushed back into the sea.

The naval part of the operation was given the code name of 'Neptune'; the landings were 'Overlord'. In retrospect, and possibly at the time, these code names seem transparently thin. For the landings two armies would be used, the American 1st Army under Lieutenant-General Omar Bradley, and the British 2nd Army under Lieutenant-General Sir Miles Dempsey. The joint armies were commanded by General Bernard Montgomery until the troops were established ashore and called 21st Army Group. After that, Eisenhower would take supreme command and Montgomery would command 1st Army only. Bradley would continue to command 2nd Army. This was a political decision, for in spite of Montgomery's greater experience it was important to have an American in eventual overall command. Eisenhower was extremely good at creating harmony between the diverse elements which made up the Allied Expeditionary Force, and equally important was the fact that he would make sure the AEF obtained its fair share of American resources; there was a well-founded suspicion that a disproportionate quantity of these was being allocated to the Pacific.

For Neptune the commanders were all British: Montgomery as mentioned, Admiral Sir Bernard Ramsay in charge of the navies, and Air Chief Marshal Sir Trafford Leigh-Mallory in charge of the air forces. The assault force was to consist of 37 divisions (each division averaging 15,000 men). The armies, of course, included much more than men: tanks, guns, and equipment for engineers, signals, medical services, and many other units all had a place in the vast armada. SHAEF (Supreme Headquarters Allied Expeditionary Force) knew that the Germans had 60 divisions to defend the coast, but they were extended over a wide area. This made the deception plan vital.

Von Runstedt felt that the German divisions were trying to cover too wide a front and suggested that they would be wise to withdraw to a shorter line just outside the German frontier. Hitler would not hear of this and sent Rommel to command the troops in France, while leaving von Runstedt in overall command. Von Runstedt believed the best policy would be to let the Allies get a large proportion of their forces ashore, then to destroy them with a massive counter-attack. Rommel would have preferred to launch the full German effort against the Allies as they came onto the beaches. The result was a compromise in which German infantry were positioned well forward, while the armour was held back. These disagreements and dispositions were known to the Allies through the Enigma intercepts.

In an invasion the incoming commander holds an initial advantage, for he can choose his entry point on a long range of coastline which cannot possibly be defended in depth along its entire length. However, once he lands, the defence will be able to mass much larger numbers than the attacker can hope to put ashore in the early stages. Knowing that Hitler had decided that the Calais area would be their designated landing area, the Allies did their utmost to strengthen that belief. One of their many ways of doing this was to arrange for a totally convincing service of messages to be sent by the XX spy 'Garbo'. In addition there was a huge radio deception plan which created mythical divisions in East Anglia and Kent; the regiment mainly responsible for this was 'Phantom', originally a 'private army' created early in the war, but now a recognised unit with the official title of GHQ Liaison Regiment. The Calais area was also closely recon-noitred by the RAF – and bombed – so that there could be no doubt in the minds of the German General Staff that the main attack would be in and around this port.

If any German aircraft had been able to penetrate the British defences and take a look at the south and west of England, a very different view would have been formed. Everywhere from Dorset to Portsmouth there were huge concentrations of troops, vehicles, tanks, and guns. Well camouflaged though these camps were, a photographic reconnaissance would probably have disclosed that some-thing very unusual was happening. In fact, the area 10 miles along the coast inland had been sealed off and elaborate precautions were taken to ensure that no secrets were betrayed by letters from soldiers to their families or girl-friends. The most difficult objects to conceal were the large numbers of ships and landing craft: 76 per cent of these were British.

The landing craft, which varied in design according to their purpose, were a British invention but had subsequently been manufactured in large numbers in the US. Some carried infantry, some tanks, some vehicles, and some dock machinery. They were flat-bottomed, so that they could come close in to the shore. The aim was to carry these landing craft across the Channel on larger ships, then unload them as close to the shore as possible, so that they could complete the journey under their own power. On the day of the landings, as discussed later, one of the American units took heavy casualties because the commander assumed that it would be better to unload from the larger ships into the assault craft while these were still out of range of the majority of the gunfire from the shore. He did not realise that the Channel can be one of the most unpredictable and dangerous seas in the world and, in consequence, a large number of Americans were drowned before they even heard a bullet.

Among the assault force were a number of Rhino ferries: these were 400-ton steel rafts which were used for unloading LSTs (Landing Ship Tanks) in deep water. The LSTs then made their way to the shore, lowered their ramps, and sent their cargoes on their way. As the ships approached the beaches they were liable to meet what was known as 'Rommel's asparagus'. This ingenious hazard consisted of numerous stakes which would be covered at high tide (when an invasion force would have to land): on to each was tied enough high explosive to sink any craft unlucky enough to encounter it, as many did. One of the first tasks of the Royal Engineers of the assault force was to swim to these stakes and immobilize the explosive charges; it was not the sort of assignment their families and friends would have cared to witness.

Before the first soldier set foot on the Normandy beaches there had been years of thought, discussion and preparation. This had eventually resulted in a plan to secure the flanks of the armies by two airborne assaults and then make the first landings on five chosen beaches. The right wing of the assault was allotted to the Americans, whose airborne forces would drop around Carentan before their armies came ashore on Utah and Omaha beaches; on the left, the British 6th Airborne would come down on the left flank, and their troops would come in on Gold, Juno and Sword beaches. The airborne forces were to protect the newly landed ground troops from a sudden assault on the flank; they were also given the task of holding certain roads and bridges so that the Germans could not blow them up and prevent the armies from advancing into the interior. In the event, both airborne forces were much disrupted by bad weather.

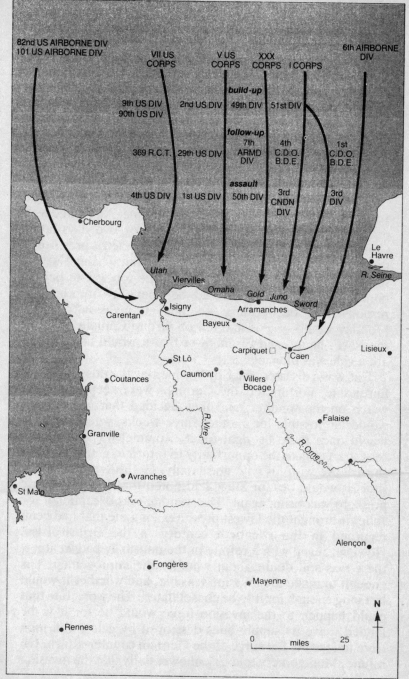

D Day Landings

Weather had been the unpredictable factor in the plan for the invasion. In theory, the beginning of June should produce long, sunny days and calm seas; in practice, it rarely does. However, June was unlikely to produce a long period of bad weather, and if the invasion could take place as planned there would, at least in theory, be ample time for the invading army to be in Germany by late autumn. With reasonable luck campaigning would be complete before the winter had set in and presumably the Germans would by then have sur-rendered.

The landing was originally planned for Monday, 5 June 1944. On that date the tide would be suitable. All looked well on 3 June, but that was no guarantee for two days later. Conditions on 5 June depended on the barometric pressure in the Azores on the 3rd: if that was low, the Channel would soon be in turmoil, the clouds would be too low to permit bombing and the wind would be above 18 m.p.h. The responsibility of deciding whether an invasion on that Monday would be possible fell on Group Captain Stagg of the RAF: he advised Eisenhower that it would not. On the 4th a gale was blowing.

This was a disaster, since by Wednesday the tides would be unsuitable. Fortunately the Germans were keeping a close watch on the weather, and they decided that no invasion would be possible for another three weeks, when the tides would once more be right for it. Rommel was sufficiently reassured to take the opportunity to return to Germany for a short leave with his wife and family. He little realised how short it would be, for Stagg had noted that the barometric pressure was rising again. The weather was exceptional for June: it brought the lowest pressures for June that had been recorded in the twentieth century in the British Isles. However, even with a respite in the unusually bad weather, there was still doubt about whether the improvement was enough to make the invasion feasible, and whether it would last long enough for it to be consolidated. The worst fate that could happen to the invasion force would be for it to be landed, have its supply lines destroyed by gales, and then have to face the full surge of the German counter-attack. On 4 June, Montgomery told Eisenhower flatly that the invasion was simply not possible and must be postponed indefinitely. Eisenhower postponed it for 24 hours. The following day at his briefing conference, he informed his senior commanders of Stagg's opinion. It was now clear that the weather was improving, but no one could predict how fast or for how long. He turned to Montgomery. 'What do you think?' he asked. 'We'll go,' said Montgomery. Eisenhower was astonished. The greatest gamble of the war was now in train.

Like the battle of Waterloo, the battle of Normandy was a very close thing. The American airborne force, consisting of 82nd and 101st Divisions, a total of 12,000 men, ran into considerable difficulties in the low cloud and even more when it landed in flooded fields. Many of the parachutists fell into mud and water and, being weighed down by their heavy equipment, were drowned. Nevertheless the divisions captured most of their objectives and prevented the German 91st Division from counter-attacking when the American landings took place on Utah beach a few hours later. The British 6th Airborne on the other flank also had its share of troubles. One of its tasks was to capture two bridges near Benouville, one over the River Orne and the other over the canal; both were vital to Montgomery's plan for breaking out of the beachhead. The bridges had been wired for demolition by the Germans: they were also strongly defended. However, in spite of strong cross winds, a force of two hundred men travelling in six gliders crash-landed on the night of 5/6 June and secured them. Other parachutists and gliders came down in the surrounding countryside and reinforced the position. Anti-tank guns were set up, to meet the expected attack from 21st Panzer Division. Five bridges over the Dives, which the Germans hoped to use, were blown up, and the Merville battery, which commanded the beaches, was also put out of action.

The fact that all this took place in the wind, rain and darkness makes it something of a miracle. A number of the 6th Airborne gliders had blown off course, high winds had deposited many parachutists up to seven miles from their planned objectives; some gliders never reached France at all, for their tow ropes had snapped in the high winds and they had come down in the Channel.

As the troops poured ashore in the early hours of 6 June, they met mixed fortunes. 36,000 Americans, destined for Utah beach on the Cotentin peninsula, relied on two patrol and one radar boat for guidance, but one patrol boat was sunk and the radar boat fouled its propeller. Without the radar boat, the American convoy was unable to fix its position and, caught by a strong tide, landed a mile south of their planned destination. This mishap turned out to be a blessing in disguise; for the loss of 12 men killed and 100 wounded they landed thousands of men and their equipment. An inspired decision by their commander, the 57-year-old Brigadier-General Theodore Roosevelt, then took them straight inland instead of trying to work back to their original destination.

Less fortunate were the Americans who tried to land at Omaha beach to the east of Isigny. Although the German High Command thought the likely invasion point would be Calais, this had not caused them to neglect the defences along the rest of the coastline facing Britain. Thousands of men of all nationalities had been conscripted as forced labour to build gun emplacements, forts, bunkers and blockhouses all along the shore and at the more vulnerable points these defences extended far inland. At Omaha there were eight concrete bunkers full of all types of guns, and in front of them 35 anti-tank guns and 85 machine-guns. Barbed wire and mines filled the gaps between the gun sites. The villages behind Omaha were also bristling with fortifications and guns.

Because of this range of firepower, the American admiral decided it would be best to lower their landing craft 12 miles offshore. Many of the boats were swamped and others were driven well off course. One of the more brilliant innovations for D Day was the DD (Duplex Drive) amphibious tank. This was an ingenious method of enabling tanks to float in the water by surrounding them with canvas. However, the canvas was not capable of withstanding the battering it received from the seas off Omaha and 27 of the 29 American tanks sank. This left the assaulting infantry without the support of armour.

That was not the only disaster which befell the Americans

at Omaha that day. A naval force which had been given the task of saturating the German defence with rockets made a mistake in its navigation and moved eastwards along the Channel when it should have been going in the opposite direction. No explanation of this appalling error was ever given, but it meant that when the ships came back, hours later, having realised their mistake, thousands of Americans had been slaughtered.

Meanwhile, 10 landing craft sank on the way in: others, driven off course by the tide, landed at points not protected by American covering fire. Even when they reached the beach in the face of murderous German fire, they were unable to force their way inland; their commanders had refused to accept the specialised British vehicles for dealing with hazards such as mine-fields, anti-tank ditches, and barbed wire. It had been thought, incorrectly, that the weight of firepower from the sea in the preliminary bombardment would have made these additions unnecessary. Although the Americans in the Pacific were making good use of flame-throwers, they had not visualized them as being necessary on the Normandy beaches. The only asset the Americans had on Omaha beach was courage, and there was no shortage of that. The American commander, General Huebner, remained cool in the face of impending total disaster. He put in more infantry and arranged for them to be given a powerful covering barrage as they edged their way inland. By the end of that long day the US forces had established a bridgehead four miles long and in places two miles deep, but it had cost 3,000 casualties. At one stage it had looked as if the invasion force might be pushed right back into the sea, but fortunately the Germans had decided that a full strength counter-attack was unnecessary. By the time they realised their mistake ammunition was running short in their forward defences and Allied bombing was preventing fresh supplies from reaching them.

The British 30 Corps had been assigned Gold beach which had Arromanches at the centre point. The sea was very rough in this area, but the troops got ashore with the minimum of dislocation. Even so, a number of their landing craft were damaged or sunk on the under-water obstacles. The initial landings were not at Arromanches itself, where the museum now stands, but came in from the left flank to capture the town. However, Arromanches would shortly become a place of enormous importance. By the end of the first day, British troops had already reached the outskirts of Bayeux, six miles inland. Juno and Sword beaches came under the command of 1 British Corps, Juno being assigned to 3 Canadian Division, and Sword to 3 British Division and 1 and 4 Canadian Brigades. This was the area which the Germans now attacked with 21 Panzer and 711 Infantry Divisions. The aim of the invaders here was to reach Caen by the end of the first day and to take it on the second; in the event, the capture of Caen took a month.

Although some of the troops taking part in the landings were what had become known as veterans, implying soldiers of some experience rather than old men, the majority were going into action for the first time. Innocence on the battlefield can be a valuable commodity. Inexperienced troops will often rush forward and capture a position – if they are not annihilated in the process – while hardened warriors will take a more cautious approach and probably fail to gain any ground at all.

The most important gain of the day was Arromanches, which was eminently suitable for one of the great engineering triumphs of the war: Mulberry Harbour. Knowing that they were unlikely to capture a substantial port immediately after landing, the Allies decided to take an artificial one with them. Mulberry, of which portions may still be seen at Arromanches today (1988), stemmed from an idea of Churchill's dating back to 1915. In 1942 he recalled his earlier thoughts and three 'Mulberries' were built. The one at Vierville which was to be used by the Americans was wrecked by a storm and one for Cherbourg was unsatisfactory and was not used. The one at Arromanches was a triumphant success. It weighed a million tons, was two-thirds of a mile long, and handled cargoes of 680,000 tons, 40,000 vehicles, and half a million men. The Germans never suspected the existence of Mulberries, which had taken eight months to build and the construction of which had employed 20,000 men. The outer line of the Arromanches Mulberry consisted of breakwaters made by filling sixty obsolete ships with thousands of tons of concrete and sinking them. Inside the perimeter was a series of caissons, weighing up to 6,000 tons each; they were towed across the Channel by powerful tugs, then sunk in position. Inside there were jetties and wharves made of pontoons. In all a Mulberry provided everything which a port could provide: even exit roads over the sands were laid and consisted either of coconut matting or prefabricated metal mats. This Mulberry could defend itself from aerial attack by means of Bofors guns, and had the storage capacity of the port at Dover.

The Mulberries were not the only miracle produced at this time. In order to supply the invasion force with the vast quantity of fuel it would require, a pipeline was built to stretch from the Isle of Wight to Cherbourg. The code name for this was Pluto (Pipeline under the Ocean). Later, one was laid from Dungeness to Boulogne.

Fortunately for the Allies, Hitler clung obstinately to his obsession that the main landings would take place in the Calais area. Even when the Normandy bridgehead was firmly established, Hitler and his obedient Higher Command were convinced that this could only be a diversion designed to draw the German army away from the Calais area. Among the nearby German troops the confusion which comes from hurried decisions reigned. It is expressed by the army as: Order, counter-order = disorder. Although 21st Panzer had begun an attack on 6th Airborne, this was changed for it to meet the thrust towards Caen. Once in its new position it held up the British advance, but by then it had failed in its primary task which should have been to drive the invaders back into the sea. Rommel, who had returned rapidly from leave, still hoped to put in a counter-attack, but the headquarters of Panzer Group West was heavily bombed on 10 June and most of its staff officers were killed. On the first day of the landings 156,000 men had come ashore for the remarkably small total of 9,000 casualties. By 12 June, the invasion force had been built up to 326,547 men with their transport and stores. However by now the German resistance was better organised and the Allies had still not reached Caen. But they were ashore, and just in time.

On 13 June at 4.13 a.m., the first flying bomb fell on British soil. It landed on agricultural land at Swanscombe, near Gravesend, and destroyed approximately 100 square yards of growing vegetables but no humans. Others followed. A few days later a bomb fell on a crowded shopping centre at Clapham and another at Balham in London. The death toll began to mount. The most dramatic incident was at the Guards Chapel at Wellington Barracks on 18 June. The bomb landed just as morning service was beginning and killed 119 people, injuring another 141. The fact that a ton of high explosive had landed within yards of Buckingham Palace, the Houses of Parliament and the Whitehall Ministries, showed how vulnerable the heart of London had suddenly become. Even the worst days of the Blitz had never caused such sudden, unheralded devastation. The Air Ministry soon discovered that the new weapon was an aircraft piloted by a robot, was 25 feet long, had a range of 200 miles and was driven by a pulsed jet engine using liquid fuel and oxygen. Its speed was only 300 miles an hour and therefore if intercepted it could be shot down by fighter aircraft. There was, however, little point in shooting it down if it was already over the target area. The name of this terror weapon was 'Vergeltung' meaning reprisal. It was said to indicate the Nazi desire to revenge themselves for the bomber attacks on Germany but was, of course, the 'secret' weapon about which Hitler had boasted so long and so often, and which he expected to win the war for him. Observers who saw V1s making their way through the sky at first thought they were ordinary aircraft which had been shot at and caught fire. Soon, like all enemy weapons, they became easily recognised by their sound: the listener would have the unnerving experience of hearing the V1 approach, then realise that its engines had cut out and that it was now making its descent. Hearing the stick of bombs dropping from an aircraft was bad, but this was worse. Even so, the British public found a humorous nickname for V1s and christened them 'doodlebugs'.

The V2, which began falling on London in September, was an even more murderously intimidating weapon. It was a rocket, rather than an aircraft, and instead of arriving slowly at a low altitude, it came in at over 2,000 m.p.h. from a height of 30 miles. Its speed was faster than the sound it created, and therefore it was not heard until the warhead had landed. Although fighters had been able to intercept and shoot down V1s, there was no defence against V2s, for an anti-ballistic missile would not be invented until after the war. The only means of reducing the toll caused by the V2 weapon was to bomb the sites from which they were launched and the factories in which they were made. In order to escape detection the launching sites were frequently changed by the Germans, but as fast as they moved to new ones these were reported back to London by local resistance agents or aerial reconnaissance. By the end of the war, V1s and V2s had killed 9,000 and injured 18,000 more. They had also caused enormous material damage. Even that was not the final bill, for countering their effects with aircraft and anti-aircraft guns, as well as diverting civil and military personnel to clear up the damage they created, involved thousands. Undoubtedly the V weapons were one of the most cost-effective inventions of the war. Even so, they should not have came as the surprise they did, for rockets had been in existence since the Middle Ages and even before the war the RAF was using a pilotless target aircraft with a range of 300 miles.

Although the V1s were too late to affect the invasion on 6 June, they played a substantial part later in delaying the progress of the attacking forces.

On 27 June the Allies gained another valuable asset when the Americans, commanded by Lieutenant-General J. Lawton Collins, veteran of the Guadalcanal campaign described earlier, captured Cherbourg. Collins' jungle experience, which might have been thought irrelevant for Normandy, turned out to be a useful asset when negotiating the *bocage* – the sunken lanes and high hedges of Normandy.

Owing to the fact that parts of the port had been damaged by Allied bombing and the defenders' demolition, Cherbourg was not immediately usable, but later proved invaluable. Unfortunately there was no similar success story on the other flank, for the Germans had concentrated most of their forces in an effort to prevent a break-out in that sector. However, this situation fitted in with the general Allied strategy, for the German concentration round the Caen area left Bradley and Patton with a two to one superiority in divisions for their break out through Avranches.

By now Hitler was beginning to have doubts about the suitability of the commanders he had appointed for the Western Front. Von Runstedt was replaced by von Kluge on 1 July. Rommel, although well out of Hitler's favour by this time, left the scene for a different reason. On 15 July, when he was on his way to visit a unit in northern France, his staff car was attacked by a British aircraft. Ironically the village to which he was carried for medical treatment was called Ste Foy de Montgommery. Within a week occurred one of the most extraordinary events of the war – a long-expected attempt to assassinate Hitler. This was organised by Count Claus Schenk von Stauffenberg. After being wounded in Tunisia, von Stauffenberg was convinced that Hitler's policies, whether successful or not, would ruin Germany in every way. He therefore organised a group of conspirators who would be ready to take over as soon as Hitler was dead. When Hitler called one of his periodic conferences at Rastenburg, East Germany, von Stauffenberg carried in a briefcase which he placed under the table near Hitler. Unfortunately for him, the briefcase was moved without his knowledge and Hitler escaped with burns and minor injuries. Four other people attending the conference were killed outright.

Hitler's revenge was swift and devastating. Eight of the conspirators were hanged on wires attached to meat hooks, watched by Hitler and filmed by a camera team as they each took about five minutes to die. Hitler subsequently amused himself by watching the film and also made it compulsory viewing in some training establishments. Eventually he tracked down and executed some 5,000 people, many of them only remotely concerned with the assassination attempt. Von Kluge and Rommel, who were under suspicion of being involved, both committed suicide, the former on 19 August, the latter in October. The plot gave Hitler the excuse to remove the last traces of independence from the army, which was now completely under Nazi control. Although he had lost none of his savagery, Hitler was becoming increasingly morose and withdrawn. He had little

to cheer him. Caen had fallen to the Allies at last on 9 July,
though a month behind schedule. St Lô fell on the 18th. On
26 July Patton broke out from the beachhead and began to
range through Brittany. On 7 August the Germans put in a
heavy counter-attack towards Avranches. Bradley checked
the German thrust at Mortain, while Patton's army curved up
north-east towards Argentan. Patton, having been given a
chance to command armies in the field again after the
incident in Sicily, was enjoying himself and had lost none of
his former self-esteem.

With the British 2nd Army and the Canadian Army now
converging on the Germans from the north, it was soon all
too clear to the German 5th Panzer and 7th Army that they
were in a trap. This was the Falaise 'pocket' and, as they
struggled to get away as many troops as possible before the
entrance to the pocket was closed, the area became one of
the greatest 'killing grounds' of the war. Day after day the
Germans were hammered relentlessly by bombers and shell-
fire, and, although they fought back, it ended with 10,000 of
them dead and 50,000 being taken prisoner. The wreckage of
burnt-out tanks, vehicles and guns was indescribable. And on
15 August, France was once more invaded, this time near
Cannes, in 'Operation Anvil'. The aim of this operation was
to clear southern France of Germans, which it did, thus
providing 10 more divisions for use against the Allied
advance in the north. The South of France was of no tactical
value to the Allies and the troops they used in its invasion
would have been more usefully employed in Italy, from
which most of them had been taken. Tactically it would have
been far more sensible to leave those 10 German divisions in
the South of France waiting for an invasion which never
came. This represented one of the many divergences in
Allied opinion on strategy. Hitler was fervently hoping that
Anglo-American-Russian differences might become so
unbridgeable that even at that late stage of the war one
partner or another would decide to give up further action and
make a separate peace. He was unduly optimistic, but
certainly feelings were running high. One of the worst
examples was over the American thrust towards Brest,
Lorient and St Nazaire. Brest held out till 18 September, its

ancient fortifications proving much more formidable than had been anticipated; Lorient and St Nazaire remained in German hands till the end of the war. Dempsey would have liked to break out from Caen in the inappropriately named 'Operation Goodwood' and advance along the Orne to Argentan. This could have been accomplished as early as 18 July, thus trapping the Germans weeks before the lengthy convergence on Falaise. Patton's army was closing in around Falaise and he was told to slow down his advance in case he should find himself confronting the British instead of the Germans. His comment did little for Anglo-American relations, for he replied, 'Let me go and we'll drive the British back into the sea for another Dunkirk.'

Although Eisenhower was no field commander, his chances of making the right decisions were further hampered by the variety and differing temperaments of his subordinates. Bradley, Montgomery and Patton all regarded each other with ill-disguised contempt. Eisenhower had the onerous task of controlling his turbulent commanders in the field and at the same time paying attention to the views of the American public and politicians. In the interests of Allied harmony it was essential that no one should seem to be receiving special favour; this may have made sense politically but it was a disaster for the war effort. Up till 1 September Eisenhower, though Supreme Commander of the Allied Armies, exercised his authority from a distance. After 1 September he took over command in the field. This was the month in which the war in Europe could have been finished, but unfortunately the opportunity was lost.

Paris was liberated on 23 August and General de Gaulle, who had landed in France the day after D Day, walked along the Champs Elysées on 26 August. De Gaulle had acquitted himself well in the 1940 fighting against the Germans, but since going into exile in Britain he had proved to be an abrasive, even hostile guest. He was to prove even more hostile in the future. By this time very unpleasant events were taking place in the newly liberated areas. Most of the French had passively accepted the occupation, but some had co-operated actively with the Germans, assisting the Gestapo and even finding Jews for the concentration camps and gas chambers. The Milice (a fascist, collaborationist police force trained by the Gestapo) had a particularly nasty reputation. Most of them had been marked down by the resistance and now their turn had come. Women who had fraternised with the Germans, or even married them, were treated with considerable brutality, some having all their hair shaved off before being paraded in the streets. Vengeance on 'collaborators' seems to have been somewhat indiscriminate. In 1940 when the Germans had swept through Europe and were deep into the Middle East, it seemed unlikely that they would ever be dislodged. In 1941, when they were clearly overrunning Russia also, many French people decided that, although they disliked the presence of the Germans, many of whom tried to make themselves liked, they had no alternative but to accept them, to trade with them and to live as normally as possible. They had no reason to expect liberation. Some of them forgot that they were in an occupied country and the war was not over. They learned a hard lesson in 1944.

However the liberation of Paris no more meant that the war was over than the liberation of Rome had done. The Germans had lost 500,000 men in Normandy, of which nearly half were prisoners. Vast quantities of equipment, including tanks, had been lost too and morale had not been improved by the fact that if Hitler had not insisted on imposing his own ideas about tactics and strategy, the picture would have been entirely different and the Allies would have been in a much worse situation.

Instead, the Allies were in an extremely strong position. Progress was being maintained along the entire front. Patton had now reached Lorraine and was pressing ahead confidently. There was general euphoria, because the Germans were now being pushed backwards and their front was crumbling. Even the normally cautious Montgomery caught the feeling. The commander of 30 Corps, which was the spearhead of 2nd Army, was Lieutenant-General Sir Brian Horrocks, who had now recovered from the near-fatal wound he had sustained in North Africa, and was proving himself as one of the most dynamic leaders of the war. Horrocks used to recall with some pleasure the reaction of the normally imperturbable Guards Armoured Division when he told them their next objective was Brussels, 75 miles away. Nevertheless they reached it by nightfall, though not without some opposition from the Germans. The following day, 11th Armoured Division reached Antwerp. The Allies were within 100 miles of the Ruhr and facing a gap 100 miles wide in the German defence. In the south Patton had reached the Moselle with six strong divisions; he was now 30 miles from the Saar. If he continued, he would soon be occupying Strasbourg.

Eisenhower was now faced with a vital decision. Owing to the fact that the Allies had moved so fast that they had outstripped their supplies, there was a serious petrol shortage. Le Havre, Boulogne, Calais and Dunkirk were still in German hands. Antwerp, though captured, would not be available for use for at least a month, and Cherbourg was so far to the rear that it could not redress the balance. Patton captured 5,000 gallons of petrol but, without disclosing this fact to the other armies, simply appropriated it for his own forces. When the information leaked out, as was inevitable, disgust with Patton was universal, not least among his fellow countrymen.

Even with windfalls such as Patton had enjoyed, there was clearly not enough fuel to keep the two columns moving forward at their present pace. But which one should now be chosen as the spearhead of the attack? If it were Patton's, he would undoubtedly thrust eventually into southern Germany. Whatever might have been felt about Patton's character faults, there was no denying that he was a brilliant and dynamic leader who would not give the Germans a chance to recover their balance. However, as Eisenhower knew, once he crossed the Rhine he would probably try to win the war on his own. That might lead to a swift victory, or to a spectacular disaster. In fact, Patton's advance was checked at Metz.

In the north, the British 2nd Army and American 1st Army were advancing side by side, with a total of 40 divisions. This looked to be an unstoppable steam roller, although the Germans, who were frantically trying to strengthen their defences, apparently did not think so. However, for this northern juggernaut to achieve what was expected of it, it needed adequate supplies of fuel. To provide all that was needed, the advance of Patton's army would have to be halted. Patton was now about 100 miles closer to Germany than the northern group was: to have halted him completely would have produced an outcry back in America which Eisenhower did not care to contemplate.

Uncertain which option to take, Eisenhower compromised. He allocated 2,000 tons of supplies a day to Patton and 5,000 to the 1st Army in the north. These were in sharp contrast to the quantities the German forces were receiving, but the latter were less extravagent in their use of them. Vast amounts of Allied supplies, including petrol, were, however, disappearing as they travelled over the long supply line to the front. Many a small fortune was being made on the black market.

Although Eisenhower's 'broad front advance' policy was mistaken, the emphasis on the northern approach was not. After the war, the German generals confirmed that if complete priority had been given to the northern front, the Allies would have been in Berlin and Prague before the Russians. During September, when it was obvious to every commander except Eisenhower that the broad front policy was a mistaken one, frustration caused bad decisions to be made. The first one was at Arnhem.

The operation, code-named 'Market Garden', aimed at out-flanking the formidable Siegfried line, which the Germans had been perfecting for several years, and capturing the most important bridges in Holland. These were at Arnhem on the lower Rhine, and over the Maas and the Waal. Capturing the bridge at Arnhem was a particularly ambitious enterprise and Montgomery's staff were distinctly unhappy over the plan.

All three key bridges were to be seized by a combination of parachute drops and land operations. Airborne attacks are unnerving for those in the target area, but depend for their ultimate success on land forces going up to consolidate the position the surprise air attack has won. This is because there is a limit to the size of weapons and quantity of ammunition which can be carried by air. If the ground forces do not arrive soon after the airborne drop, the parachutists and gliders will

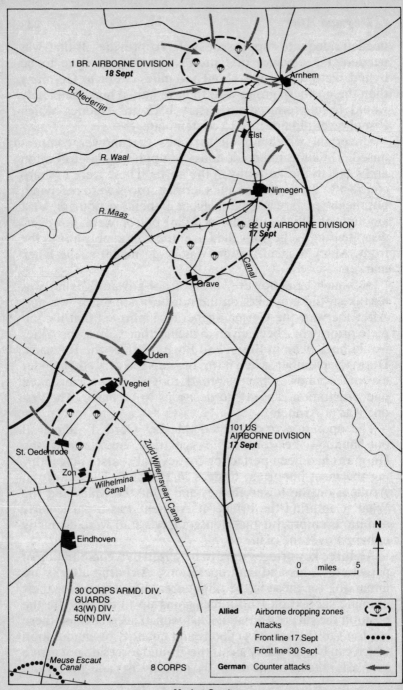

Market Garden

1 BR. AIRBORNE DIVISION
18 Sept

R. Nederrijn

Arnhem

Elst

R. Waal

Nijmegen

R. Maas

82 US AIRBORNE DIVISION
17 Sept

Canal

Grave

Uden

Veghel

101 US
AIRBORNE DIVISION
17 Sept

St. Oedenrode

Zon

Zuid Willemsvaart Canal

Wilhelmina
Canal

Eindhoven

N

0   miles   5

30 CORPS ARMD. DIV.
GUARDS
43(W) DIV.
50(N) DIV.

8 CORPS

Meuse Escaut
Canal

Allied	Airborne dropping zones
	Attacks
	Front line 17 Sept
	Front line 30 Sept
German	Counter attacks

be overwhelmed by the enemy's heavy artillery and tanks. This is what happened at Arnhem. Undoubtedly, this was Montgomery's greatest tactical mistake. There were, of course, factors other than purely military ones which caused him to take the fatal decision. By this stage in the campaign, his health had deteriorated: the responsibility of command, even without the conflict of views at high level, would have exhausted anyone. His spearhead general, Brian Horrocks, who would be commanding the land forces, had never fully recovered from his war wounds, but at that moment seemed to be in better health than previously and than he would be later. De Guingand, Montgomery's Chief of Staff, was also showing signs of strain.

Two other factors may have influenced Montgomery. One was the fact that the first V2 had fallen on England on 8 September and its destructive power had shown that the sooner Germany itself could be invaded, the less chance there was of the V2 tipping the balance even at this late stage. The second was the existence of 1st Allied Airborne Army, commanded by Lieutenant-General Lewis Brereton, United States, which was in Britain, longing to be involved in the war. 1st British Airborne, destined for Arnhem, was particularly anxious to distinguish itself and thus match the performance of 6th Airborne on D Day. The American 82nd and 101st Airborne Divisions could take a less anxious view: they had been in action on D Day and they knew their turn would come again. In the event, 82nd and 101st attained the less ambitious objective which had been assigned to them, though not without more difficulties than had been expected. Unfortunately for 1st British Airborne it ran into total disaster, and out of the 10,000 men landed at Arnhem, 1,130 were killed and 6,450 captured. The remaining 2,163 managed to make their way back across the Rhine when the order to do so was given.

There were several reasons for the disaster. The principal was that the 9th and 10th Panzer Divisions were in the Arnhem area when the drop took place. Both had been badly mauled in the Normandy battle and were making their way back to Germany for a refit. However, although below the level of peak efficiency, both divisions had a plentiful supply of tanks and self-propelled guns, and both were trained in anti-parachute defence. Making matters potentially worse for the British parachutists was the fact that, on the day the drop took place, General Model, Commander-in-Chief of the German Forces, was lunching at Oosterbek, six miles west of Arnhem. When he looked out of the window and saw British parachutists coming down out of the sky his reaction was swift. In addition to the bonus of 9th and 10th Panzer, he already had four divisional battle groups and an infantry division in the area. He ordered them all to converge on Arnhem. Meanwhile, 1st Airborne was landing on a dropping zone eight miles from the bridge. This DZ had been chosen because it was considered more suitable than any nearer territory would have been. Unfortunately this meant that its leading detachments did not reach the vital bridge until half an hour after soldiers from 9th Panzer had reached it. Only half the men of 1st Airborne's first drop could be used because the other half had to stay and guard the DZ, which was needed for supplies and reinforcements. The result was that for the following seven days 1st Airborne fought a gruelling battle against greatly superior forces. The US 82nd and 101st did their utmost to come to the rescue of 1st Airborne, but in vain. Meanwhile 30 Corps was trying to force its way along a narrow road which threaded its way past dykes and water, all the time under German air and artillery attack. The attempt failed: not only had an entire airborne division been lost but the Germans had now been given a useful respite in which to redeploy their forces and organise a strong defence. Montgomery's gamble had failed. Any hopes he might have had of bouncing forward towards Berlin, and thus making Eisenhower discard his disastrous 'broad front' policy had now been lost.

Discussion and analysis of what had gone wrong at Arnhem continued for years after the war. The subject was revived again when a gripping film entitled *A Bridge Too Far*, based on a best selling book, was made with a galaxy of acting talent. Montgomery insisted that the operation had been a justified enterprise. Few people could be found to agree with him. A disconcerting piece of information came to light later when it was learnt that the Dutch resistance had warned

British Intelligence that General Model was in the Arnhem area and had strong Panzer support. For some unexplained reason, the report was neglected. This was explained by the fact that the Dutch resistance had never been fully trusted since the *Englandspiel* incident long before; however, it seems more likely that so much intelligence information was pouring in at that time, much of it out of date, that several vital pieces of information were overlooked. Perhaps the *Englandspiel* traitor was involved. At this time the Enigma information was of minor value, for the battlefield situation was changing so rapidly that intercepts were usually out of date before they were decrypted.

Another misjudgement which contributed to the failure concerned the flooded road along which 30 Corps struggled to reach Arnhem. It was thought that the verges were mined. They were not, and if this had been known, perhaps 30 Corps would have arrived in time.

At this point we will leave the north-west European campaign and look at the wider scene. We left the Red Army at the point where it had re-entered Poland and was poised to capture Warsaw. On 1 August the inhabitants of that city, in happy anticipation of the arrival of their liberators, rose in rebellion against the German occupation force and looked forward to the gratitude they would receive from the Russians for making their task easier. However, the Russians failed to arrive, as confidently expected. This may have been due to the fact that their armies were exhausted by their recent enormous drive forward and needed time to refit and regroup: they had been fighting for two months continuously and had recently had a setback, being pushed back 65 miles. This was not the explanation which many Western writers gave for the Russian delay. Sovietologists were clear in their own minds that Stalin had no intention of having local national leaders, however communist, in power in the territories which would now become part of the new Russian empire. Whatever governments Poland, Bulgaria, Roumania, Hungary, Czechoslovakia, and perhaps Austria, Yugoslavia and Finland would have, would be chosen by the Russians and not by local patriots. In the event, the Russians did not reach

Yugoslavia, where Tito's independent stance certainly gave no pleasure to the Russians.

Unfortunately for the Poles in Warsaw, the Germans had strong forces around Poland, which was on the direct route to Germany. The Poles, as might be expected from their record elsewhere in the war, fought the German occupiers with great courage and skill. The Germans put one of the most brutal and sadistic commanders in charge of operations, a member of the SS (Schutzstaffel), which was renowned for its brutality. From the SS came the concentration camp guards and although some of their regiments were formidable fighters, others were made up of opportunist volunteers from occupied countries or criminals whose sentences had been commuted for military service. Every form of barbarism, such as bayoneting babies and burning people alive with petrol was used to terrorize the population into submission. The Poles would not be intimidated and held out for a whole month; in the final stages they were fighting in the city's sewers. Guderian, the German tank commander, heard of the atrocities and protested to Hitler, an act of considerable moral courge, as Hitler knew well enough what was going on. Before the end of the fighting the atrocities had been stopped through Guderian's intervention, but when it was all over, and 300,000 Poles were dead, Hitler ordered that the entire city of Warsaw be demolished. When the Russians finally arrived in January 1945, they found that the order had been almost completed. Subsequently the Russians claimed that they were not ready to take Warsaw and the rising should have been co-ordinated with them.

Although pausing in this sector, the Russians were consolidating their position elsewhere. In the south they drove into Roumania where some of the defending forces were Roumanian troops who had been made Hitler's unenthusiastic allies. Roumania was an example of what can happen to a small state with valuable assets if it is situated between two great powers. Roumania had been made independent (from the Turks) in 1878, but had a tradition of oppressive governments both before and after that date. When the country was forcibly occupied by the Nazis, her great grain wealth was immediately at their disposal and her valuable oil wells at

Ploesti made her a regular target for Allied bombing. Many of her troops had been forced to fight for the Germans in Russia, where they were less well clothed and equipped than the Germans. Some turned on the Germans and assisted the Russians in April 1944. The Russians pressed on through Roumania to Bucharest and Ploesti, and beyond into Bulgaria.

In September Estonia and Latvia were cleared of Germans: the Russians did not occupy Finland but signed an armistice with that country. This reassured Sweden and Norway, who were apprehensive of Russian ambition in that area. Although Sweden was neutral, she had been supplying Germany with valuable war materials and was not sure how the Russians would view this form of neutrality. The Western Allies were also watching the area carefully, wondering whether the Russians might soon replace the Germans in Norway and Denmark. However, even with all these defeats Germany seemed far from collapse. There was more hard fighting when the Red Army invaded Hungary in October, and they made little progress in Czechoslovakia: Prague itself would not be freed of the Germans until 2 May 1945. In that month the citizens rose against their occupiers with happier results than the Poles had known in Warsaw five months earlier.

Although prisoners were taken on the Eastern Front, little mercy was given or expected. The German invaders had used ruthlessness and terrorism as deliberate policy in 1941, hoping to prevent the Russians destroying their crops in a 'scorched earth' campaign. Although the Russians had not planned a programme of terrorism, their military efficiency had embodied a considerable degree of ruthlessness. Subsequently the Russians claimed the war had cost them 20 million lives; when the time for revenge came, they were hardly likely to be moved by feelings of charity and forgiveness.

12

CLOSING IN ON JAPAN

In mid-1944, the Americans were still 2,000 miles from Japan and the Japanese decided they must be prevented from making any further advances. The next stage for the Americans would be the acquisition of bases in the Marianas and the Philippines. It would not be easy, for the Japanese still controlled a formidable navy, an air force with a considerable number of suicide aircraft and a ground army which would never surrender willingly. However, by now, in addition to their carriers, the US navy had ocean-going submarines which were playing havoc with Japanese plans by sinking urgently required reinforcements; furthermore they had developed an ingenious system known as 'the fleet train', by which damaged ships were repaired at sea. Japanese calculations that damaged American carriers would need to go all the way back to Hawaii or America were being proved seriously wrong.

In mid-June, after a heavy bombardment from carrier-borne aircraft, the Americans put 18,000 troops ashore at Saipan, losing 2,000 in the process. The Japanese had superior numbers on the island, as well as 7,000 sailors, and set about trying to put the Americans off again.

While the ground troops were locked in this life and death struggle, the Japanese navy commander, Admiral Toyoda, decided that this situation offered an excellent opportunity to destroy supporting American carriers. Numerically he was slightly inferior, except in heavy cruisers: the US navy had seven fleet carriers to his five, and eight light carriers to his four. In aircraft Toyoda was at an even greater disadvantage, having 473 to meet 956. As well as the valuable base at Saipan the Americans were also keen to reoccupy Guam, one of their former possessions, to the south of the group. However, the Japanese also had another fleet under Vice-Admiral Ozawa with 100 aircraft, and this now engaged the Americans who were attacking Guam.

This particular battle became known to the Americans as 'The Great Turkey Shoot'. It was a superb performance on the part of the American pilots. Using Grumman 'Hellcat' aircraft, they shot down 42 out of 69 Japanese aircraft in the first wave of the Japanese attack. While this was going on, American submarines sank two Japanese carriers. In the second Japanese attack the Japanese lost 98 out of 130 aircraft. The third Japanese raid failed to find its targets and returned unscathed. The fourth lost 73 planes out of 82. In these battles the Americans lost a total of 30 aircraft.

Ozawa now withdrew, but the Americans followed him relentlessly. They shot down a further 65 Japanese aircraft and sank one carrier, losing 20 more planes in doing so. Unfortunately the pursuit had taken the American aircraft well beyond their safety margin and on the way back, trying to find their parent carriers in the dark, 80 crashed into the sea, having exhausted their fuel. But it had been a remarkable achievement for the American airmen for although they had lost 130 planes, the Japanese had lost 395; a figure they could not afford.

Although this battle, officially the Battle of the Philippine Sea, ended on 22 June, the struggle for Saipan continued until 9 July. When the fighting was over, the Americans had had 14,000 casualties, the Japanese 24,000. Saipan had been a Japanese mandate before the war began and when it was lost hundreds of Japanese civilians committed suicide by jumping off the cliffs into the sea. Japanese who felt themselves to be dishonoured or to have failed in some way, had a traditional form of suicide which is known as *hara-kiri*, meaning literally 'to cut the stomach'. In its most spectacular form this meant the suicide would dramatically disembowel himself with the sword of his ancestors. This form of death was excruciatingly painful and slow and therefore seemed a suitable act for a soldier who was punishing himself for his disgrace. Sometimes a small ceremonial cut was made and then a revolver bullet would do the rest. Considerable numbers of Japanese committed suicide before the end of the war, although those who omitted to do so did not seem to be particularly affected by remorse subsequently. A feature of the Japanese, which made them difficult opponents in wartime, was that they never considered anything impossible, and they had no hesitation about using tactics which were in themselves suicidal. They would cross terrain which other armies might consider vitually impassable and would run on to machine-guns in the expectation that however many of them might be killed – and thus attain immortality in Nirvana – some would survive to overwhelm the position. Soldiers would strap explosives on their backs and dive between the tracks of oncoming tanks. So anxious were they to kill the enemy that if a Japanese was wounded and a British soldier stopped to give him a drink of water or otherwise help him, the Japanese would pull out the pin from his last grenade and blow the pair of them to pieces.

Suicidal attacks were known as *kamikaze* (literally 'divine wind') and usually came from small suicide aircraft, which, loaded with high explosive, would dive on to enemy surface ships. *Kamikaze* submarines were midget craft which were vitually manned torpedoes. Even larger aircraft and submarines would often try to crash land on to their targets. This indifference to death made the Japanese particularly inhuman to those whom they took prisoner, or who lived in the territories they had overrun and which they claimed to have 'liberated'. In July 1944, when the Japanese empire was shrinking into 'fortress Japan', they sent home unescorted convoys of cargo ships, loaded well beyond the safety limits with tin and other goods from the territories they still controlled, such as Indonesia and Malaya. On these boats were also loaded survivors of the Burma 'railway of death'. There was no marking on these ships other than Japanese merchant navy flags and, in consequence, many of them were sunk by Allied submarines. Most PoWs simply drowned, if not killed in the explosion, as they were usually locked in the holds below decks, but a few escaped and survived.

As the American forces drew nearer to Japan, there was some division of opinion over the best direction for the next attack. Admiral Nimitz would have preferred to capture Taiwan (Formosa) and, with that as a main base, to work up the coast of China. This plan was opposed by MacArthur, who felt that it was incumbent upon him to liberate the Philippines at the earliest possible moment. Furthermore, recapturing the Philippines, which is a group of islands 7,000 in number, looked an easier option than finding a way through the concentrated defences of Taiwan. In addition, the Philippines were familiar territory to the US Forces; Taiwan was not.

The next operation showed that Japanese opposition was likely to become even more obstinate as their total of defeats mounted. To the west of the Carolines, and therefore a useful base for an attack on the Philippines, was a group of islands known as the Palau group. The Japanese had established a garrison of 5,000 on the island of Pelelieu, which the Americans assaulted in September. This event passed virtually unnoticed in Europe, where attention was diverted by the capture of Antwerp and Brussels, the arrival of the first V2, the disaster at Arnhem and the regaining of Boulogne, Brest and Calais. When the US Marines landed on Pelelieu they lost 1,000 men on the beaches and when they fought their way inland they found the Japanese had dug themselves into a hillside and made a series of interlocking defence points in caves. There was nowhere for them to retreat to, even if that had been their intention; all they were concerned about was killing the maximum number of Americans. It took the latter two months to eliminate the last of the Japanese, a gruesome process achieved by long-range flame-throwers. By then, their commander had committed *hara-kiri*, 5,000 Japanese had been killed and nearly 2,000 Americans had died as well. However, now that the assault on the Philippines had begun, the newly acquired base at Pelelieu would be a useful asset, instead of a dangerous liability in the rear areas.

In the 7,000 islands which comprise the Philippines two islands, Luzon (containing the capital Manila) in the north and Mindanao in the south are the largest, Luzon being 40,422 square miles in area and Mindanao 36,538. In between there are the sizeable islands of Panay, Mindoro and

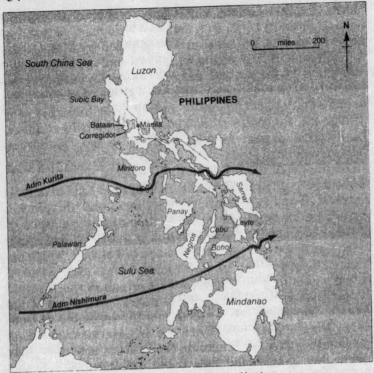

The Philippines – The Battle of Leyte

Leyte. Leyte, on the eastern side, was chosen for the landings. For these, the Americans assembled an armada of over 700 ships, which included seventeen carriers. They began by pounding the Japanese-held airfields in Taiwan and China, destroying in the process over 500 Japanese aircraft for the loss of less than 100 of their own. They then proceeded to land 132,000 men on Leyte, together with essential stores. All this was done by 21 October. However, it was one thing to put a force of this size on shore and another to keep it supplied at such a vast distance from its main bases. The Japanese were aware of the situation and therefore felt that the occasion represented an opportunity to catch the Americans in a position where they would have little room for manoeuvre. Although the Japanese navy had been unable to replace the aircraft it had lost in earlier battles and could not deploy more than 116 carrier-borne machines, the presence of land-based aircraft on Japanese airfields in the Philippines gave them confidence that they would not be out-fought in the air.

The tactical plan was that Admiral Ozawa, who had been in command during the Japanese defeat in the Battle of the Philippine Sea, would venture out from Japanese waters and lure a substantial portion of American naval strength away from the area of the landings. Once this had happened, the bulk of the remaining Japanese naval strength would approach Leyte Gulf from the south in a two-pronged attack, the prong from the north coming via the San Bernardino Strait and the southern one through the Surigao Strait. The northern prong would be commanded by Admiral Kurita, the southern by Nishimura: together they mustered seven battleships and an impressive number of cruisers and destroyers.

Kurita was followed by American submarines, which sank a heavy cruiser, and by American aircraft which sank a battleship. Halsey decided that these losses would be enough to discourage Kurita from any further adventures and set off to find Ozawa. However, Ozawa proved an elusive quarry and 24 hours later Halsey was still looking for him. In the meantime, Kurita, far from breaking off the action, was pressing ahead at full speed towards Leyte. Nishimura was also making good progress towards Leyte when he met six American battleships and eight cruisers in the Surigao Strait. He lost a cruiser and a battleship, and had other craft badly damaged. Prospects seemed better for Kurita when he emerged from the San Bernardino Strait and met a much smaller force under Admiral Sprague. In the ensuing battle, in which the outclassed American ships all performed superbly, one destroyer, the USS *Johnston*, was outstanding. *Johnston*, commanded by Ernest E. Evans, put itself firmly in the way of four battleships, seven cruisers and 12 destroyers. Before she was sunk three hours later, *Johnston* had torpedoed a Japanese cruiser, damaged a battleship and another cruiser and had had a very disheartening effect on Kurita's fleet. Evans went down with his ship and 185 of his crew. Sprague's force lost five ships in all, one due to a *kamikaze* air attack, but had done enough damage to persuade Kurita to break off the action. The latter may have been influenced by thinking of the possibility of an early return of Halsey's carriers, but more probably had decided that if this was the outer fringe of the battle, he would be unwise to go further in at this moment. It seems that his lookouts had identified American destroyers as cruisers and assumed also that the escort carriers, which were converted merchant ships with small numbers of aircraft, were in fact their bigger sisters.

While this was happening, Halsey had at last caught up with Ozawa. He sank all four of the latter's carriers and a destroyer. Unfortunately for the follow-up, he then misinterpreted a message from Nimitz and wasted an hour before returning to Leyte. In consequence he missed the chance of intercepting and destroying Kurita's force as it came back through the San Bernadino Strait. It seems that the escape of the rest of Kurita's force made the Americans overestimate the remaining strength of the Japanese. It was, in fact, almost exhausted and if this had been realised the US navy would have sailed much closer to Japan without relying on captured island bases. Meanwhile, the fighting for the Philippines was not going as well as had been hoped. The Japanese speedily brought in all the forces they could muster from nearby islands and turned the area into a major battlefield. American efforts to put more men ashore were met with vigorous resistance, including a number of successful *kamikaze* attacks. General Yamashita, victor of Singapore and later to be hanged as a war criminal, had been put in command of the defending Japanese forces and, although unable to prevent the landings, continued to fight on the defensive until the end of the war. Establishing themselves on Leyte cost the Americans heavily in casualties from tropical diseases, though only 2,260 were killed in the landings, against 24,000 Japanese dead.

Having achieved a presence on the islands, MacArthur proceeded to strengthen it by landings at other points. There was much more hard fighting to be done. American forces landed on Mindoro on 15 December and then moved north to Luzon. By now the Japanese had realised how expensive they could make this onslaught for the Americans if they developed their *kamikaze* attacks. To the Japanese the loss of aircraft or pilots was immaterial: all that mattered was crippling the US Fleet and they inflicted many damaging blows. By the end of the year the two forces were locked in a struggle which would culminate in the battle for Manila in the following month.

At this stage in the war few except the scientists working on the atomic bomb thought it would end by any other means than a prolonged and bloody struggle. Even when the US forces in the Pacific eventually stormed the islands of Japan, there would still be millions of Japanese soldiers determined to carry on the fight elsewhere. There were Japanese soldiers in Borneo, Indonesia, Malaya, Indo-China, Thailand, Okinawa, China and Burma. In Japan itself, which consisted of four main islands, Hokkaido, Honshu, Shikoku and Kyushu, every male, whether fit or not, had been trained for military service, and in addition women and children were undergoing basic military training. The war in the East looked set to last for years.

An example of the problems which would be encountered in freeing Japanese occupied countries of their armies of occupation could be seen in Burma. In 1942 the Japanese had been at the frontiers of India, and the threat had not been entirely lifted even by the following year. Wingate had made a spectacular foraye in 1943 but, although the effect on British morale had been excellent, the losses had been too high for this sort of expedition to offer a long-term solution. Meanwhile, fighting around Akyab and along the Arakan had not produced the results hoped for. General 'Bill' Slim was a magnificent, dogged commander, immensely popular with his troops, but his day-to-day activities left him no time to look at the wider issues. In consequence, a new command, SEAC (South-East Asia Command), was formed in August 1943 and Admiral Lord Louis Mountbatten made Supreme Commander. Mountbatten was a flamboyant figure but he had a good record in Combined Operations and his close connection with the British Royal Family gave him prestige which was valuable in international conferences. Mountbatten was able to emphasise the need for air supply and also the importance of establishing a link with China. Unfortunately, to reach China aircraft had to make a dangerous journey over the range of mountains known to aviators as 'the Hump'. This route would not be necessary if the Allies could capture the town of Myitkina in Burma, which had three good airfields, and use it as a staging post.

But in the early months of 1944 the armies in Burma had too much to contend with to see the capture of Myitkina as anything but an optimistic, long-term prospect in a complicated campaign, which would involve an army, comprising of Chinese and Americans, approaching from the north and the recapture of Akyab in the Arakan by 15 Corps of the 14 Army. At the same time Wingate would take in another, larger force of Chindits and cut the communications of the Japanese facing the northern invasion force. This northern group was commanded by General 'Vinegar Joe' Stillwell, who was an excellent and tough leader but so abrasive that he was violently unpopular even with his own countrymen. He was also extremely anti-British. General Chiang Kai-shek was also scheduled to join in with a Chinese force coming south-west over the river Salween, but this development failed to materialise.

However, the Japanese had their own ideas about what should happen next and, as the British offensive in the Arakan began in February, it quickly ran into serious trouble. Instead of approaching head on, the Japanese flowed round the British positions getting into the rear areas and causing considerable dismay and confusion. Previously the 14 Army would have retreated and tried to re-establish a line further back, but on this occasion they withdrew into 'boxes' where they held out in self-contained groups, each supplied by air drops. Slim now gradually withdrew to create shields round the key positions of Kohima and Imphal. The contribution of the US Air Force to the success of these manoeuvres was considerable: 615,000 tons of supplies and 315,000 reinforcements were flown in, three-quarters by the US Air Force and one-quarter by the RAF which had heavy commitments elsewhere. The Americans were also flying in substantial quantities of supplies to China in arduous and dangerous journeys over 'the Hump'. Not least of the virtues of this massive air support was in evacuating casualties, of which the Burma campaign produced more than its fair share. Apart from casualties produced by what the army describes as GSW (gunshot wounds), there were tropical diseases of every type from malaria to typhus. Cuts and scratches became infected immediately; insects, leeches, bugs and lice were always present, and the heat, relentless rain and gruelling terrain added their quota to the total of discomforts.

On 5 March 1944 the second Chindit expedition set out, this time on a much larger scale than the first. Auchinleck, now Commander-in-Chief, India, and in that post organising supplies to Burma, had doubts about the cost-effectiveness of this enterprise. Wingate himself was killed in an air crash on 24 March, but his Chindits had by this time established themselves along the main Japanese line of communications to Imphal. Their jungle stronghold became known as 'White City' from the number of parachutes in the trees around, although many of the occupants had come in by glider. After Wingate's death command of the Chindits was taken by General Lentaigne. The army, which tends to be sceptical of the value of special forces, felt that the soldiers concerned would have been put to better use if employed normally, notably around Kohima.

On 15 March 1944, the Japanese launched an offensive designed to reach India. They aimed at the Brahmaputra Valley in Assam, which entailed passing Kohima and Imphal. In the ensuing battles at these two places, the fighting was as bitter as anything seen during the entire war. At Kohima the two armies were separated by the width of the tennis court outside the District Commissioner's bungalow. Grenades were being flung back and forth through air which had previously experienced nothing more lethal than tennis balls. At the end of a series of desperate battles, the Japanese could do no more and retreated back over the Chindwin. One of the most remarkable V.C.s of the war was won at Kohima by the 19-year-old Lance Corporal Harman of the Royal West Kent Regiment, who did not live to receive it. Harman, a well-built soldier, ran up to a Japanese machine-gun, shot the crew and brought the gun back to his own lines on his shoulders. At this time the Japanese were occupying a field-service supply-depot bakery. Harman stormed it on his own with grenades and having set it on fire came back to his section with a wounded Japanese under each arm.

But although they had failed to invade India the Japanese still had plenty of fight in them. In consequence, Stilwell's army from China did not take Myitkina until August. In addition to his Chinese troops he had a commando force known as 'Merrill's Marauders', which took a valuable but exhausting part in the campaign. By December 1944 Slim was strong enough to cross the Chindwin, thus causing the Japanese to take up position behind the Irrawaddy. Hardly had they done so than Slim crossed that river too, south of Mandalay. The 14 Army was now poised to attack Meiktila, a town which was a vital pivot in the Japanese defence. They would have to fight every inch of the way to capture it, as they knew from past experience. But at least they had reached Christmas 1944 with the best prospects since the war in Burma began.

13

EUROPE: SOME FURTHER SURPRISES IN STORE

The catastrophe at Arnhem, although a setback, did not alter the Allies' conviction that they would be arriving in Germany in the near future and that the end of the European war was in sight. Montgomery was still emphasising that the northern thrust should be given full priority but Antwerp, which few people had seemed to realise was 50 miles inland and thus needed its approaches cleared, was not usuable until the end of November. In the circumstances, it seemed that the war would settle into a stalemate for the winter.

On 16 December 1944 that view was abruptly changed when 6th SS Panzer Army launched a ferocious attack on US 5th Corps and headed for Liège. Simultaneously 5th Panzer Army fell on US 8th Corps and drove for Namur. The folly of the 'broad front' policy was now only too clearly exposed. The American 1st Army was trying to hold 85 miles of front with only five divisions, of which three were under strength. A corps is unlikely to withstand the approach of an army which may be from two to three times its strength. Added to this were the factors of deception and surprise. Where had these new German armies come from? Not only 5th and 6th Panzer, but also 7th German Army was involved.

Unsuspected by the Allies, the Germans had been gradually withdrawing troops from other sectors and building up a force of 250,000 men behind the German border opposite the Ardennes sector. This plan, it seems, was Hitler's, and showed a streak of genius which still enabled him to retain control of his armies even after the long chain of disasters everywhere else. Complete secrecy had shrouded the operation: radio contact had been entirely banned. This last

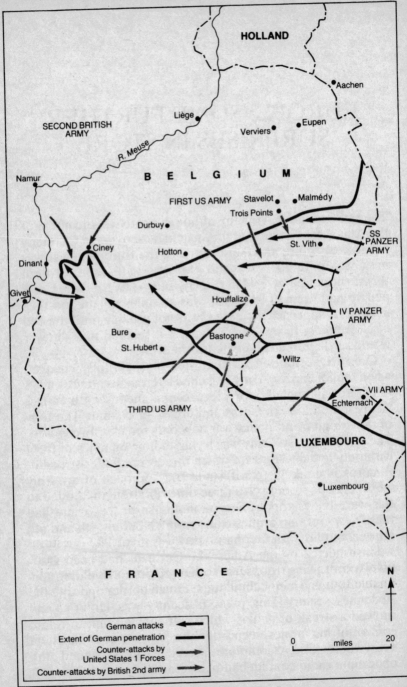

The Ardennes Battle 1944–5

HOLLAND

Aachen

SECOND BRITISH ARMY

Liège

Verviers • Eupen

R. Meuse

Namur

B E L G I U M

FIRST US ARMY

Stavelot • Malmédy

Trois Points

Durbuy •

SS PANZER ARMY

St. Vith •

Ciney

Hotton •

Dinant •

Givet •

Houffalize

IV PANZER ARMY

Bure •

Bastogne

St. Hubert •

Wiltz •

VII ARMY

THIRD US ARMY

Echternach

LUXEMBOURG

Luxembourg •

F R A N C E

N

German attacks
Extent of German penetration
Counter-attacks by
United States 1 Forces
Counter-attacks by British 2nd army

0   miles   20

reason explains why no giveaway messages had been intercepted by Ultra, which, of course, had no means of tapping in on land lines, still less on manually transmitted material. Reports from local agents of the Germans massing huge numbers of troops had been dismissed as fantasy, presumably because they did not accord with official ideas.

Added to the surprise of an attack coming in winter through a sector believed – even after the 1940 experience – to be unsuitable for tanks, and from an army which was presumably trying to repair the ravages of recent defeats, was a remarkable piece of deception. Otto Skorzeny, whom we last spoke of as snatching away Mussolini by a brilliant airborne swoop on his mountain prison, now proceeded to play havoc behind the American lines. For this he infiltrated members of his 150 Panzer Brigade, whom he dressed up in American uniforms. In this guise they acted as military police, putting up false direction boards and altering existing ones to point in different directions. American drivers who already found signposting in Europe a problem were thrown into complete confusion by this new hazard. False radio messages, purporting to come from American sources, added to their problems. It was a high risk adventure for Skorzeny's men, for the conventions of war agree that, whereas wounded or surrendered enemy servicemen will be regarded as prisoners-of-war, those masquerading in the uniform of the opposition may expect to be shot summarily if captured, which they were likely to be. However, the results for Skorzeny were as gratifying as they were irritating for the Allies. In order to distinguish between friend and foe, American military police tested everyone they did not recognise by asking them questions to which the answers would show they were genuine Americans. Most of these questions were totally baffling to the British when they became involved; Lieutenant-General Brian Horrocks was quite unable to name the second largest town in Texas; a number of Americans would have been equally floored by the same question.

Eisenhower now showed qualities as a field commander which neither his adversaries nor even his friends would have expected. He sent 18th Airborne Corps to assist Hodges, whose US 1st Army was blocking the German drive towards Antwerp. He gave Bradley's 12 Army Group the task of checking any German breakthrough and also put him in charge of the forces in the south. He put the US 1st and 9th Armies, in the northern sector, under the command of Montgomery, and told Patton to drive north-east towards Houffalize, which was in the centre of the German breakthrough. Meanwhile the German attack had driven as far west as Dinant, where their spearheads were counterattacked by the British 2nd Army. In reaching that point, the Germans had passed on each side of Bastogne, thereby isolating it. However, by this time 101st Airborne had dropped near the town and settled in and, further north, stubborn American resistance was bringing the German columns to a halt.

Bastogne was isolated, completely surrounded and miles behind the German lines. Its American commander, Brigadier-General Anthony McAuliffe, was invited by the Germans to surrender on 22 December but, not being a talkative man, replied simply with the word 'Nuts'. Other British or American commanders might have chosen a less printable word.

Although the Germans had been frustrated in their attempt to reach Antwerp and cause devastation beyond, the 'Battle of the Bulge' was by no means over and unless the situation was restored rapidly the fighting in the area could prolong the war considerably. Some of the German commanders even thought that it could swing the war back permanently in the German favour. As their forward units were within three miles of the Meuse by 24 December, their view seemed to have some substance.

However, in spite of atrocious weather conditions, the Allied air forces were now relentlessly pounding the German spearheads and rear areas. That 'white Christmas' was not a happy time for the Germans. The 7th German Army was stopped on the 25th, and on Boxing Day 4th Armoured Division reached Bastogne. Even so, there were still two German corps threatening the town, and on 30 December von Manteuffel's 7th Army and Patton's US Third met head on. For seven days they slogged it out in the snow in the rugged Ardennes countryside but then the Germans had shot their bolt. The great gamble had failed and reluctantly Hitler agreed to a retreat, so that 6th Panzer Army could be used against the Russians. Bastogne was finally relieved on 9 January but, as the Germans were withdrawing in disciplined order, the final shots in the battle were not fired till 28 January. The victory had been won, as Montgomery acknowledged, 'by the staunch qualities of the American fighting soldier'. Although initially caught napping, the Americans had fought back with dogged courage. Both armies had had to defy the worst of weather conditions: fog, rain, snow, bitter cold. The Allies had had 77,000 casualties, 7,000 more than the Germans, but 50,000 Germans had also been taken prisoner. They also lost over 500 tanks and 1,500 aircraft, which they could ill afford, but Allied losses in material had been nearly as heavy.

For those who had thought the German army, now drawing on its last reserves, was a spent force, this winter battle had come as a sharp shock. There would be no easy end to the war. The German resistance would have been admirable if it had not been defending a system in which unspeakable horrors and atrocities were being committed as a daily routine. Within a few months the evil of Nazi Germany would be revealed to the world.

Surprises were not, however, limited to France and Belgium in 1944. As if in another world, a very different type of war was being fought in Italy and the Balkans. We left it with the Allies weakened by the need to send troops to invade the South of France but with Rome now behind their lines, and the German army, under Kesselring, on a line between Pisa and Rimini. Like the 14th Army in Burma, the Allies in Italy felt they were a forgotten army, with all the public attention being focused on the fighting in France. They were not flattered when people at home congratulated them on not being involved in the Normandy invasion and cynically christened themselves 'the D Day Dodgers'. In fact, just as it is as easy to be killed by a rifle bullet as with a hydrogen bomb, so was it as easy, if not easier, to be killed in Italy as in Normandy. In September 1944 the Germans were firmly entrenched in what came to be called the Gothic Line. This

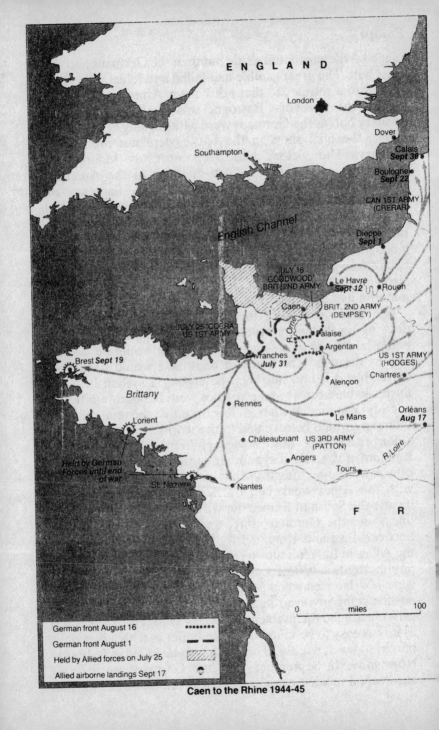

ENGLAND

London

Dover

Calais *Sept 30*

Boulogne *Sept 22*

Southampton

CAN 1ST ARMY (CRERAR)

English Channel

Dieppe *Sept 1*

JULY 18 'GOODWOOD' BRIT. 2ND ARMY

Le Havre *Sept 12*

Rouen

Caen

BRIT. 2ND ARMY (DEMPSEY)

JULY 25 'COBRA' US 1ST ARMY

R. Orne

Falaise

Argentan

Avranches *July 31*

US 1ST ARMY (HODGES)

Brest *Sept 19*

Alençon

Chartres

Brittany

Rennes

Le Mans

Orléans *Aug 17*

Lorient

Châteaubriant

US 3RD ARMY (PATTON)

Held by German Forces until end of war

Angers

Tours

R. Loire

St. Nazaire

Nantes

F   **R**

0   miles   100

German front August 16   ••••••••

German front August 1   — — —

Held by Allied forces on July 25   ////

Allied airborne landings Sept 17   ◒

Caen to the Rhine 1944-45

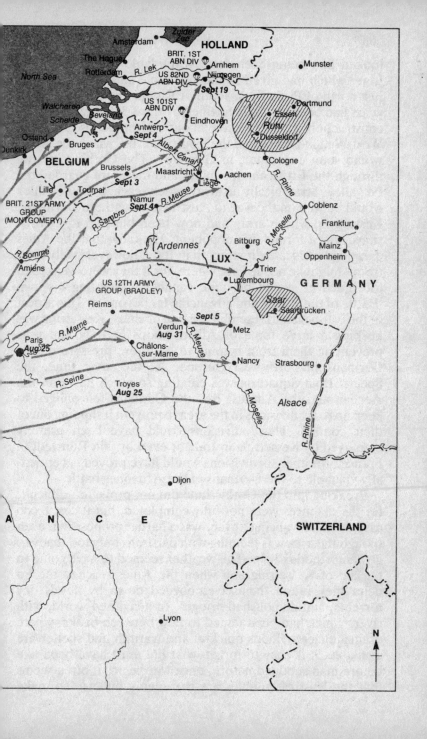

North Sea

Amsterdam
Zuider Zee
HOLLAND
The Hague
Rotterdam
R. Lek
BRIT. 1ST ABN DIV
Arnhem
US 82ND ABN DIV
Nijmegen
Sept 19
US 101ST ABN DIV
Munster
Walcheren
Scheldt
Beveland
Eindhoven
Ruhr
Essen
Dortmund
Dusseldorf
Ostend
Dunkirk
Bruges
Antwerp
Sept 4
BELGIUM
Albert Canal
Brussels
Sept 3
Maastricht
Aachen
Cologne
R. Rhine
Lille
Tournai
Namur
Sept 4
Liège
Coblenz
BRIT. 21ST ARMY GROUP (MONTGOMERY)
R. Sambre
R. Meuse
Frankfurt
R. Somme
Amiens
Ardennes
LUX
Bitburg
Mainz
Oppenheim
R. Moselle
Trier
Luxembourg
GERMANY
US 12TH ARMY GROUP (BRADLEY)
Reims
Saar
Saarbrücken
R. Marne
Sept 5
Verdun
Aug 31
Metz
Paris
Aug 25
Châlons-sur-Marne
R. Meuse
Nancy
Strasbourg
R. Seine
Troyes
Aug 25
Alsace
R. Moselle
R. Rhine
Dijon
F R A N C E
SWITZERLAND
Lyon
N

looked like being even more formidable than the Gustav Line, which had given so much trouble earlier. It ran from just north of Pisa to just south of Rimini and for nearly two years had been carefully fortified by the Todt organisation, a construction team of forced labour which had also built the West Wall in France and the Siegfried Line, which the Allies would soon encounter, in Germany. The Gothic Line ran through the Etruscan Appenines and therefore guarded the Po valley. Strategically an army which reached the Po valley would be well on the way to Austria and southern Germany. Kesselring, whose army had now been built up to 25 divisions, was a formidable opponent. He knew that the Allies dared not reduce their strength in Italy, however badly their troops might be needed elsewhere, for if they were weakened too much he would be quite capable of creating his own 'Battle of the Bulge' and advancing far beyond it. This aspect of the war began to resemble a game of chess. Kesselring was keeping a large force of Allied troops in Italy and thus preventing them from helping to put more pressure on the Germans in north-west Europe. At the same time, the Special Boat Squadron was creating so much havoc in the Aegean and the Adriatic that the Germans felt obliged to keep up to six divisions in the area to prevent it slipping out of their control. Those divisions could have been usefully employed by Kesselring in Italy or even by von Runstedt in France. Another six divisions would have proved exceptionally valuable to the Germans in the Ardennes battle.

Breaking into the Gothic Line did not prove too difficult, for the defences were not fully completed, but it cost 8,000 casualties. Advancing further was a harder proposition, even though the area was teeming with partisans only too ready to give unorthodox help. The weather seemed to have come to the aid of Kesselring and when the Allies reached the Po delta they found themselves bogged down by floods, icy torrents, and demolished bridges. In a civilised world, with rivers which had been tamed to flow between banks, where drainage clears floods quickly, and warmth and shelter are available, it is easy to forget what life must have been like before man subdued nature; once war begins it often seems that the least of troubles are the enemy bullets. To make matters worse for the Allies, they now began to run seriously short of ammunition. Ravenna was captured but Bologna held out. Showing unseasonable spirit, the Germans counter-attacked at Christmas, but after some rapid Allied deployment this dangerous thrust was held.

By spring 1945 the Allies felt in a position to resume the offensive. Allied air superiority, combined with heavy artillery bombardments, enabled the infantry to force back the German army. Bologna was taken on 21 April, Verona and Genoa on 26 April. On 2 May 1945 the Germans formally surrendered in Italy.

It had been a long and exhausting campaign, costing the Germans 536,000 casualties and the Allies 312,000. Fought over exceptionally difficult terrain, it had brought out brilliant tactical skills on both sides. The chief sufferers had been the Italian people, who had been dragged into German battles in other lands, had lived in an occupied country in which they had tried to liberate themselves by a civil war, and had had their country fought over from one end to the other for two long years. Not surprisingly, when the Allies reached Milan, and Mussolini was discovered attempting to escape to Switzerland with his mistress, the Italian people took savage revenge on the cause of all their troubles. The mutilated corpses were hung upside down in a public place in the town.

But even as the war in Italy was ending there were clear signs that a new conflict was beginning nearby. Tito's army, well supplied by the Allies, had every intention of extending his control as far north as possible and, if permitted, of annexing the whole of Trieste. In Greece, the clash between rival political systems seemed likely to be resolved by bloodshed rather than the ballot box. All over the region, from Sicily to the Adriatic and across to Turkey, large numbers of German and other weapons had fallen into communist hands. The long, gruelling war which was finishing in Europe had not taught people the wisdom of the biblical saying: 'All they that take the sword shall perish with the sword', but had apparently left them believing, like Clausewitz, that 'War is a continuation of policy by other means'.

14
THE FINAL ROUNDS

On 12 January 1945, in spite of the winter weather, the Russian armies once again took the offensive. On 17 January 1945 they were in Warsaw – five months later than the wretched inhabitants of that city had anticipated. Russian armies were now driving towards Germany. In the north, Rokossovsky was heading for Danzig, Cherniakhovsky was in East Prussia, Zhukov was coming through the centre of Poland, and Petrov was in the Carpathians. When the Red Army reached the Oder on 3 February, Germans of all types tried to leave Berlin, mostly on foot, fearing Russian vengeance for the crimes committed by their own fellow-countrymen. The weather was bitterly cold, but that seemed less important than the fact that the Red Army was less than 40 miles away.

But the German army still had the intention and the ability to fight on and make the Allies pay dearly for final victory. As we saw earlier, they still held a strong position in Italy and the Allied armies in the west had still not crossed the Rhine. In order to do that they had first to win what became known as the Reichswald Battle. The brunt of this fell on the Canadians. They had the task of crossing the polder (reclaimed land) which had now been flooded again by the Germans, making it into a huge lake, and after that fighting their way through the Hochwald Forest which was bristling with fortifications. The battle lasted five weeks and, owing to the mud, rain and deliberate flooding, bore a close resemblance to the gruelling battles of World War I, particularly Passchendaele. At times the Germans, who had some of their best paratroop units fighting as infantry here, counter-attacked and were held with difficulty. By 10 March, when the battle was over, the Germans had had over 70,000 casualties, of which 17,000 were prisoners. British and Canadian losses were 16,000; although the Allies had found this one of their most difficult battles, air superiority, which had enabled them to saturate the German defences with bombs and massive artillery barrages, had helped to limit their casualty figures. In this sector the Allies were now on the bank of the Rhine, though not across it. The first crossing came further south at Remagen, much to the satisfaction of Bradley. A platoon of the US 9th Armoured Division had made an unexpected rush across the Ludendorff Bridge, which lay south of Cologne. The Germans were caught by surprise and failed to explode the demolition charges in time. The German officer responsible for destroying the bridge was subsequently taken prisoner, but Hitler was so enraged that he promptly court-martialled and shot four others who were in no way to blame. Although the Germans made desperate efforts to seal off this bridgehead by shelling the bridge itself, they failed to destroy it before the Americans had put several divisions on the other side. Unhappily for Bradley, he was not allowed to exploit this Remagen triumph: it did not fit in with Eisenhower's tactical plans, which involved a mass crossing by Montgomery at Wesel on 24 March. To occupy Patton's Third Army, Bradley agreed that it should sweep up the river, clearing the west bank and therefore cutting off any German troops in the area. This he did, over a 70-mile stretch, and on 22 March sent his own troops across at Oppenheim, between Mannheim and Mainz; they met no German opposition.

On the night of 23 March Montgomery began his assault with 24 divisions along a 35-mile stretch of the river. The crossing was preceded by a huge aerial and artillery bombardment, but the Germans could only find five tired divisions to oppose it. The need to build up adequate supplies of materials and ammunition had delayed the crossing, for it was thought that these might well be needed, if not in the crossing, then very soon on the other side. The crossing was made by infantry units in swimming tanks, and to make sure that a counter-attack did not push them back into the river, two airborne divisions were dropped ahead of them to clear

the way. This massive display of strength would have been
necessary if Hitler had not decided to move the bulk of his
best remaining troops to try to hold the Russians on the
Eastern Front: he was under the impression that the Western
Allies were exhausted by their recent efforts and that the
greatest danger came from the Red Army.

Casualties were light, but there were small pockets of
strong resistance consisting of fanatical Germans. Montgomery built up a force of 20 divisions and 1,500 tanks in this
area before he pressed on, but when he did the Germans
were beginning to surrender in numbers so large that
prisoners-of-war were now a hindrance. Hitler issued orders
that all water supplies, electricity plants, gas works and food
stores ahead of the Allied armies must now be destroyed.
Albert Speer, his Minister of War Production, who subsequently claimed that he realised that Germany had lost the
war in early 1943, secretly countermanded Hitler's order.

The US 1st and 9th Armies now encircled the Ruhr and
met near Paderborn, trapping 400,000 Germans. Further
south Patton reached Frankfurt. When, on 12 April, the US
9th Army reached the Elbe near Magdeburg, they were
within 60 miles of Berlin. Elsewhere other bastions of
German resistance were now crumbling: Danzig fell on 30
March and on 13 April the Russians entered Vienna. Hitler
was later reported to have been scarcely sane at this time,
studying horoscopes and issuing orders to armies which no
longer existed. Goering and Himmler were both now trying
to negotiate a surrender to the Allies to prevent Berlin being
taken; it was, of course, a futile effort. On the night of 28
April, Hitler married his mistress, Eva Braun (she committed suicide by poison on 30 April 1945), and on 29 April he
named Admiral Doenitz as his successor, poisoned his dog
and disappeared. It was thought that he had shot himself in
the bunker below the Chancellery where he had spent his last
days and that his body had been burnt beyond recognition
but rumours that he and his deputy Martin Bormann had
escaped to South America persisted for many years. Another
improbable hypothesis was that he had been captured by the
Russians, who were holding him in secret for reasons best
known to themselves. There can be little doubt however that

this evil man, with his strange magnetism and malevolent influence, died by his own hand in the ruins of the capital city of the country he had brought to total destruction.

The war in Europe was not quite over. Russian troops were still fighting their way street by street into the heart of Berlin. On 2 May, British, American and Russian troops met on the shores of the Baltic and at Torgau on the Elbe. There was considerable anxiety in the West as to whether the Russians were going to continue their thrust into the Scandinavian countries and stay there, but this fear proved groundless. On 4 May the unconditional surrender of the German armed forces was made by representatives of Admiral Doenitz to Field-Marshal Montgomery on Luneburg Heath. The European war was formally ended on 7 May at Reims, when a document to that effect was signed by Air Chief Marshal Tedder, representing Eisenhower, by Field Marshal Keitel, representing Doenitz, and by Marshal Zhukov, representing Stalin. In the general rejoicing which took place in the capitals of the West it was forgotten that this was only the European part of World War II. Millions of men were still fighting each other in the Far East and nothing in that theatre indicated that there would be a less gruelling conclusion there.

The final stages of the war in Europe, as the Allied armies made their way across Europe, provided all the evidence which was needed that this really had been a just war. Soldiers in the armies which crossed Germany saw sights they could scarcely believe and could never forget. It was known that Hitler's rantings about a pure Nordic race, and his freely expressed hatred of certain minorities had caused those who could to flee from his power and find shelter in other countries, but few realised the horrors of what became known as 'the Holocaust'. Thousands of innocent people had been arrested in the middle of the night, taken away, and interrogated with the most barbaric forms of medieval torture. In huge camps there were barracks filled to the roof with emaciated corpses, who had died of starvation, beatings, in medical experiments and in the gas chambers. While they were waiting for cremation, their teeth and hair were removed for industrial use. Those too weak to work in armaments factories had often been shot, beheaded or simply tumbled alive into deep mass graves. Eisenhower insisted that every American soldier should be shown these camps so that he would never forget what he had been fighting against. Films of the camps were made compulsory viewing for German civilians. The vast majority of the victims were Jews, and were said to number as many as six million, though later, in a macabre argument about statistics, it was claimed that the figure should be two million less. They had been brought in from all over Europe from the countries which the German armies had overrun. People asked how it was that a country which had produced the musicians and culture for which Germany was famous could have done such things. There was no satisfactory answer. Most Germans said they were unaware that these camps ever existed, but few outside Germany believed them. They probably knew but were powerless to invervene and hoped that before long it would all stop, perhaps when the war ended and Germany had won. A complete and documented account of Nazi atrocities both inside and outside the concentration camps is given in Lord Russell of Liverpool's book *The Scourge of the Swastika*; a similar account of Japanese war crimes is given in his *The Knights of the Bushido*.

Not surprisingly, surviving Jews did everything in their power to reach the country of Palestine, which had been created out of part of the Turkish empire in 1919 and had been administered by the British under a League of Nations mandate which was due to end with an independent Israel in 1948. But that is another story.

Sadly, President Franklin D. Roosevelt, the man who had done so much to win the war and end the Hitler tyranny, had died on 12 April. He had never lost faith in Britain's ability to hold the Nazi enemy until his own countrymen recognised the danger, abandoned their neutrality and took a full part in the war. Roosevelt never left the United States in any doubt of what it was fighting for once the die had been cast. The Allies owed him a great debt. Unfortunately his great service was marred towards the end by his mistaken belief that he could trust Stalin and that the best way to develop a friendship with the Russian dictator was to appear to see his viewpoint instead of Churchill's. Not until it was too late and Stalin had extended his empire into central and southern Europe was it recognised by many Americans that Stalin was the imperialist, not Churchill.

After 1945 it was realised that Stalin had been the man with the clearest vision of what might happen when the war was over and how it might be turned to the advantage of the person with foresight. He had observed with interest the way in which the Allies hoped to bring Russia into a community of great powers, living in amity. He had been astonished by Eisenhower's 'broad front' policy and delighted when he saw that the Allies were being held back from their advantageous position so that the Red Army could reach Berlin first. He had agreed readily to the four-power occupation of the city, which was firmly inside the Russian occupation zone of Germany (later to become East German). He had assumed that this minor nuisance of four-power occupation of the city could be ended later when all the other armies had demobilized. As far as Russia was concerned the moment seemed to have come in 1948, but the Berlin Air Lift quickly proved that he was wrong. Stalin's aim was simple and straightforward: he wanted a communist world which would look to Russia as its leader. But he was prepared to wait. In time, he knew that, as was written in the works of Marx and Lenin, the capitalist world would tear itself apart and collapse. He would never trust anyone, however much he might appear to do so. Even while he was consolidating his grip on Bulgaria, East Germany, Poland, Roumania and Czechoslovakia, he was encouraging and supplying Mao Tse-tung in China and negotiating with the Allies the price he would require for entering the war against Japan. Japan and Russia were old adversaries. So far Russia had been able to concentrate its whole effort against Germany, giving the Russians a numerical advantage of five million to two million on the Eastern Front. Stalin had not been required to send troops to North Africa, Sicily, Italy, France or the south Pacific. He wished to see Japan defeated, but only at great cost to America and with the proviso that, for Russian help, he would obtain the strategic island of Sakhalin and share in the occupation of Japan itself. In the event he left Russia's entry into the war

against Japan too late, coming in only four days before Japan
capitulated, but even then he managed to extract useful
territorial gains.

We left the 14th Army on the approaches to Meiktila on
28 February 1945. The Japanese fought stubbornly to retain
this key communications point; they even managed to cut off
General Cowan's 17th Division temporarily, but air supply
enabled Cowan to keep moving forward, and Meiktila was
taken on 3 March. The Japanese now fell back on Mandalay,
where there was an ancient fortress palace which in the
nineteenth century had been christened Fort Dufferin. Fort
Dufferin was a hard nut to crack. The RAF bounced bombs
at it across the water in front of it, and it was shelled
repeatedly. Fortunately the Japanese decided to leave of
their own accord and Mandalay was occupied on 20 March.
The next step was Rangoon, but the monsoon was now
imminent and once that began movement would be severely
restricted. Rangoon was three hundred miles from Meiktila.
However, the Japanese army, though still ready to fight and
die, was now in a sorry state, underfed, and ravaged with
malaria and other tropical diseases. On 3 May the Allies
entered Rangoon. Although by this time the most effective
Japanese troops and aircraft had been withdrawn to take part
in the defence of Japan itself, there were still numbers of
armed Japanese scattered through the jungle, posing a threat
as guerrillas. A long period of what the services call 'mopping
up' ensued before the last of them laid down their arms.

Two outposts needed to be captured before the Allies
could begin their final assault on Japan. One was Iwo Jima,
an island in the Bonin group, 750 miles from Japan which,
although measuring only four-and-a-half by two-and-a-half
miles, would provide a useful staging ground for the US
bombers, or a dangerous fighter base if retained by the
Japanese. However, at this moment it was garrisoned by
20,000 fanatically determined Japanese who had skilfully dug
fortifications in the extinct volcano Suribachi. The US Air
Force pounded Iwo Jima with nearly 7,000 tons of bombs and
shelled it with 22,000 shells before the soldiers set foot
ashore. Unfortunately the massive bombardment had had
virtually no effect, and the ensuing battles have rightly

become an American epic. Underfoot was volcano ash, which hampered both foot-slogging infantry and amphibious tracked vehicles. As 30,000 US Marines stormed ashore, the Japanese met them with concentrated mortar-fire from their concealed positions in the tunnels, costing the Americans 2,400 men. The battle lasted from 19 February to 16 March, with the Marines having to conquer every yard of the slopes before even entering the tunnel defences. By the time the island was in American hands, one-third of the Americans had been killed or wounded, but of the 20,000 Japanese only 216 remained. As well as their land casualties, the Americans had suffered badly from two *kamikaze* attacks, which damaged several ships and sank the *Bismarck Sea*, a light carrier.

The next outpost, Okinawa, looked no less formidable and so it proved to be. The word means a 'long rope' and is a fair description of an island 67 miles long which varies in width from three to 20 miles. It lies in the Ryuku group and is only 350 miles from Japan itself. In the last days of March 1943, Okinawa had the usual saturation bombardment. Here the garrison was larger, initially numbering 100,000 men, but this time the Americans had assembled 300,000 troops for the assault. They landed 60,000 of them on 1 April 1945, and quickly captured two airfields. But on this occasion the Japanese had varied their tactics. They did not intend to slog it out with the Marines on the shore line while their back-up was being pounded to fragments by massive American air and naval bombardment. Instead they put up a token resistance on the beaches. Six days later they launched a huge counter-attack, every aspect of which was suicidal. 353 *kamikaze* aircraft were aimed at the American ground forces and their support, and into this maelstrom went the *Yamato*, the world's largest battleship, weighing 72,000 tons and carrying nine 18-inch guns. Almost unbelievably this giant ship had been given only sufficient fuel for the outward journey; it also lacked adequate air cover. Inevitably it was sunk by a succession of bombs and torpedoes on 7 April. A new weapon, the baka (which means 'fool') was first seen here. It was a glider packed with explosives which, after being towed to the target by a bomber, was released for its *kamikaze* pilot to use a rocket motor to take it to its destination. The first Japanese counter-attack met with limited success, but the battle continued in the manner with which the Americans were now only too familiar; it did not end till three months later. By that time the Americans had had 12,000 killed and 36,000 wounded; 34 American ships had been sunk and 368 damaged. There were 127,000 known Japanese dead, including their commander, who committed *hara-kiri* when the battle was clearly lost.

With an adequate supply of air bases within easy reach of the Japanese mainland, the US Air Force now intensified its attack. Its four-engined B29s (*B Ni-ju kus* as the Japanese knew them) became a familiar and dreaded sight as they cruised over the islands with long vapour trails behind them. Everything proceeded as if a normal invasion would now take place, but America had other plans to stun the Japanese into surrender. If 12,000 men had been killed on Okinawa, the thought of the casualties likely to be incurred in invading the mainland was a daunting thought.

In other parts of south-east Asia there were still groups of Japanese continuing to fight in mountains and jungles. On Luzon resistance would continue until the end of the war. Similarly, although Mindanao had been captured by 17 April there were still isolated groups of Japanese who refused to surrender. Borneo, whose oilfields had been so vital to the Japanese, was re-taken by Australian forces, although the campaign there was not concluded until 21 July, thereby almost coinciding with that on Okinawa.

All through that last summer of the war, American aircraft pounded Japan methodically. There was worse to come. On 16 July 1945 an explosive atomic device had been successfully tested at Alamogordo, New Mexico. The resulting explosion was the equivalent of 15,000 tons of TNT.

This was clearly a new dimension in warfare, with potential for destruction on such a scale that it involved a moral dilemma. Although it was realised that thousands of soldiers and civilians would be killed if Japan was invaded with what from now on would be called 'conventional' weapons, the devastating power of the atomic bomb might easily result in (another new word) overkill. And if the Japanese still did not surrender but decided to fight on, would the rest of the world permit the incineration of the entire Japanese population? In fact, the power of the atomic weapon was severely limited, for there were only two bombs available by August.

From 17 July to 2 August a conference involving Churchill, Truman and Stalin was held at Potsdam to decide on policy towards the defeated countries when the war was finally over. Japan was subsequently informed that if she surrendered immediately the Japanese people would not be made slaves, but their nation, though not their empire, would remain intact. War criminals would be prosecuted and there would be a temporary military occupation. In view of Japan's record, these terms seemed fair and generous to the Allies, but were received without enthusiasm in Japan. There had, in fact, been several feelers for peace put out by Japan earlier, but these had demanded far more generous terms than the Allies were prepared to agree. The Japanese had given no sign that they could be trusted and after Pearl Harbor the United States was likely to require more than bland promises: furthermore there were still Japanese armies occupying Java, Sumatra, Singapore, Malaya, Thailand, Indo-China, Taiwan and substantial portions of China. It was clear than nothing less than a massive demonstration of invincible power would be necessary to bring the war to an end forthwith. Nothing smaller would do. The previous November their aircraft carrier, the *Shinano*, newly built and the largest in the world, had been torpedoed and sunk by the American submarine *Archerfish* in Japanese territorial waters, before she could fire a shot or launch an aircraft. If an unsinkable, invulnerable ship like this could be destroyed without denting Japanese confidence in their ability to win the war, something of almost supernatural power could be the only resort.

So on 6 August 1945 an atomic bomb with the explosive power of 20,000 tons of TNT was carried by a B29 and dropped on Hiroshima, the seventh largest town in Japan. The decision to drop the bomb was not taken without considerable debate even though at that stage the implications of radiation were not fully appreciated. Hiroshima was a military target, containing the headquarters of five armies, with a garrison of 150,000 soldiers and a population of 343,000 civilians. It was a harbour and was crammed with oil refineries, workshops, warehouses and armaments factories. When the bomb, which descended on Hiroshima by parachute, exploded, it killed 70,000 people, injured 70,000 more, and flattened four-and-a-quarter square miles of the city. There would be other deaths later from radiation sickness. After the explosion there was a wave of suffocating heat and then a hurricane-force wind. Around the central zone of the explosion, trees and buildings suddenly caught fire and the flames quickly swept over anything which was burnable. When night came the fires died down, for there was nothing left to burn.

The Allies then sent an ultimatum to the Japanese government in Tokyo, informing them that if they did not now surrender, further bombs would be dropped. The ultimatum was ignored. Two days after Hiroshima had been incinerated, the Soviet Union declared war on Japan and invaded Manchuria. On 9 August a second atomic bomb was dropped on Japan, this time on Nagasaki, a port on Kyushu. This was a place of 250,000 inhabitants, of whom 35,000 were killed and 60,000 injured. The area devastated was approximately one-third that of Hiroshima.

On 10 August the Japanese government agreed the Potsdam terms, but requested that the Emperor should retain his sovereign status, subject to the orders of the Allied Supreme Commander. This was agreed and the Emperor Hirohito issued an imperial rescript informing his people they should now surrender. The following day, when the rescript had reached most of its far-flung destinations, the war was over. A few isolated Japanese units continued to fight on in ignorance of this, others decided to ignore it, and certain extremists planned to kill the newly appointed Prime Minister.

On 2 September on the US flagship in Tokyo Bay the formal surrender was signed. General Douglas MacArthur was now commanding the Allied army of occupation. MacArthur subsequently issued various decrees which restored civil liberties, created adult suffrage, abolished the secret police, changed the system of land tenure and generally prepared Japan for the democratic constitution which was approved in 1946 and introduced in 1947. The Emperor retained his position as a symbol of state although the sovereign power now rested with the people.

On 9 September 1945, a separate ceremony took place in Nanking to conclude Japan's war with China. Meanwhile the war in Korea had ended less tidily. Korea, as we saw earlier, had been annexed to Japan and was at first thought of as being a suitable area for four-power occupation. However, after Soviet troops had invaded Manchuria and entered North Korea, it was decided that the best solution would be for the Soviet Army to occupy North Korea, down to the 38th parallel. This part of the agreement was implemented promptly and the Russians installed their communist supporters in positions of power. The Americans did not arrive in South Korea until nearly a month later and a formal surrender of their 'zone' was made on 9 September. The Russians then supplied their satellite zone with arms and encouragement, and in 1950 the North decided that the time was opportune to invade and occupy the South. They had not reckoned with the quick decisiveness of President Truman, the man who had authorised the dropping of the atomic bomb: he responded by spurring the United Nations into action and sending an American force to defend the political integrity of South Korea. It was an interesting example of the seeds of the next war being planted by the peace treaties of the last. The war did not end till 1953 and the ensuing peace has always been an uneasy one.

15
AFTERMATH AND HINDSIGHT

The destruction and confusion caused by the six-and-a-half year world war had been unprecedented, and neither victors nor vanquished would be able to put matters right for many years, if at all. The exact toll of the dead is unknown, but Russia was said to have lost 11 million military and seven million civilians. Poland had lost nearly six million civilians and soldiers, nearly half of them being Jews killed in the Nazi death camps. Approximately three million German military had been killed and three million civilians. The Japanese were said to have had 1.3 million military and 670,000 civilians killed. China's losses almost defied calculation, but were not less than a million combatants and 20 million civilians. Britain had lost 264,443 military and 92,673 civilians. The United States had lost 292,131 military and 6,000 civilians.

One of the first tasks of the victors was to bring to justice all war criminals. In the event, a large number undoubtedly escaped the fate they deserved, particularly in Japan. However, from 20 November 1945 to 1 October 1946 an international tribunal sat at Nuremberg to try the most prominent Nazis. Like all Germans, most of them denied all knowledge of the concentration camps, but Goëring, von Ribbentrop, Keitel and Jodl were sentenced to death by hanging. Goëring managed to escape by poisoning himself. Doenitz, the submarine commander and Hitler's successor, was sentenced to 20 years imprisonment, as was Speer, who had been responsible for war production. Krupp, the multi-millionaire in whose factories thousands of prisoners from concentration camps had been worked to the point of death, was found to be unfit to plead. Rudolf Hess was sentenced to life imprisonment, which he served in Spandau prison until his death in 1987. Of the 24 major defendants at Nuremberg, three were acquitted. The process of finding and trying other war criminals, such as the concentration camp SS sadists, doctors who had conducted medical experiments on the living and mass murderers has been continued ever since.

Although many people thought that the emperor Hirohito should be tried as a war criminal, this idea was not considered, partly because he was an instrument of the war policy not an instigator, and partly because his continued presence at the head of the Japanese nation would help preserve order and prevent it sliding into chaos. Others were not so lucky. Prince Konoye, who had been Prime Minister when the Japanese massacred 60,000 men, women and children in Nanking, committed suicide. Tojo, who had been the real ruler of Japan and the originator of the war policy, tried to commit *hara-kiri* but failed. He was hanged, completely unrepentant for the damage he had caused to his own country and others. General Yamashita received short shrift, as the atrocities committed by his troops were too well authenticated. He was hanged in December 1945. Many lesser performers were brought to trial and some executed, but undoubtedly even more escaped than had done in Germany.

This time there were to be no huge war reparations, only certain reparations in kind: instead the victors would try to rebuild the defeated countries into prosperous democracies, fit to take their proper part in the comradeship of nations. American businessmen, who had profited considerably during the war, now saw unprecedented investment opportunities in the defeated countries, mainly Germany and Japan. They were immensely successful in reviving those two economies and within a few years were so alarmed by the prosperity and enterprise of their former foes that they were seriously discussing tariff barriers. Japan, in fact, killed off the British and German motor-cycle industries and within a few years was dominating not merely the older industries in America, such as optics, but also the new ones such as electronics.

France emerged from the war with a sense of humiliation and resentment, but revived more quickly than expected. Much of her self-respect came back when de Gaulle was elected President. Unfortunately, de Gaulle never felt any gratitude to his British hosts, whose determination had saved his life and his country, and Britain and France continued to be divided by 21 miles of water and an ocean of political distrust.

For a victor, Britain came off remarkably badly, worse in fact than defeated countries such as Italy which benefited hugely from American money. In July 1945 the British people had discarded Churchill and elected a socialist government with Clement Attlee as Prime Minister. For the next six years Attlee's government tried to turn Britain into a socialist state, and was much assisted in this by the preservation of the multitude of controls which had been necessary for a nation fighting for its life in a world war. In order to create what was thought by the government to be a fairer society, various forms of control on food, clothing, fuel and employment were continued for years after the war. Much private industry was nationalized. Many returning servicemen were astonished to find that Churchill, the symbol of all their hopes for many years, had been relegated to a secondary position and the wartime drabness and shortages which they had hoped would have ended were as strongly entrenched as ever. However, it would be unfair to blame the socialists for all the miseries of post-war Britain, underfed, exhausted, materially battered, financially almost bankrupt and with shortages everywhere owing to the war: whatever government Britain had had at that time would have been in difficulties not of its own making.

During the war, even in the darkest days, there had been much thought about the future. In Britain in 1944 parliament had passed the Butler Education Act (R. A. Butler was Minister of Education), abolishing the fee-paying grammar schools (at which there were many free places) and putting in their place a structure of free grammar schools, to which education admission could only be gained by passing an examination at the age of 11 (the 11 plus). Those unable to pass were relegated to Secondary Modern Schools of all-round lower standard, unless their parents had the money or they themselves the ability to win scholarships to enable them to attend the independent schools: these varied from Eton and Harrow to very minor schools, equally jealous of their status and independence. This was state education with a vengeance.

At the same time, planning was made for a 'Welfare State', in which a person would be looked after from the cradle to the grave. This came in in 1948, with family allowances, funeral grants, unemployment and incapacity pay, and a free National Health Service.

Welfare was also being implemented on a wider, international scale. Wartime conferences had stressed the need for post-war economic planning, financial stability, and assistance to less fortunate nations. Above all, there had been a demand for an organisation to replace the League of Nations which, having failed, had virtually fallen apart. The new body was the United Nations and one of its first tasks was to help the survivors of concentration camps, refugees and other victims of the war. It incorporated a Security Council in which the great powers, the United States, Great Britain, France, the USSR and China, would check any aggression. Its successes and failures lie outside the province of this book.

The creation of the United Nations had been discussed at Yalta, in the Crimea, in February 1945, when Roosevelt, Stalin and Churchill had met to discuss the action which should be taken at the end of the war. The conference decided that Germany would be divided into four zones which would be administered by Britain, France, Russia and America. An Allied Control Commission was to be set up in Berlin, which would be administered in sectors. Austria was also divided into four zones. Like Berlin, the capital Vienna also fell into the Russian zone and again required a four-power administration. Austria was considered to be an innocent victim of German coercion, rather than a defeated enemy and was soon granted its own elections.

Although the rest of the Allies were not interested in extracting reparations from the defeated countries, Russia took a different view and removed considerable quantities of material goods from Germany and Austria. The biggest factor in setting the defeated countries back on the road to recovery was the generous financial allocations made by the US government in support of relief and rehabilitation. America was, of course, the only country able to provide such help, but it needs to be noted that American aid was extremely generous. Unfortunately Britain, although a victor was virtually bankrupt and the Lend-Lease Agreement by which the US had supplied Britain with goods as payment for the lease of bases was abruptly terminated on 24 August 1945 by President Truman. However, although Lend-Lease had stopped, Britain was still under contract to receive large quantities of American goods for which she now had to pay in dollars. Three years later, America realised that a harsh economic policy towards European countries was a road to disaster and introduced the European Recovery Programme (Marshall Aid) on very generous terms.

Although America's contribution to the war had been decisive, she herself had hardly suffered at all in it. The total war casualties had amounted to only 292,000 military and 6,000 civilians, which was less than those incurred in the Civil War nearly 100 years earlier. Yet 16 million Americans had been called up, eleven-and-a-quarter of these in the army, four million in the navy, and 670,000 in the Marines who had fought so well in the Pacific. They had also called up 216,000 women and a number of auxiliaries. America produced nearly half the arms used by the Allies, without materially affecting home consumption of goods. There was a form of rationing and price control, but it caused little hardship. America was so generous with the pay of her own troops, with everyone receiving several times that of their Allies, that considerable resentment was created. In Britain, American troops were also supplied from servicemen's shops (the PX), which stocked goods which had long disappeared from the British market or were heavily rationed if available at all. American troops with their high pay, glamorous reputation, appearance and accent were extremely popular with women, much to the fury of those competing. This fact often led to open hostility and fights. In the same way the British had been paid higher rates than the French in both world wars.

There are some problems which are beyond the power of politicians to solve.

One of the most valuable and popular American contributions to the war was the jeep, the small, versatile vehicle which could be used for almost everything almost everywhere. Jeeps were general purpose vehicles (GPs); the men who used them were mainly GIs, so nicknamed because the term 'General Issue' was the American equivalent of 'soldiers for the use of'.

Thousands of Americans married British, Australian and New Zealand women, and later French and German women. Thousands of lasting friendships were made between Americans and Britons of both sexes and of all types. Thousands of British service people visited the United States and made friendships and marriages. Whatever frictions there were between British and Americans were overwhelmingly outweighed by the mutual respect and friendship which grew up between the two allies.

Nearly 50 years later we can look back on World War II and draw certain conclusions from the facts we now know. We must not, however, forget that there are still facts we do not know and perhaps never will. Nevertheless we can now give an account which is broadly accurate.

It is a mixture of success and failure, of luck and stupidity, of unexpected disasters, and occasions when defeat came perilously close. In 1939 Britain was pushed into a war for which she was unprepared mentally and materially. Fortunately her opponent was not quite ready either, not having expected Britain to react so strongly to the attack on Poland. Although prepared to challenge Britain later, Hitler did not expect to be in a position to do so until 1944. However, after his easy victories in Scandinavia and France in 1940 he decided it would be wise to obtain a quick victory over Russia. Having failed to do this, he then found that the ambitions of his Axis partner Japan had brought America to the aid of both Britain and Russia. The naivety of the British government about Hitler was disclosed in the Colville Diaries. John Colville was in the Foreign Office and later became Churchill's private secretary.

As early as October 1939 the Diaries reveal that the

Cabinet was under the impression that Hitler could be deposed, Goëring put in his place and a negotiated peace arranged. By June 1940 these optimistic views were seen for the rubbish they were, but the end of the Dunkirk evacuation found Britain and France both resentful of their mutual failure to keep the Germans out of France. Clearly the French had done little to help themselves, but British tactics had not been over-intelligent either. At this stage the Ultra project was of little help, but radar was playing a very important part.

Hitler's insistence on bombing London undoubtedly helped the RAF win the Battle of Britain, as described earlier. His insistence on making military decisions was sometimes helpful to the Germans, sometimes disastrous. When he launched the German army into Russia in 1941, he was ignoring available knowledge about the developments which had taken place in the Russian armaments industry, with which Germany had once been closely linked. In December 1941, when the Japanese attacked Pearl Harbor without warning, they assumed that their own navy would be more than a match for anything the Allies could bring against them in the future. Their success in sinking the British *Prince of Wales* and *Repulse* four days later, which so appalled Britain, should really have been a warning to the Japanese of the vulnerability of their own capital ships.

Mussolini was soon shown to have miscalculated regarding the fighting qualities and enthusiasm of his own forces as well as his ability to be an equal partner to Hitler. Hitler had also miscalculated in thinking that he could use the Italian armed forces without a strong stiffening of German troops. However, the Italian military were undoubtedly a very useful asset when firmly under German control, as they showed with Rommel in North Africa. By 1943 Ultra and Magic were both producing invaluable information. However, it must not be forgotten that there were many Japanese and German messages which could not be decrypted, and that frequently a knowledge of the enemy's intentions did not mean you could take effective counter-measures.

1944 saw the war turning in the Allied favour in spite of the V1 and V2 rockets. The Ardennes counter-attack was a setback and, if it had not been contained, could have lengthened the war.

The atomic bombs which ended the war against Japan did not cause as much material damage nor as many casualties as the previous incendiary bombings. In April 1945 a raid on Tokyo was said to have killed 189,000 people, well over double the total of the two atomic bombs. Other raids on cities such as Osaka and Kobe had also caused enormous death tolls. The reason why the atomic bombs convinced the Japanese government that surrender was necessary was probably the fact that during an ordinary bombing those privileged enough to be in deep shelters could escape. With an atomic bomb a shelter would need to be deeper than any existing at that time in Japan. Tokyo could well have been the recipient of a third atomic bomb. By surrendering when they did, the Japanese saved the lives of many of their citizens and soldiers who would have been killed if Japan had fought to the end. All Allied prisoners-of-war held by the Japanese would have been killed in cold blood before an invasion actually took place. Arrangements for these massacres had already been made: many of them would have been burnt to death in places from which there was no escape and the rest would have been finished off by machine-guns. 33,000 prisoners had died of malnutrition and overwork when building the Bangkok-Moulmein railway and thousands more in Burma, Borneo and other territories which the Japanese had overrun when at the height of their power. All the survivors of the Japanese prisoner of war camps came home with some ill effects from disease, starvation and brutality, and many died soon after reaching home, but the only compensation they received from the Japanese for their treatment was £78 per man, and to pay that the Japanese had been allowed to sell the 'Railway of Death' to the Thais, using the proceeds to pay the compensation. The British government showed little interest in the fate of British PoWs, either during or after the war, but the American government showed considerable generosity to their PoWs.

The impression that the British miner and factory worker slaved for long hours doing his best to provide materials for the lads at the front is, sad to say, mistaken. Some, of course, did, usually paid at rates many times that of the serving soldier whose life was at greater risk. Trade unions fought tenaciously to retain the old restrictive practices. In Wales in 1944, 70,000 miners went on strike and there were strikes in aircraft factories, engineering works and, of course, the docks. Output in quantity and quality was approximately half that of the German and American worker. This sad story is carefully documented in Correlli Barnett's book, *The Audit of War*. A go-slow in 1943 in Liverpool cost 57 vitally needed aircraft, a strike in the November of that year cost Rolls Royce in Glasgow 730,000 man hours. There were strikes all over the country in 1944, but perhaps the most despicable was the one at Southampton when, four days after D Day, dockers refused to load desperately needed tanks. Although the 'workers' and the trade unions were clearly behaving irresponsibly, the managers, employers and government information services were also to blame. The only way to get men to work harder in some factories was to tell them their work was helping Russia: nobody told them what would have happened to them if they had tried to go on strike in the Soviet Union.

And yet, at the end of it all, in spite of incompetence, bad management, poor generalship, avoidable mistakes, and traitors in high places, the war was won. It was then learnt that if Hitler had invaded Britain he would have deported every male between the ages of 16 and 45 to work on the continent; no doubt he would have carried out similar policies in the United States. All Jews and infirm or elderly people would have been killed. In the circumstances it was not a war the Allies could afford to lose.

FURTHER READING

The following books provide more material on the subjects described in the text:

Alanbrooke, Viscount *Diaries* (2 vols) Collins 1979
Alexander, Field-Marshal Earl *Memoirs 1940–45* Cassell 1962
Allen, L. *Burma: The Longest War* Dent 1984
Ambrose, S. E. *Pegasus Bridge* Unwin 1985
Auphan, P. and Mordal, J. *The French Navy in World War II* Greenwood 1976
Barnett, Correlli *The Audit of War* Macmillan 1986
Becker, C. *Hitler's Naval War* Corgi 1976
Beevor, J. G. *S.O.E.* Bodley Head 1981
Bird, E. *Hess* Sphere 1976
Bradford, E. *Siege: Malta 1940–3* Penguin 1985
Calvocoressi, P. *Top-Secret Ultra* Cassell 1980
Carr, W. *Poland to Pearl Harbor* Arnold 1985
Cave-Browne, A. *Bodyguard of Lies* Allen 1976
Chamberlin *Life in Wartime Britain* Batsford 1972
Churchill, Winston *The Second World War I–VI* Cassell
Colville, J. *The Fringes of Power Vols I and II* Sceptre 1987
Cookridge, E. H. *They Came from the Sky* Corgi 1976
Cruikshank, C. *SOE in the Far East* OUP 1983
Ellis, J. *Cassino* Sphere 1985
Erickson, J. *The Road to Stalingrad* Panther 1985
   The Road to Berlin Weidenfeld 1983
Fitzgibbon, C. *Secret Intelligence in the 20th Century* Panther 1978
Fleming, P. *Invasion 1940* Panther 1959

Foot, M. R. D. *S.O.E.* B.B.C. 1984
  Resistance Paladin 1978
Garlinski, J. *Intercept* Dent 1979
Grigg, J. *1943: the Victory that Never Was* Methuen 1980
Hamilton, N. *Monty* (3 vols) Sceptre 1987
Hampshire, A. C. *Undercover Sailors* Kimber 1981
Hastings, M. *Bomber Command* Pan 1981
  Overlord M. Joseph 1984
Hibbert, C. *The Battle of Arnhem* Fontana 1975
Hinsley, F. H. *British Intelligence in the Second World War*
  H.M.S.O. (4 vols) 1979, 1981, 1984, 1988
Holbrook, D. *Flesh Wounds* Buchan & Enright 1987
Howarth, P. *Special Operations* R.K.P. 1955
Howarth, S. *Morning Glory: the Story of the Imperial
  Japanese Navy* Arrow 1985
Jefferson, A. *Assault on the Guns at Merville* Murray 1987
Keegan, J. *Six Armies in Normandy* Cape, 1982
Kennedy-Shaw, W. B. *Long Range Desert Group* Collins
  1945
Lamb, R. *Montgomery in Europe 1943–45* Buchan & Enrigh
  1984
Liddell-Hart, B. H. *History of the Second World War* Cassell
  1970
  The Other Side of the Hill Pan 1978
Longmate, N. *The Doodlebugs* Hutchinson 1981
MacDonald, C. B. *The Battle of the Bulge* Weidenfeld &
  Nicolson 1985
McElwee, W. *Britain's Locust Years* Faber 1962
McKee, A. *Caen: Anvil of Victory* Papermac 1985
Middlebrook, M. *The Nuremberg Raid* Penguin 1987
Montagu, E. *Beyond Top Secret U.* Corgi 1979
Padfield, P. *Dönitz: the last Führer* Panther 1985
Peniakoff, V. *Private Army* Cape 1950
Piekalkiewicz, J. *Secret Agents, Spies and Saboteurs* David
  and Charles 1969
Pimlott, J. *World War II in Photographs* Orbit 1985
Pitt, B. *The Crucible of War* (3 vols) Papermac 1986
Poolman, K. *Periscope Depth* Sphere 1984
Rhodes-James, R. *Chindit* Murray 1980
Roberts, G. P. B. *From the Desert to the Baltic* Kimber 1987

Ryan, C. *The Longest Day* N.E.L. 1962

Salisbury, H. E. *The 900 Days* Papermac 1986

Saward, D. *'Bomber' Harris* Buchan & Enright 1984

Shackman, T. *The Phony War 1939–40* Harper & Row 1982

Slim, Field-Marshal Viscount *Defeat into Victory* Papermac 1986

Smiley, D. *Albanian Assignment* Sphere 1985

Sweetman, J. *Operation Chastise* Jane's 1982

Swinson, A. *Defeat in Malaya* Macdonald 1969

Terraine, J. *The Right of the Line* Sceptre 1988

Thomas, G. and Morgan-Witts, M. *Ruin from the Air* Panther 1985

Tuchman, B. *August 1914* Macmillan 1987

Turner, E. S. *The Phoney War on the Home Front* M. Joseph 1981

Warner, P. *Alamein* Kimber 1979
The D Day Landings Kimber 1980
Invasion Road Cassell 1980
Auchinleck Buchan & Enright 1981
Phantom Kimber 1982
The S.A.S. Sphere 1983
Horrocks Hamish Hamilton 1984
The Secret Forces of World War II Granada 1985

Welchman, G. *The Hut Six Story* Penguin 1984

Young, P. *World War 1939–45* A. Barker 1966
Storm from the Sea

INDEX

Index